IMAGES
of America

CARROLL COUNTY

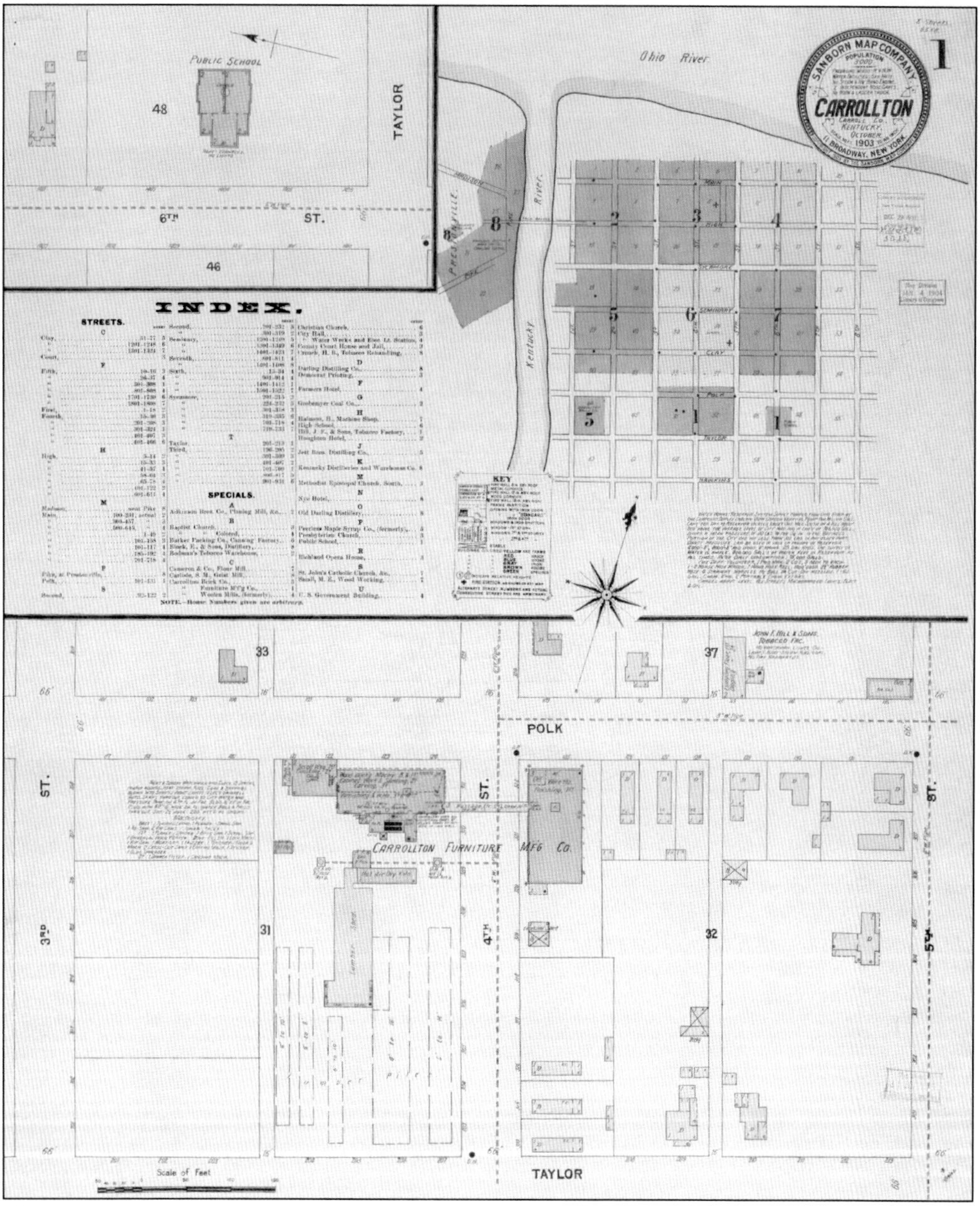

This 1903 Sanborn insurance map shows the location and layout of the Carrollton Furniture Factory, which takes the entire block between Third and Fourth Streets and Polk and Taylor Streets, plus some property in the next block to the east. Also shown are the John F. Hill & Sons Tobacco Factory, a school at Sixth and Taylor Streets, and the Old Darling Distillery in Prestonville. (Courtesy of Library of Congress.)

On the Cover: Florence Tull (right) and friends "slide the apron" of the dam at Lock One of the Kentucky River in Carroll County, Kentucky, about 1915. The lock and dam were built in the early to mid-1880s to accommodate barge traffic that brought necessities to Carrollton and Prestonville, located where the Kentucky meets the Ohio River, as well as to ship products south to Frankfort and other locations. (Courtesy of Rebecca Morgan Tull.)

IMAGES
of America

CARROLL COUNTY

Phyllis Codling McLaughlin

ARCADIA
PUBLISHING

ISBN 978-0-7385-9092-9

Published by Arcadia Publishing
Charleston, South Carolina

Printed in the United States of America

Library of Congress Control Number: 2012944675

For all general information, please contact Arcadia Publishing:
Telephone 843-853-2070
Fax 843-853-0044
E-mail sales@arcadiapublishing.com
For customer service and orders:
Toll-Free 1-888-313-2665

Visit us on the Internet at www.arcadiapublishing.com

To my husband, Andrew "Patter" McLaughlin, who encouraged me every step of the way along this journey and remained supportive even as dust and piles of laundry accumulated when deadlines approached.

Contents

ACKNOWLEDGMENTS

This project was made possible by the people who donated images from their private collections. I thank each and every person who came forward to share his or her images and knowledge of life and times in Carroll County, including Gary Ford, John and Carolyn Glauber, Rebecca Morgan Tull, Cathy Gilbert, Jim Fothergill, Nancy Jo Grobmyer, Ann Deatherage, Carolyn Stout, Don Mougey, Ben Collett, Robin Caldwell Welch, Ernest "Junior" and Donna Welch, Deborah Garrett, Ida Lewis, Linda Chandler Banks, Darrell Maines, Bill Davis, Daisy Hughes, the City of Ghent (for lending me James Bond's image collection), Ghent mayor William Mumphrey, Carrollton United Methodist Church, Susan McEuen of Carrollton Christian Church, Amy Baglan, and Tanya Supplee of General Butler State Resort Park.

I wish to thank the Port William Historical Society for the use of photographs in its collection; and the Carroll County Public Library for contributing images and for allowing me the use of the Genealogy Room, where many contributors met with me so I could scan their images.

Thanks also go to Jeff Moore, publisher of the *News-Democrat* (and my boss), for allowing me to write columns about the project to encourage submissions, for giving me full rein of the paper's archives, and for giving me the time I needed to complete this project.

I wish to extend my deep appreciation to the late Kathryn Salyers and the late Evelyn Welch. These women had a deep love and devotion to Carroll County and its history; they would have been great supporters of and contributors to this project, far beyond the scope of the work they left behind.

Finally, I thank my acquisitions editor at Arcadia Publishing, Liz Gurley, for her guidance and extensive patience in helping me to get this project completed.

INTRODUCTION

One of the first known explorers to visit the area that eventually would become Carroll County, Kentucky, was James McBride, who canoed down the Ohio River from Pittsburgh to the mouth of the Kentucky River in 1754. He carved his name and the date into a tree near the confluence of the Kentucky and Ohio Rivers. The tree remained a landmark for 30 years. Still wilderness, Kentucky soon became a county of Virginia, and settlers started arriving. In 1789, Gen. Charles Scott, a veteran of the French and Indian Wars and later governor of Kentucky from 1808 to 1812, built a blockhouse on the east side of the mouth of the Kentucky River (now known as Point Park). Similar to a fort, the blockhouse was intended to protect settlers in the area from Indian attacks.

In 1805, the Point House was built in its place and became a well-known tavern, frequented by George Rogers Clark and others who came to explore and trade.

In 1794, Benjamin Craig Sr. and James Hawkins bought 613 acres of land from the 2,000 acres awarded to Col. William Peachy in 1753 for his military service. Craig and Hawkins founded the town of Port William, which soon spread to the south and east along the banks of the Ohio River. The first town clerk was Percival Richard Butler, who had served in the Revolutionary War at Valley Forge with Gen. George Washington. His sons followed in his military footsteps: Maj. Thomas Butler served as an aide to Gen. Andrew Jackson at the Battle of New Orleans; Percival Pierce Butler served as the first adjutant general of Kentucky; and Maj. Gen. William Orlando Butler, for whom General Butler State Resort Park is named, was commander in chief of US forces during the Mexican War.

In the early 1790s, Richard and Sarah Masterson built a two-story brick house just a few miles upriver of the blockhouse. At that time, this area was part of Gallatin County, and in 1799 the Masterson's home served as the first meeting place for the Gallatin County Court. It also was the meetinghouse for the Reverend Henry Ogden and others from their Methodist congregation—before a church was built in 1810 on Ogden's nearby property. Historians believe it is the oldest existing two-story brick house on the Ohio River between Cincinnati and Louisville and one of the two oldest between Pittsburgh, Pennsylvania, and Cairo, Illinois. In 1979, the house on US 42 East was donated to the Port William Historical Society by what was then M&T Chemical. Listed in the National Register of Historic Places, it was restored by the society and serves as a museum and meeting place.

In 1838, Carroll County (named in honor of the last surviving signer of the Declaration of Independence, Charles Carroll of Maryland) was carved out of portions of Gallatin and Trimble Counties by the Kentucky Legislature. Port William was renamed Carrollton and established as the county seat. The county's population in 1840 was 3,966. In 2010, the population was 10,811.

Through the decades, other towns were founded in the county. Prestonville, just across the Kentucky River, was established about the same time as Port William. The city is the namesake of Col. William Preston and was built on a portion of the property he was awarded by land grant for his service in the Revolutionary War.

In 1900, a toll bridge was opened to replace the ferry that connected the two cities; in 1952, a newer bridge was built to accommodate the increasing volume of automobile traffic.

At one time, Prestonville actually was the larger community, with the Darling whiskey distillery, warehouses, shipping operations, a flour mill, and other businesses. Prestonville's demise began with the completion of the Kentucky Central Railroad in 1854 and a series of floods in the 1900s. Carrollton emerged as the county's commercial and industrial center and remains so today.

To the east is the city of Ghent, said to be named in 1815 by Henry Clay for the Belgian city where, three years earlier, he had participated as a member of the peace commission that ended the War of 1812. Ghent also had a booming economy from the late 1800s into the 1900s. A ferry took travelers across the Ohio to Vevay, Indiana; it operated under various owners until 1977, when the Markland Dam Bridge, just over the Gallatin County line, opened. One of Ghent's most famous sons was James Tandy Ellis, a renowned columnist and poet who also served as Kentucky's adjutant general.

South of Ghent was a city named Rislerville, which was later renamed Liberty Station. Since 1874, the city has been known as Sanders. After the railroad came through, the city and its neighbor to the west, Worthville, became bustling towns. Thousands of visitors flocked to these towns each year to stay at the resorts and take in the healing waters of their sulphur springs.

Carrollton's downtown was a thriving business district, with shoe stores, department stores, men's and women's clothing stores, taverns, restaurants, drugstores, groceries, barbershops and salons, banks, and two movie theaters.

Both Ghent and Carrollton benefited when US Highway 42 was built in the early 1930s, linking Cincinnati to Louisville. The drive brought tourists from the big cities to General Butler State Resort Park, which was established in 1933. Its stone shelter houses, roads, and other structures were built by the Civilian Conservation Corps. Its centerpiece is the Butler-Turpin State Historic House, built in 1859 and restored in the 1930s.

For decades, Butler Park's 30-acre, man-made lake drew thousands of people each summer for swimming, canoeing, and fishing; the park also featured horseback riding. For a few years in the 1980s, wintertime tourists took to the slopes of Ski Butler. Today, the park offers paddleboats, canoes, miniature golf, a nine-hole golf course, and several miles of hiking trails.

Carrollton has survived numerous floods, the worst of which was in 1937 when the waters of the Ohio River crested as high as the second floor of most downtown buildings. Other substantial floods occurred in 1945, 1964, and 1997.

Though still thriving, Carrollton's downtown began to wane after the completion of Interstate 71, which passes through the county about three miles south of the city. The thoroughfare made traveling to Louisville and Cincinnati easier for shoppers and created a competing commercial district in the county.

Fire also destroyed several downtown landmarks. In 1937, arson destroyed the Richland Theater building, which once housed Carrollton's opera house and was owned by James Howe. Rebuilt, it met a similar fate in 1977, when it and an adjoining building were destroyed by a fire started by children playing with matches. But most of the old buildings survive, and several blocks of downtown Carrollton were designated a National Historic District in the 1980s.

Since the mid-1960s, the US 42 corridor between Carrollton and Ghent has become a dynamic industrial center, including Dow Corning's Carrollton Plant (which, since 1966, has manufactured silicone) and a massive facility built in the early 1990s and owned by North American Stainless (one of the top steel-producers in the world).

One

The County Seat

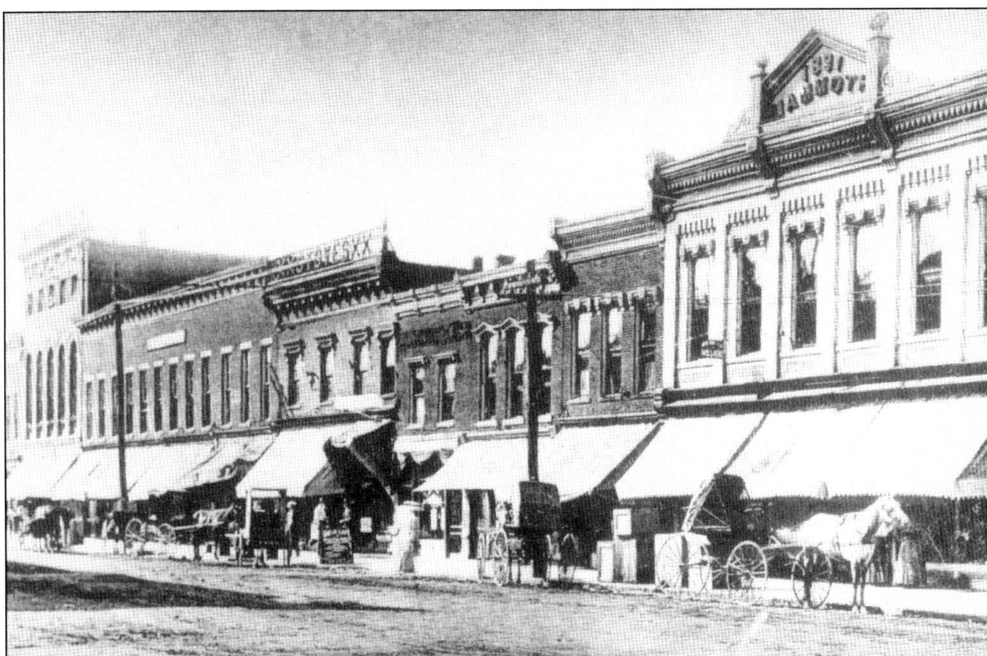

Originally known as Port William, Carrollton became the county seat when Carroll County was created in 1838. Main Street stretched east from the convergence of the Ohio and Kentucky Rivers, an area today known as Point Park. It grew into a bustling commercial district, with dry goods stores, drugstores, shoe stores, grocers, an opera house, several newspapers, and eventually movie theaters. Many of the buildings built in the mid-1800s remain, having survived a number of major floods. (Courtesy of Jim Fothergill.)

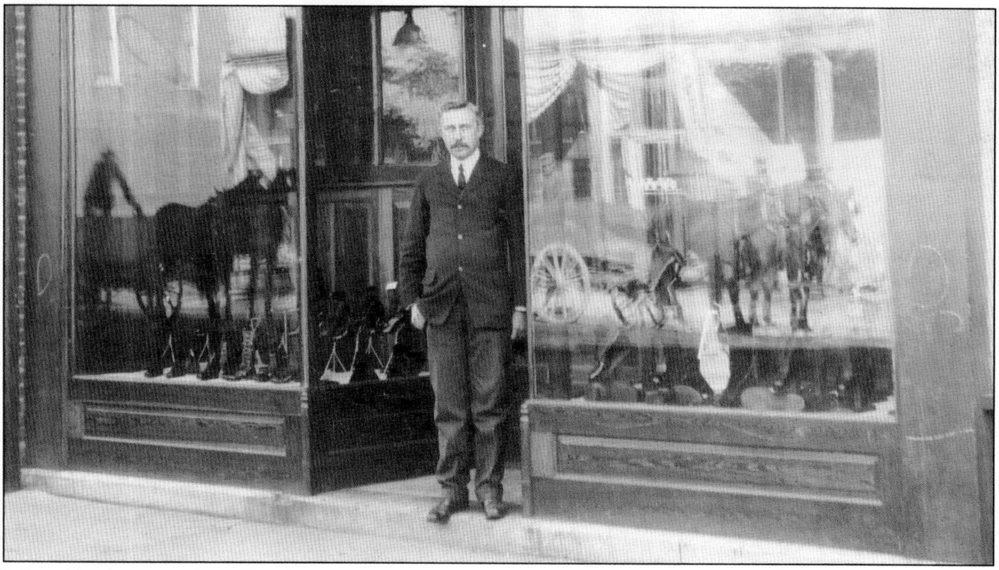

John Glauber stands in the doorway of his shoe store, founded in 1863. A cobbler himself, Glauber employed five others who manufactured and repaired shoes for his customers. During summers, when shoe sales slumped, employees offered on-site repair service for sewing machines as well. The store remained open through four generations, closing in 2007. (Courtesy of Carolyn Glauber.)

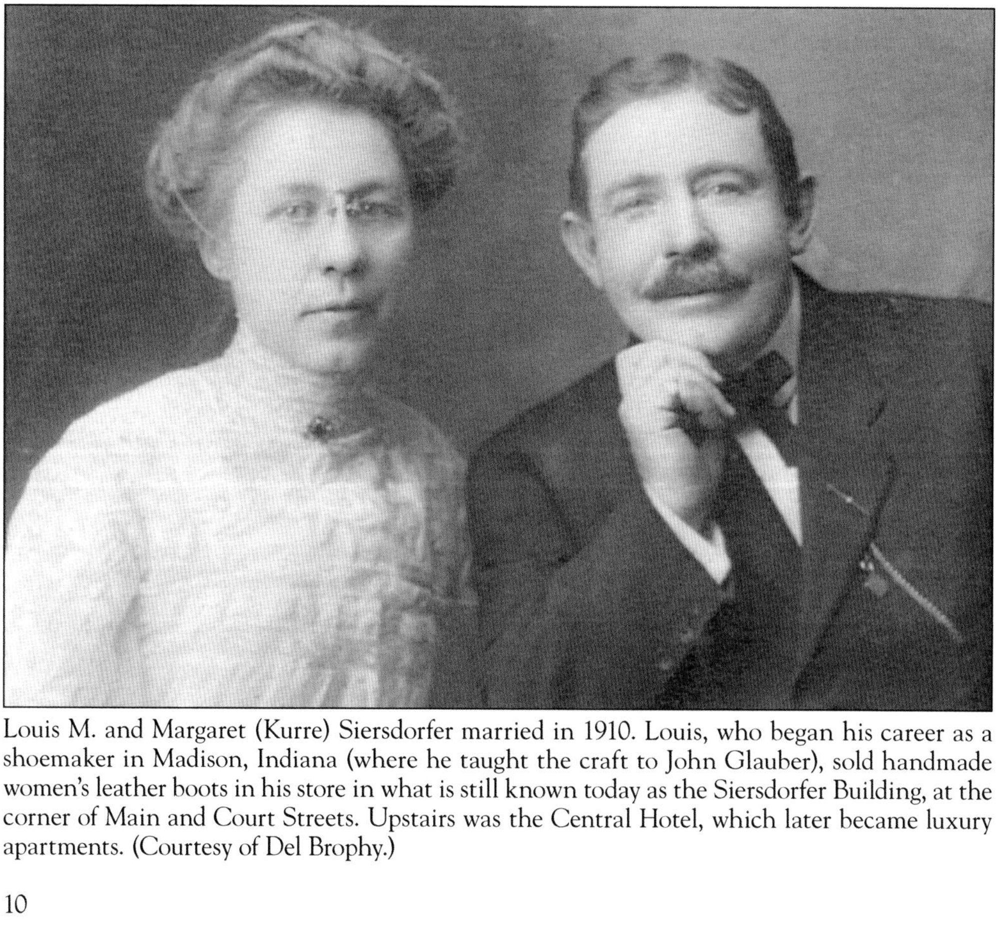

Louis M. and Margaret (Kurre) Siersdorfer married in 1910. Louis, who began his career as a shoemaker in Madison, Indiana (where he taught the craft to John Glauber), sold handmade women's leather boots in his store in what is still known today as the Siersdorfer Building, at the corner of Main and Court Streets. Upstairs was the Central Hotel, which later became luxury apartments. (Courtesy of Del Brophy.)

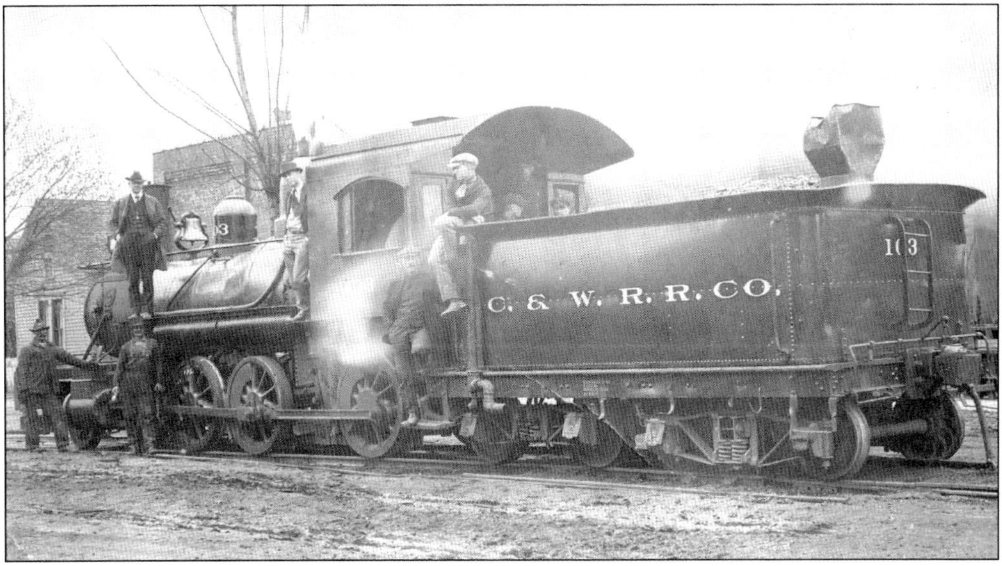

The Carrollton and Worthville Railroad was a 10-mile line running south and connecting the two cities. In Worthville, the line connected with the Louisville & Nashville Railroad. Completed in 1905, the line was used by freight cars to transport goods in either direction. Some folks jokingly referred to it as "Come and Wait" or "Careworn and Worthless," but jitneys, like the one below, also transported people and mail between the two cities eight times a day at the railroad's peak. Passenger service was suspended in 1926. In 1930, it was acquired by L&N and renamed the Carrollton Railroad. Portions of the line remain in use under CSX. (Both, courtesy of Darrell Maines.)

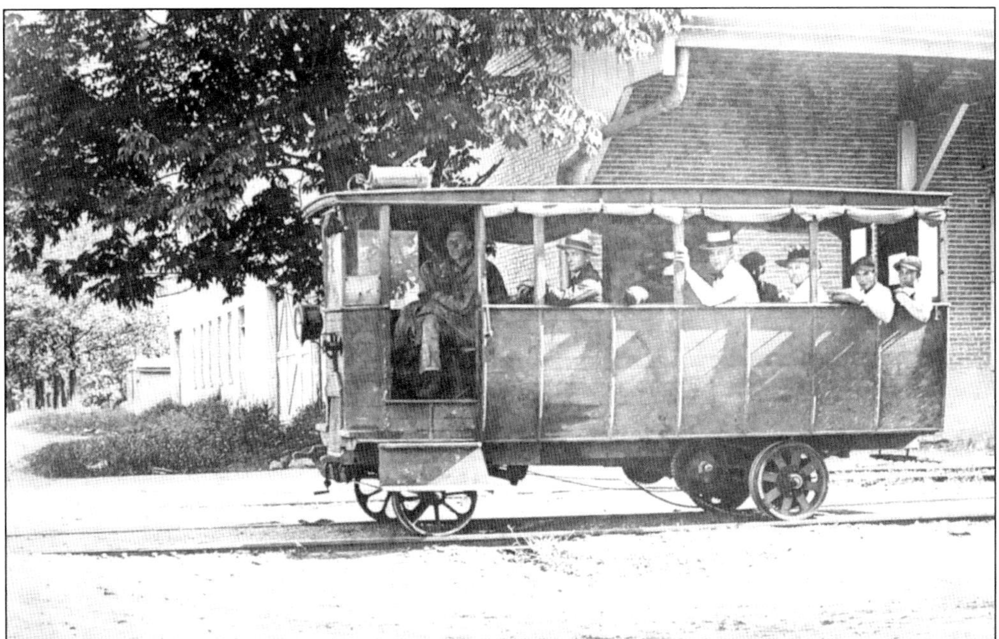

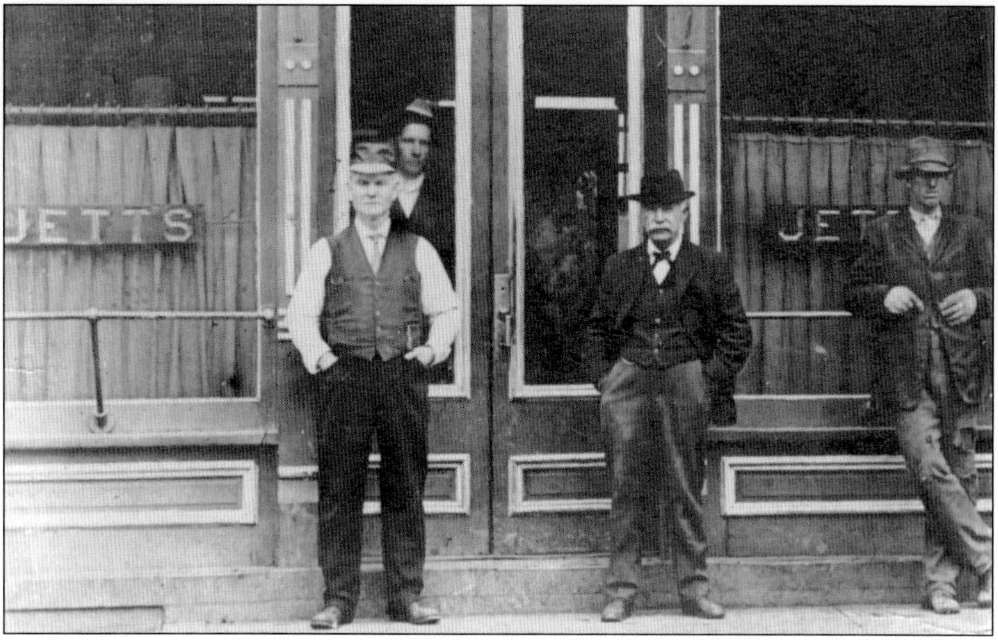

Brothers James and Joseph Jett stand in front of their saloon, once a fixture on the north side of Main Street in Carrollton. The Howe Brothers Department Store next door housed the Carrollton Opera House, on the second floor of the Howe Building. Both structures were destroyed by fire in 1977. (Courtesy of Jim Fothergill.)

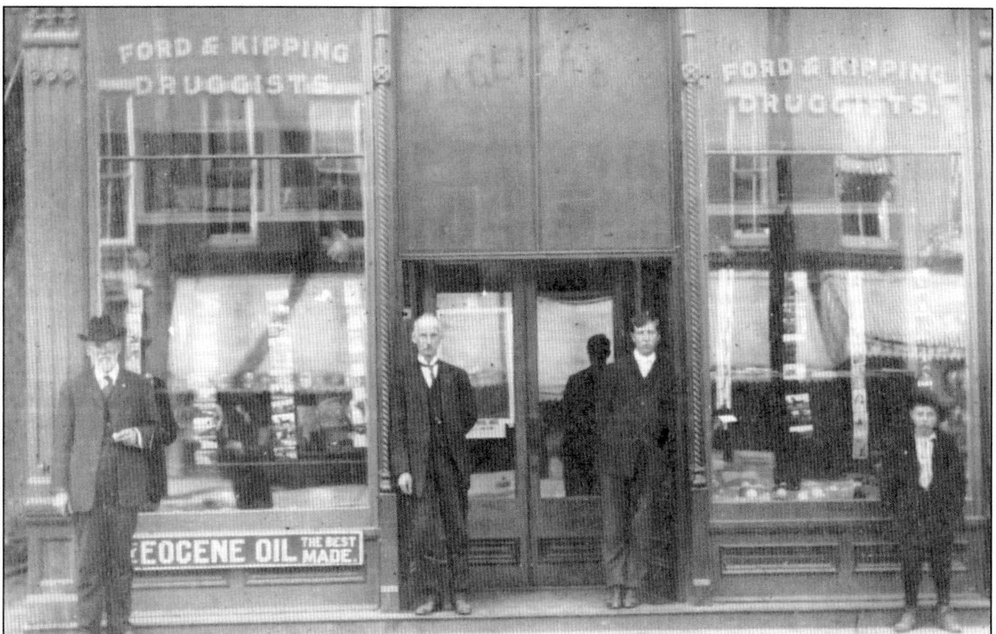

Waller E. Ford (left) and Charles T. Kipping (second from left) were the men behind Ford & Kipping Druggists, one of many drugstores that were located in downtown Carrollton through the decades. Here they pose with Edward Powers and an unidentified lad in front of the store, possibly on Fifth Street. (Courtesy of Kathryn Salyers Archives.)

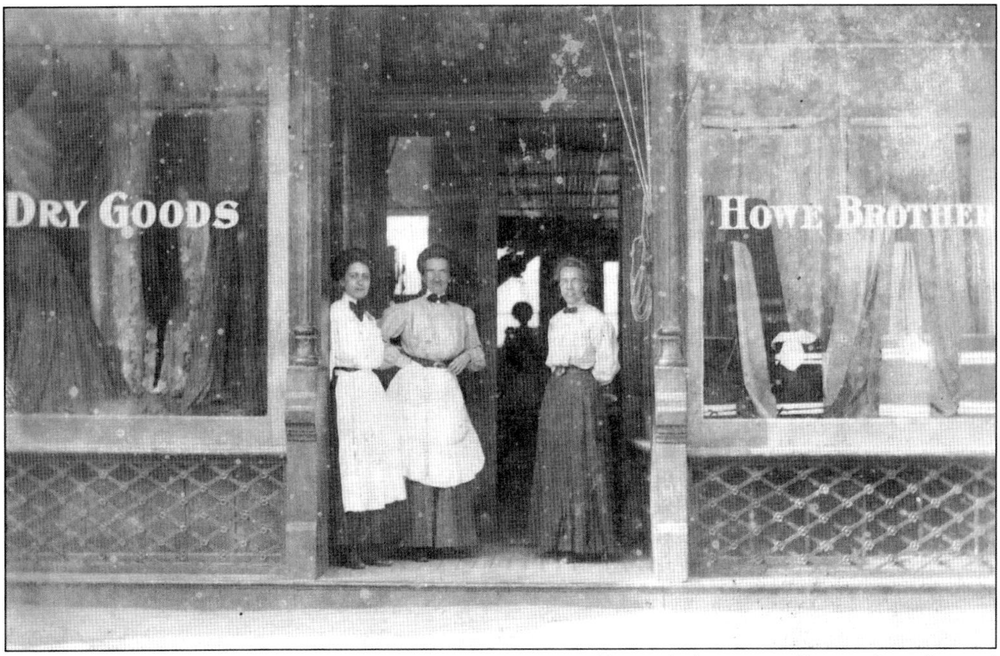

John Howe moved from Ireland to America and eventually settled in Carrollton, where he and other family members became prominent businessmen. A tailor by trade, he was well known for the quality of his men's suits. With his son William F. Howe, he branched out into banking and later founded the Carrollton National Bank with partner Henry M. Winslow. The Howe family also owned Carrollton Woolen Mills; in 1876, output at the mill was 700,000 yards of cloth and 50,000 pounds of yarn. After the elder Howe's death, his dry goods store was renamed Howe Brothers Department Store, which survived the 1937 flood only to be destroyed by arson later that year. (Both, courtesy of Ben Collett.)

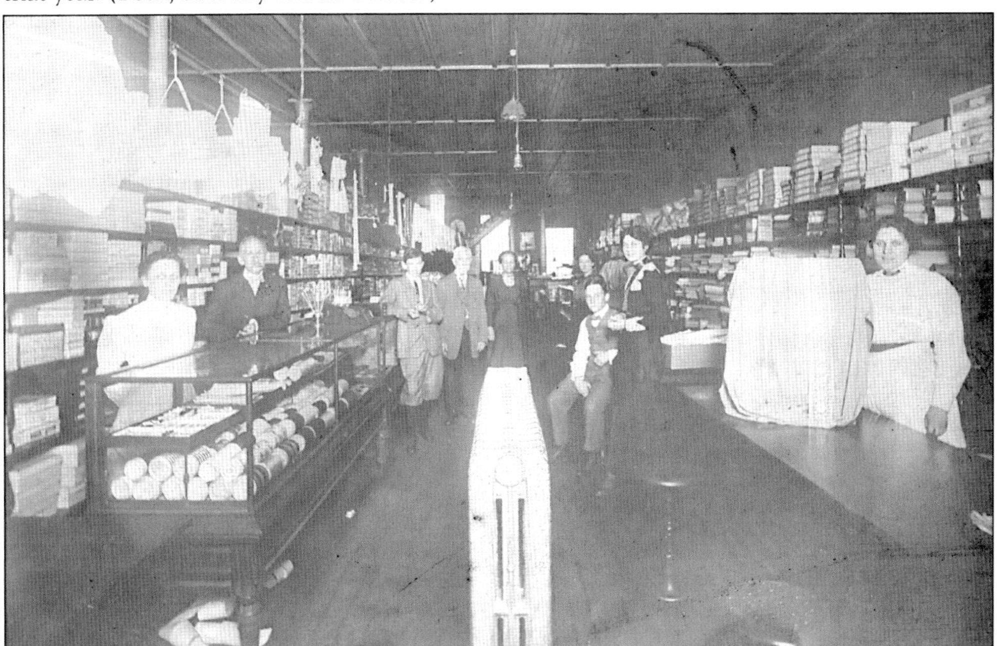

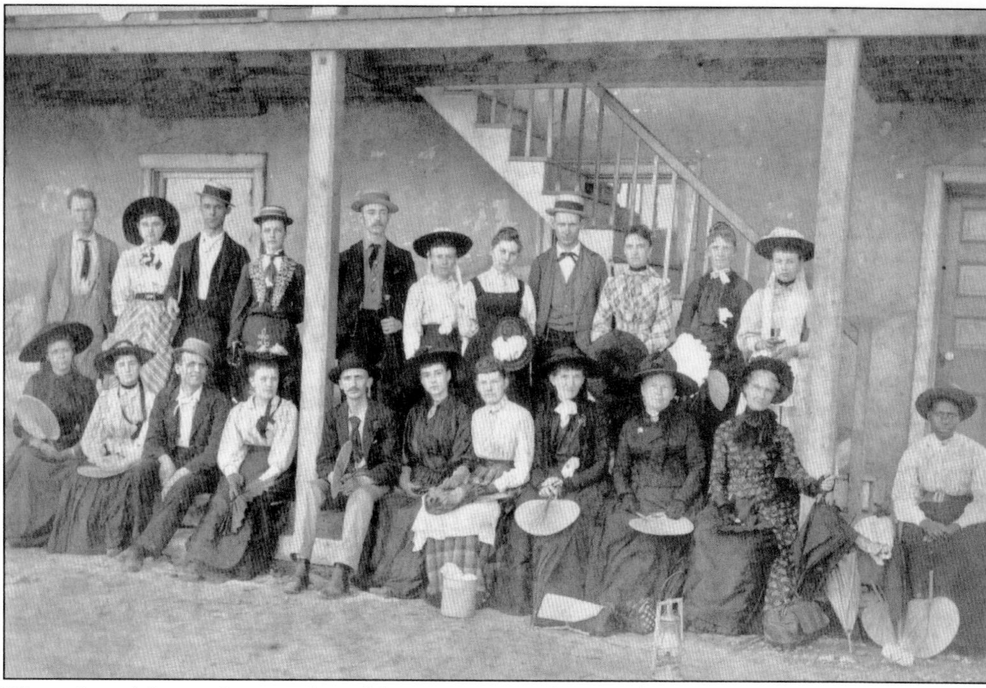

The rich and famous have gathered for a portrait at the Houghton House at Third and Main in Carrollton. They include writer James Tandy Ellis, seated third from left; members of the Masterson and Winslow families; and Maria Coburn (1819–1907), seated second from right—putting the date of the photograph at about the turn of the 20th century. The earliest inn was the Point House. (Courtesy of Kathryn Salyers Archives.)

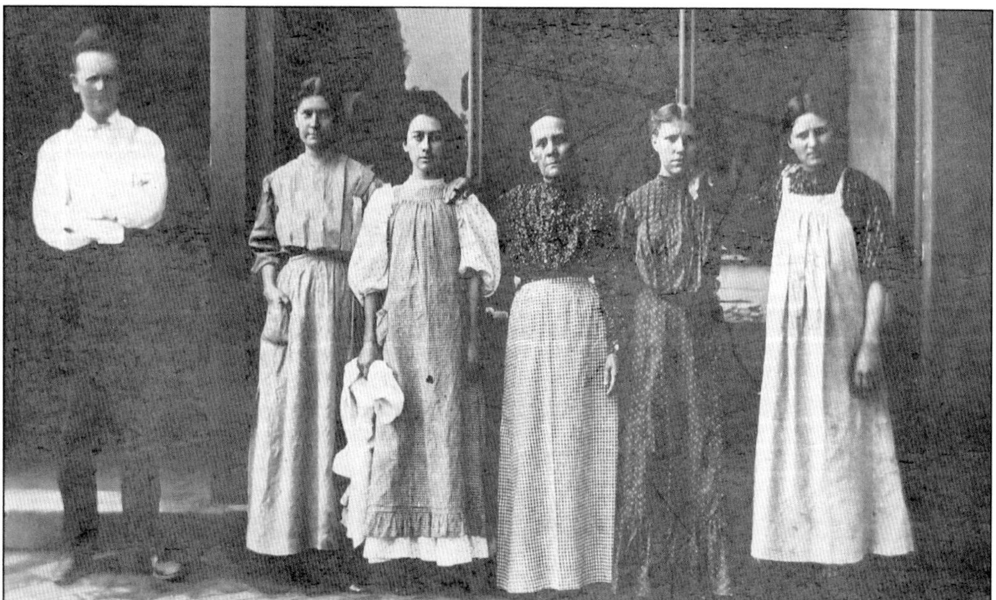

Lucinda "Cindy" Cole Dunn (third from left) worked at a laundry in Carrollton owned by a Mr. Vanmeter. From left to right are Georgia Scandrett, ? Dunn, Mrs. H. Grasmac, Lydia Russell, and Mary Hill. (Courtesy of Jean Dunn Yager.)

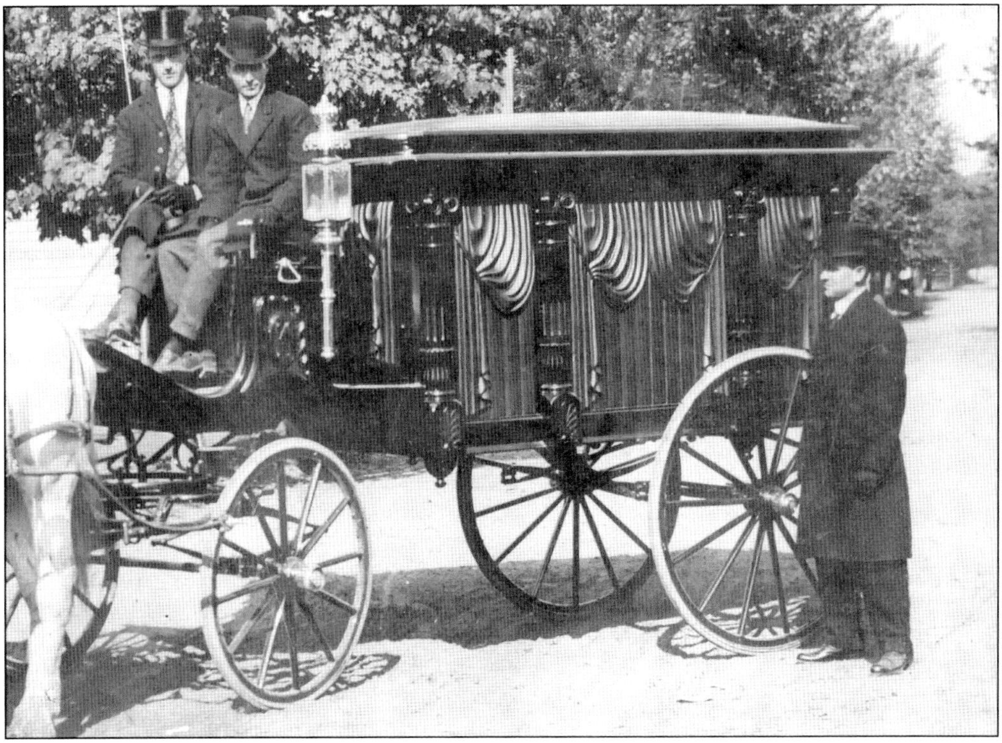

In 1907, Oscar Geier Kipping (right) took over the Kipping Funeral Home, established in 1863 by his father, Abraham F. Kipping, a German immigrant. Later, Oscar's son-in-law Carroll D. Graham became a partner. Kipping & Graham moved to Fifth Street. In 1974, employee James Dunn took over and renamed it Graham-Dunn. Also county coroner, Dunn owned it until he died in 2008. (Courtesy of Jane Graham Arnold.)

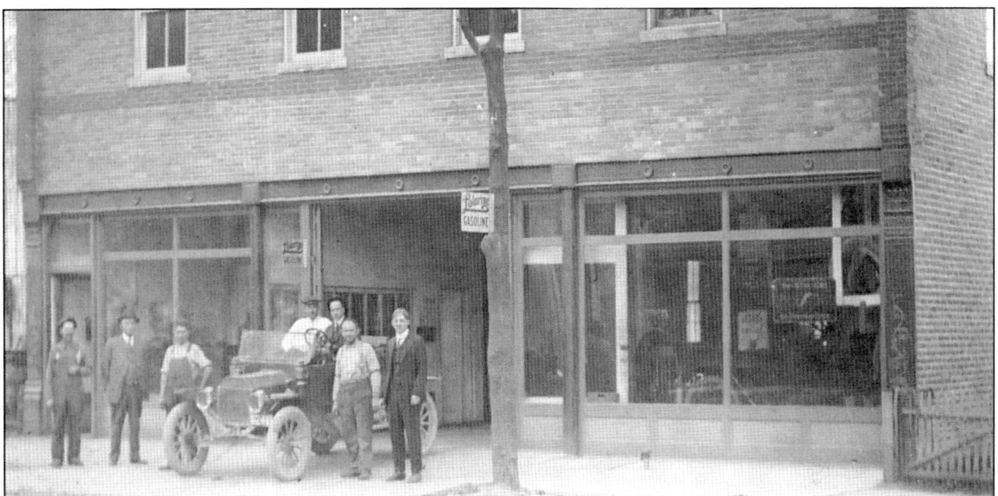

William Wood stands to the right of the driver of the automobile in this image of his garage. Wood was the first auto mechanic in Carrollton, and the photograph may show one of the first residents in the city to own a car. According to the 1920 census, Wood previously was a blacksmith. (Courtesy of Rebecca Morgan Tull.)

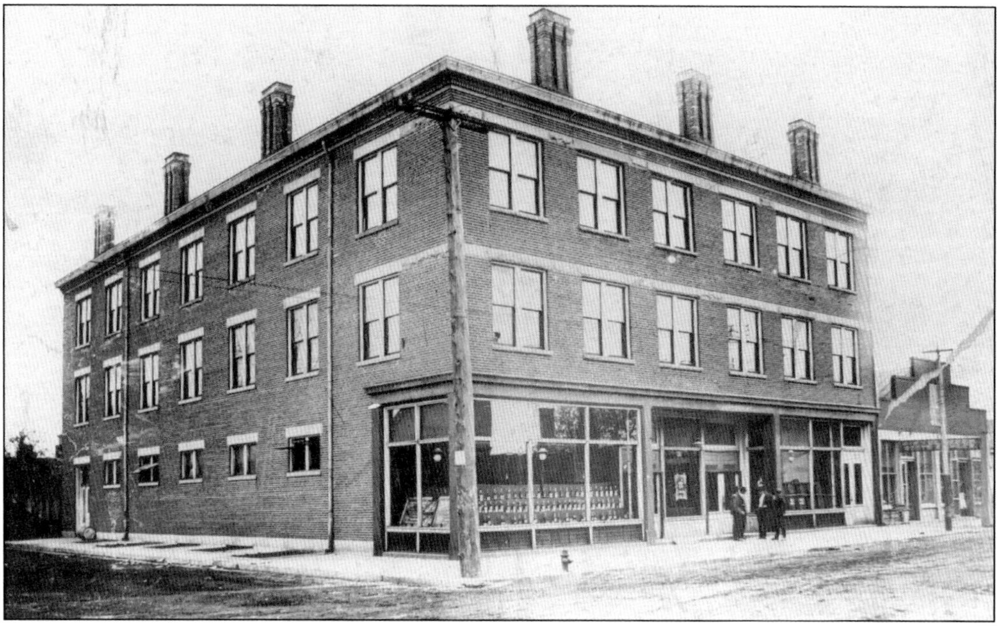

Tobacco tycoon Ralph Malcolm Barker's building at Fourth and Main Streets housed a liquor store on the first floor and the Barker Telephone Exchange (Carrollton's early phone service, which Barker brought to town) on the third. At right is John Glauber's shoe store. (Courtesy of Don Mougey.)

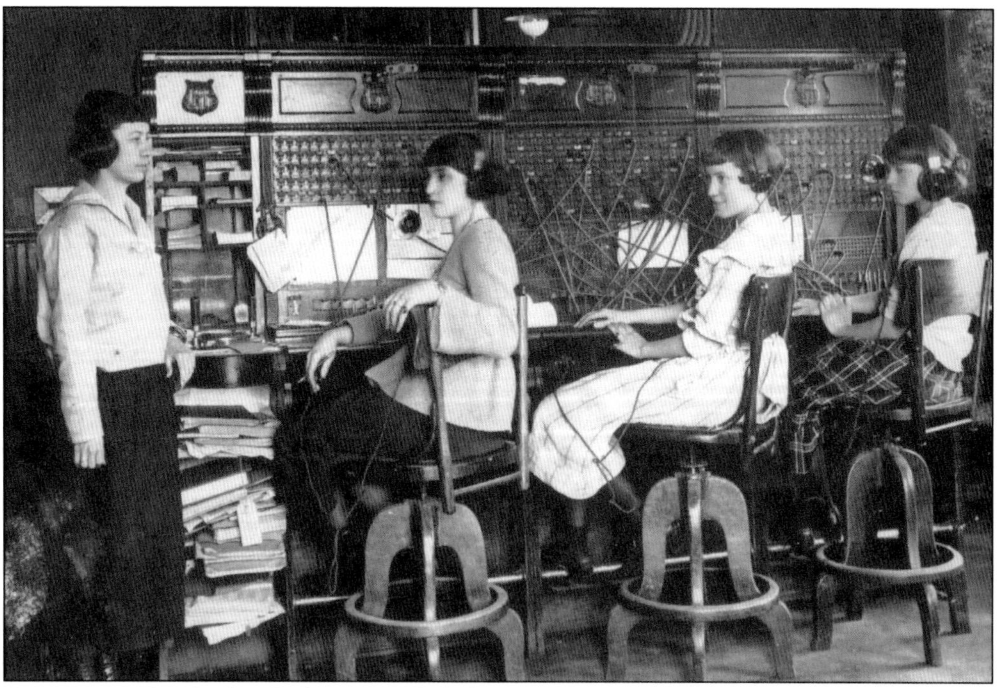

Operators in the "Barker Exchange" included, from left to right, Martha Bonta, Irene DeMint, Marie Steele, and Marie Howe, who later owned the Richland Theater. The Barker Building was home to the Lerman's department store in the mid-1900s and became home to Jefferson Community College's Carrollton campus in 1993. (Courtesy of Linda Chandler Banks.)

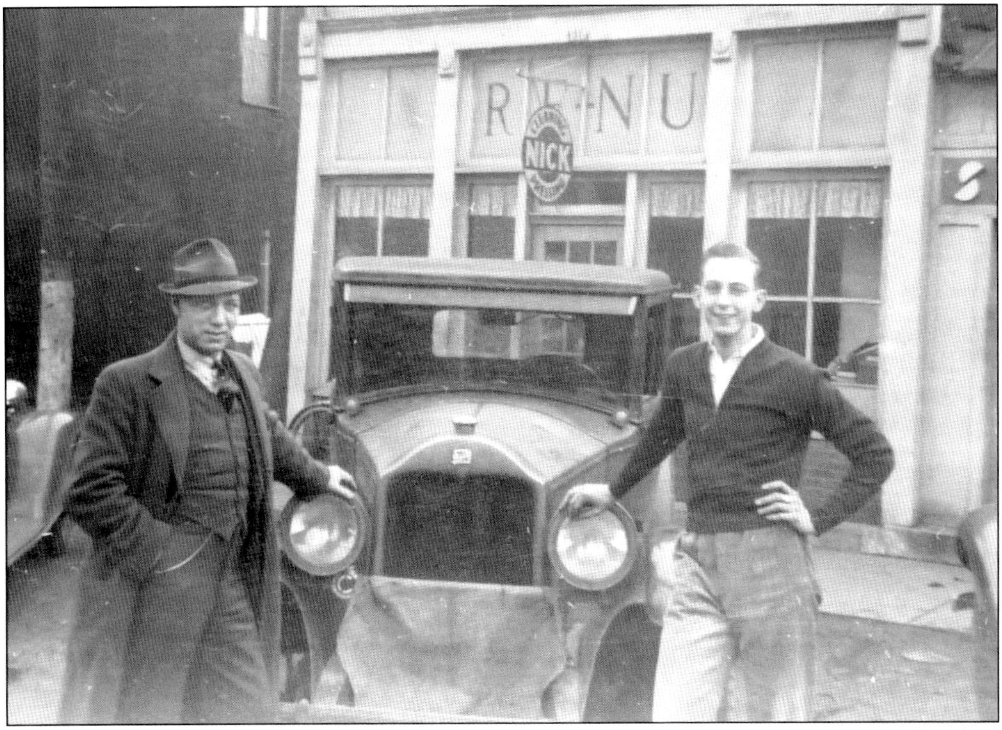

John Wessel (left) and Enos Baglan pose in front of Nick's Cleaners, owned by Enos's brother, who later was also president of Carrollton Federal Savings and Loan. Enos worked for Nick; in his US Army enlistment papers from World War II, his given occupation is "laundering, cleaning, dyeing, and pressing apparel." (Courtesy of Amy Baglan.)

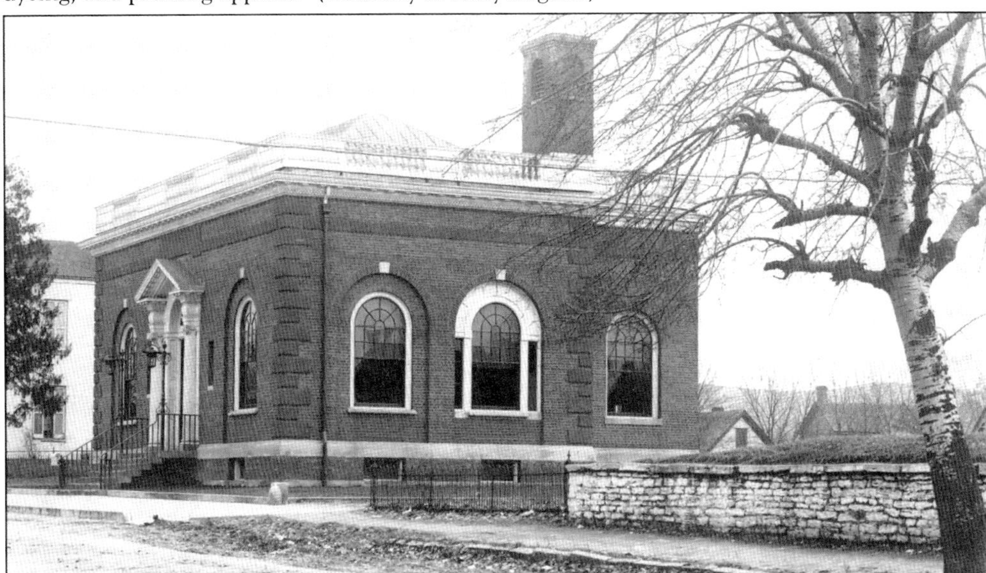

Built between 1901 and 1902, the Carrollton Post Office was constructed on the site of what had been known as the Lewis House, later owned by the Darling family, who sold the house and lot to the federal government. Still in use today, this was the city's first permanent postal facility. (Courtesy of Darrell Maines.)

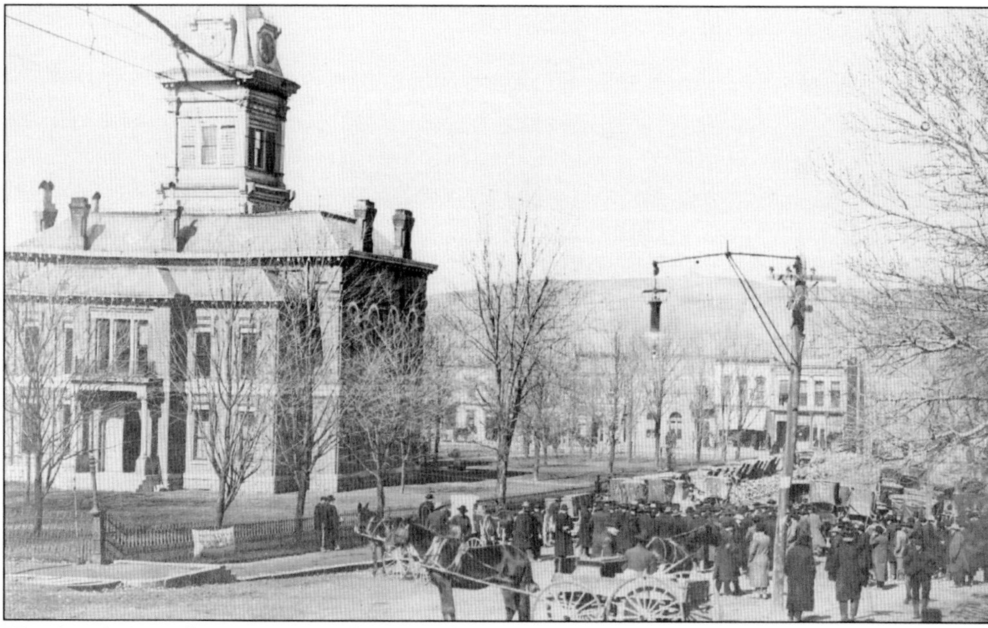

The fourth Carroll County Courthouse in downtown Carrollton was built in 1884, with a stone jail being added on the southwest corner of the lawn in 1899. This photograph shows an electric streetlight. The Jett Brothers brought gas streetlights to downtown in the mid-1800s; they then built an electric generating plant for Carrollton, along with 26 arc lamps, in 1897. (Courtesy of Darrell Maines.)

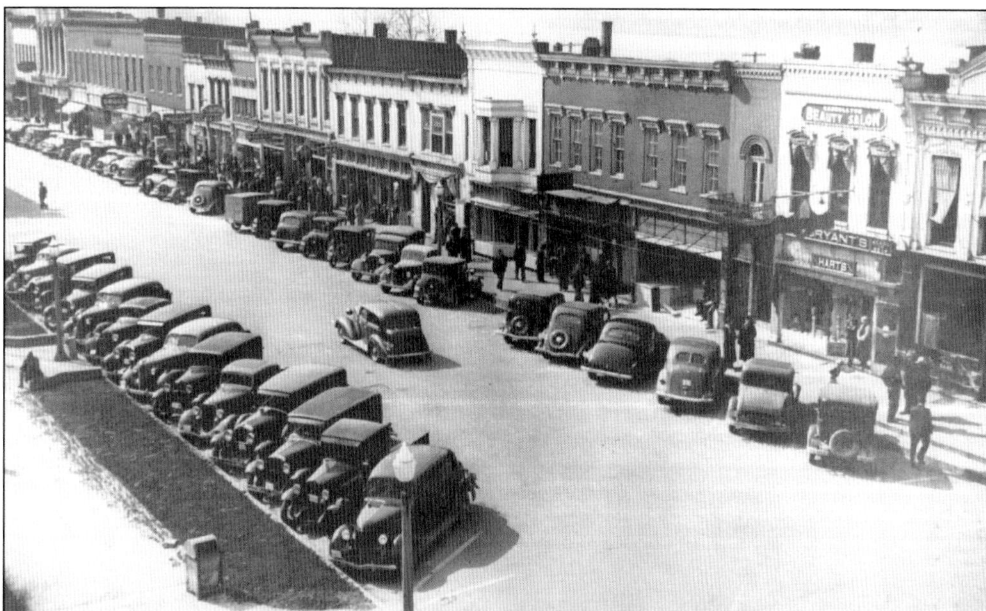

Downtown Carrollton about 1930 was a bustling shopping district. This image shows Main Street before the devastating flood of 1937. At right is the Carrollton National Bank, founded by Henry Winslow and John Howe, with Howe's department store near the far left. After a 1937 fire, the Howe Building was rebuilt and Marie Howe opened the Richland Theater there. (Courtesy of Darrell Maines.)

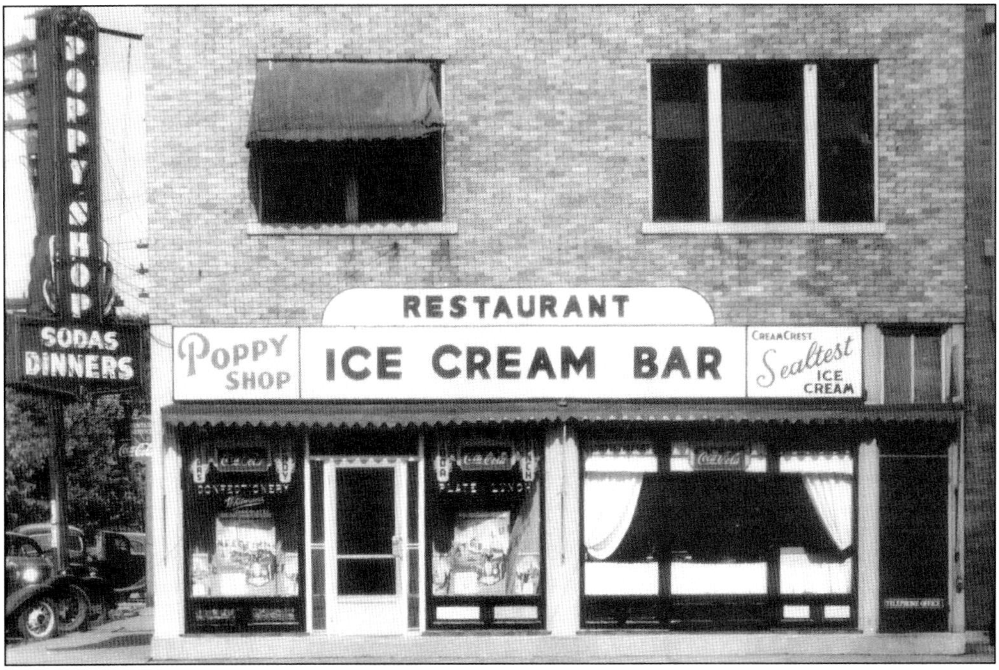

The Poppy Shop restaurant, confectionery, and ice cream bar was a popular spot on the corner of Fifth and Main Streets. Later, Bessie Boulton, owner of the Powder Puff Beauty Shop on Main Street, and Lelia Long turned the store into the Be-Leah Shop, a women's boutique. Bessie and husband Warren also operated the *Gallatin County News* in the 1930s and the *News-Democrat* in the 1940s. (Courtesy of Darrell Maines.)

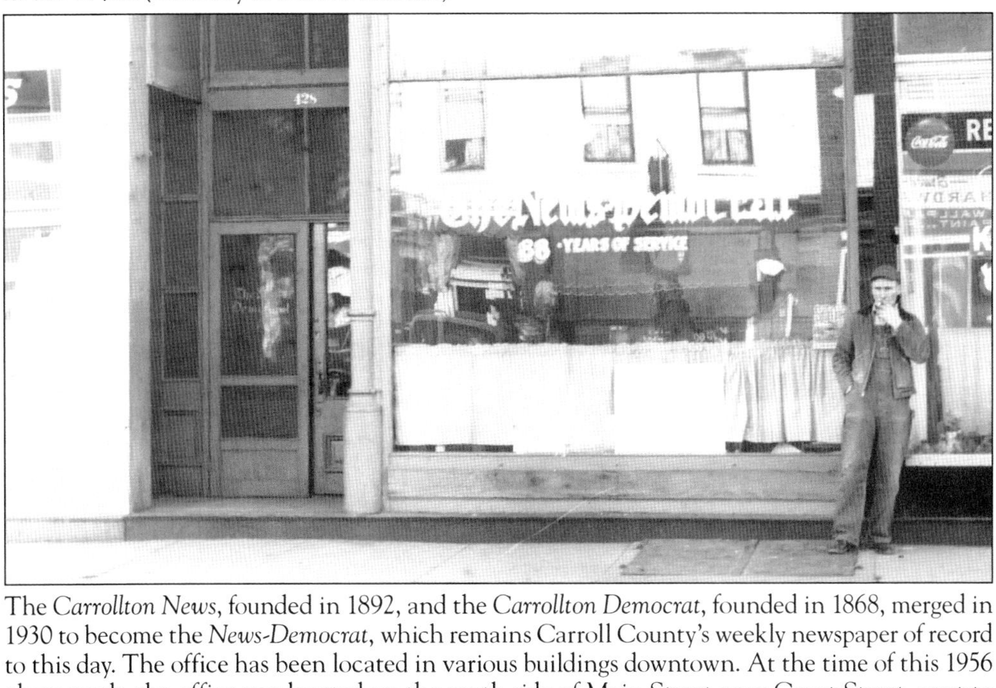

The *Carrollton News*, founded in 1892, and the *Carrollton Democrat*, founded in 1868, merged in 1930 to become the *News-Democrat*, which remains Carroll County's weekly newspaper of record to this day. The office has been located in various buildings downtown. At the time of this 1956 photograph, the office was located on the south side of Main Street near Court Street, next to the K-Dell Restaurant. (Courtesy of *News-Democrat*.)

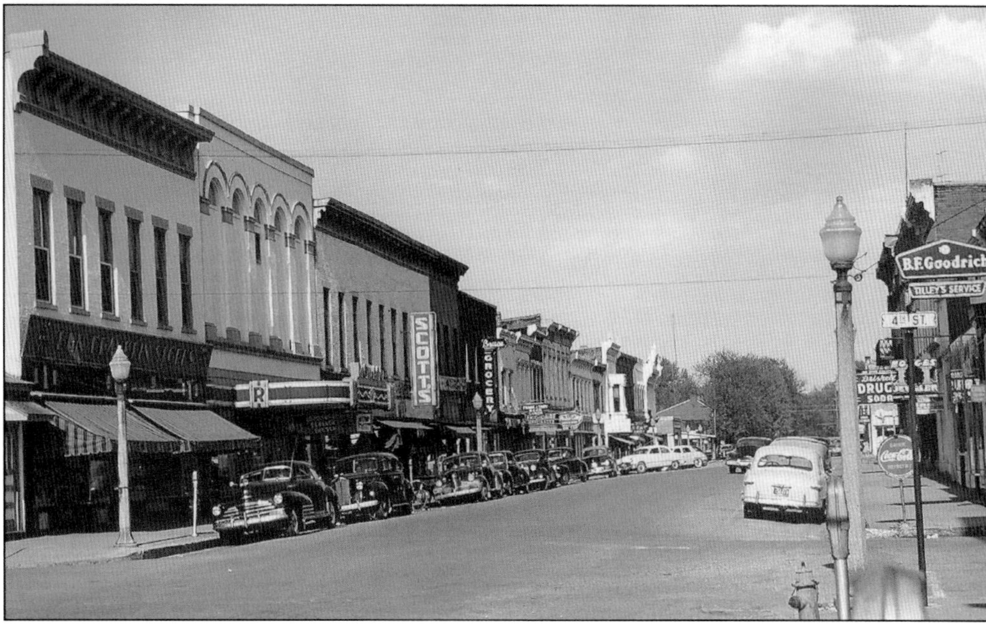

This is another view of downtown Carrollton about 1953. At far left is the Ben Franklin Store next to the Richland Theater, which is showing *City Beneath the Sea*. Both buildings were destroyed in 1977 by a fire that was started, according to the *News-Democrat*, by children playing with matches. The lot now stands empty. (Courtesy of David Renschler and Betty's Collectibles.)

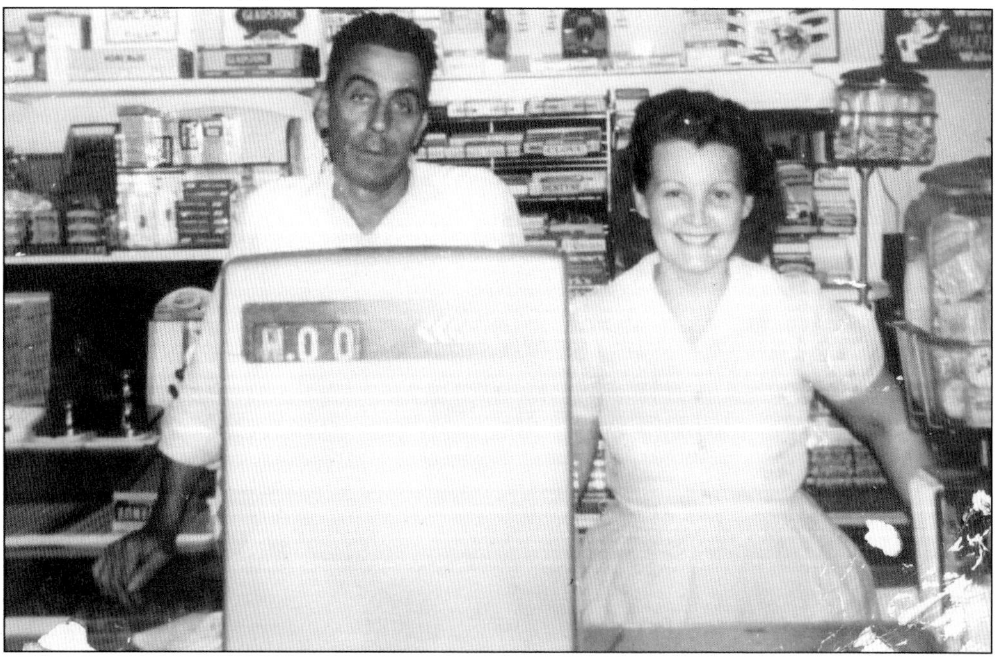

Forrest and Corrine Welch established Welch's Riverside Restaurant two blocks east on the north side of Main Street. Forrest's sister Della Kendall was proprietor of the K-Dell, which was another popular eatery on Main Street. Welch's is still the place where locals congregate daily for diner-style breakfasts, buffet lunches, and dinners. The Welches' nephew Ernest "Junior" Welch and his family manage the restaurant. (Courtesy of Welch's Riverside Restaurant.)

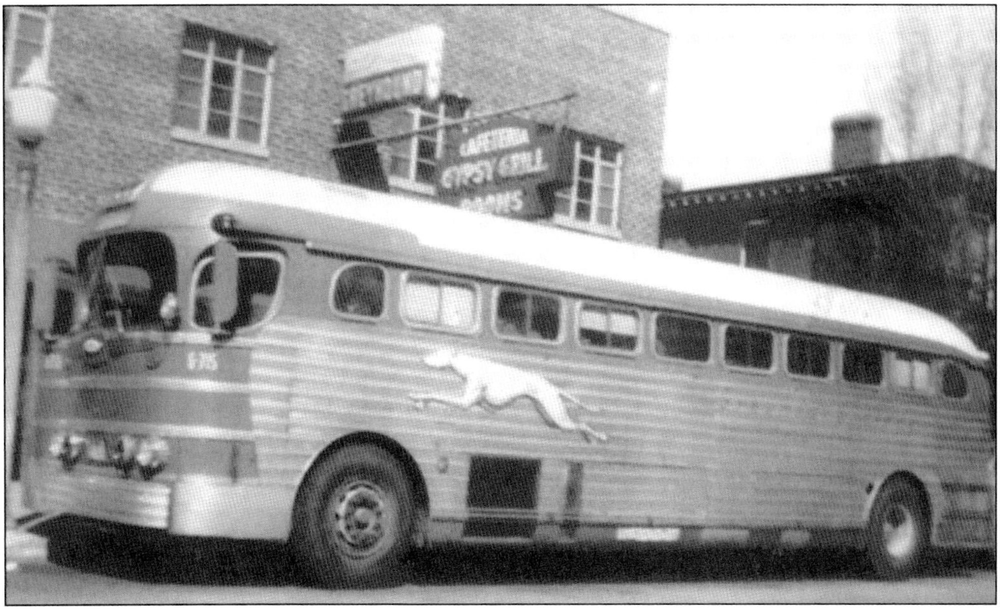

The Gypsy Grill was a popular eatery located on the north side of Highland Avenue, between Fifth and Sixth Streets. The restaurant also served as the Greyhound bus stop into at least the late 1960s. The business included a downstairs banquet room. Owners Sy and Rosemary Duvall bought the restaurant in 1940 from Nellie Lee, who also served as the *News-Democrat*'s first female editor. (Courtesy of Darrell Maines.)

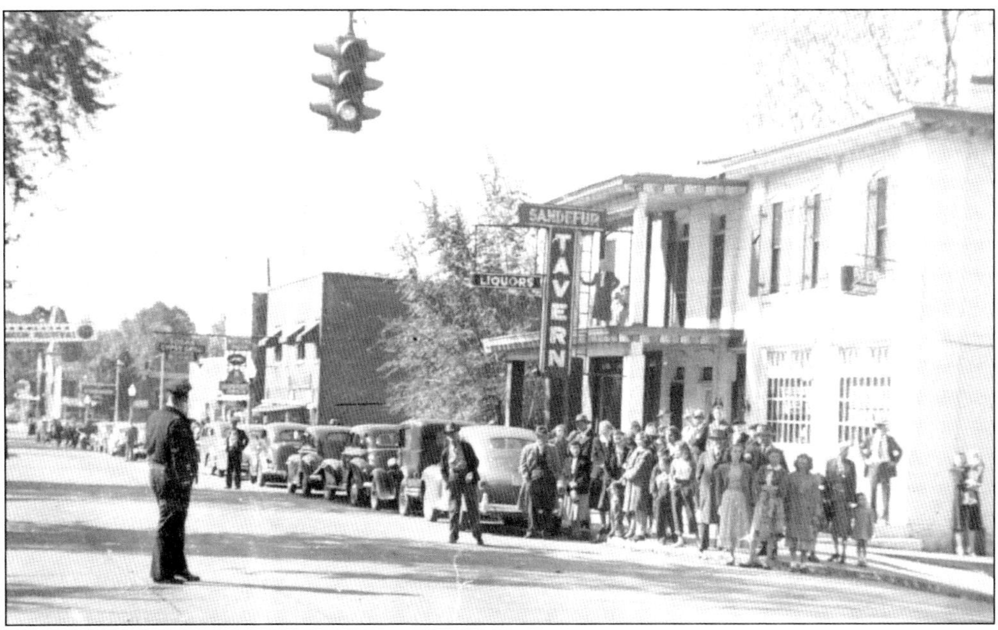

A crowd gathers in front of the Sandefur Tavern, waiting for the start of the 1948 Carrollton Tobacco Festival parade down Highland Avenue. The parade remains the highlight of an event (now known as the Carroll County Tobacco Festival) that celebrates the county's agricultural heritage. (Courtesy of Amy Baglan.)

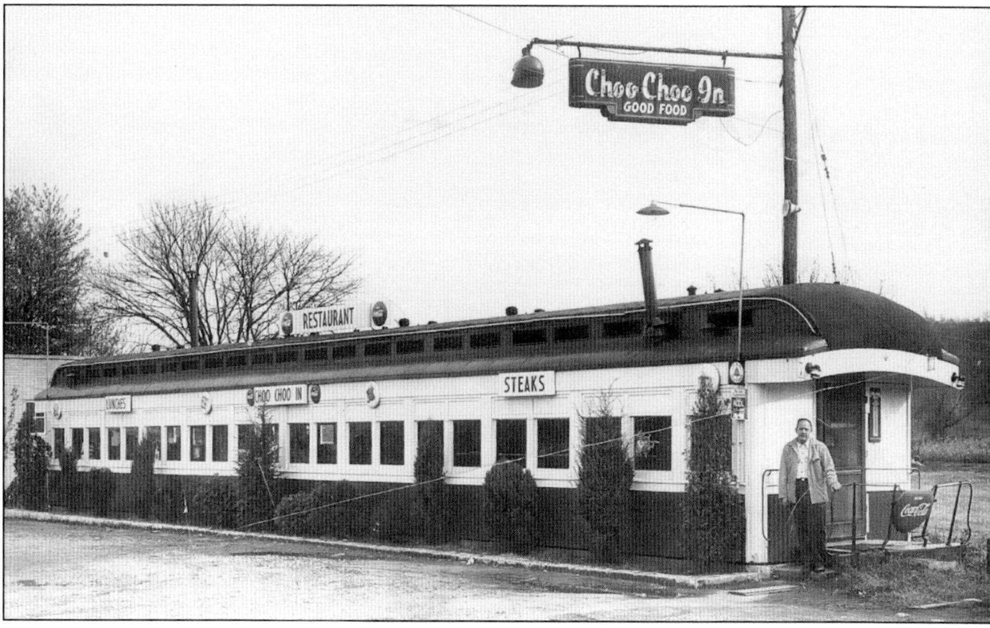

Proprietor J.E. McHatton stands outside his Choo Choo In diner in November 1951. Originally a 68-seat passenger car built and put into service by the Louisville & Nashville (L&N) Railroad in 1907, the structure came to rest on Highland Avenue, where it became a well-known eatery. Below is an interior shot with McHatton and employees Emma Hicks (left) and Lola Stockdale. It later became Katrina's Diner. (Both, courtesy of Welch's Riverside Restaurant.)

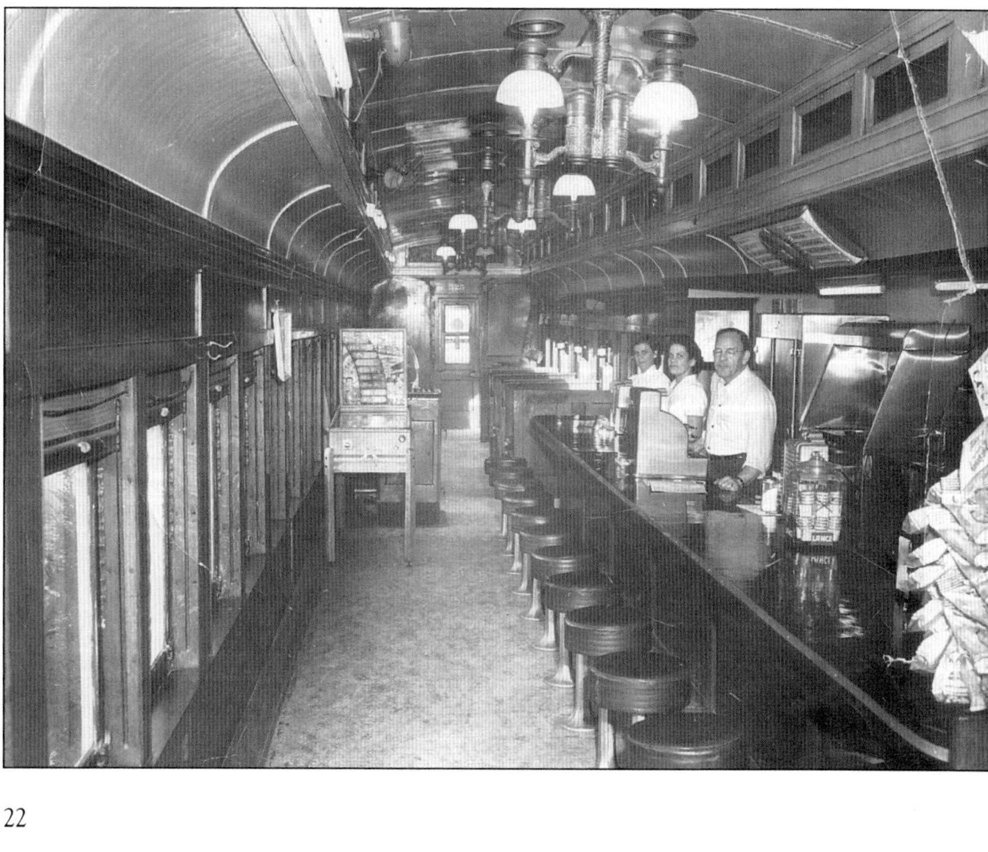

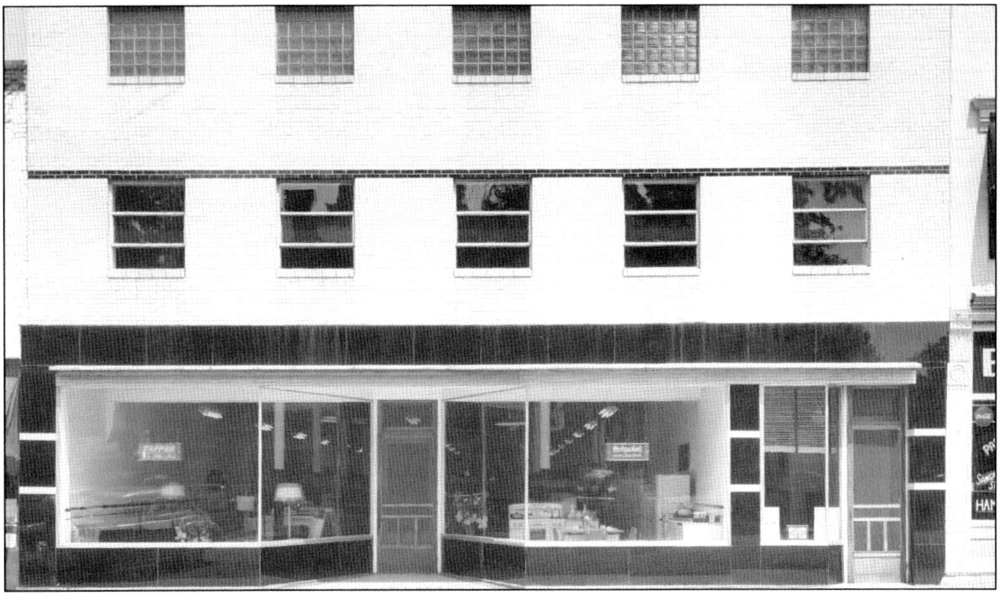

Another thriving downtown business was Wood's furniture and appliance store, located on Fifth Street across from the county courthouse. Originally Grobmyer Livery Stables, in the 1950s the building housed Wood's, which sold stoves, refrigerators, hardware items, and bicycles on the first floor, and an array of household furniture on the second. Today known as McNeal's, the store is owned by Brad McNeal and sells mostly the same wares as Wood's. (Both, courtesy of Carroll County Public Library.)

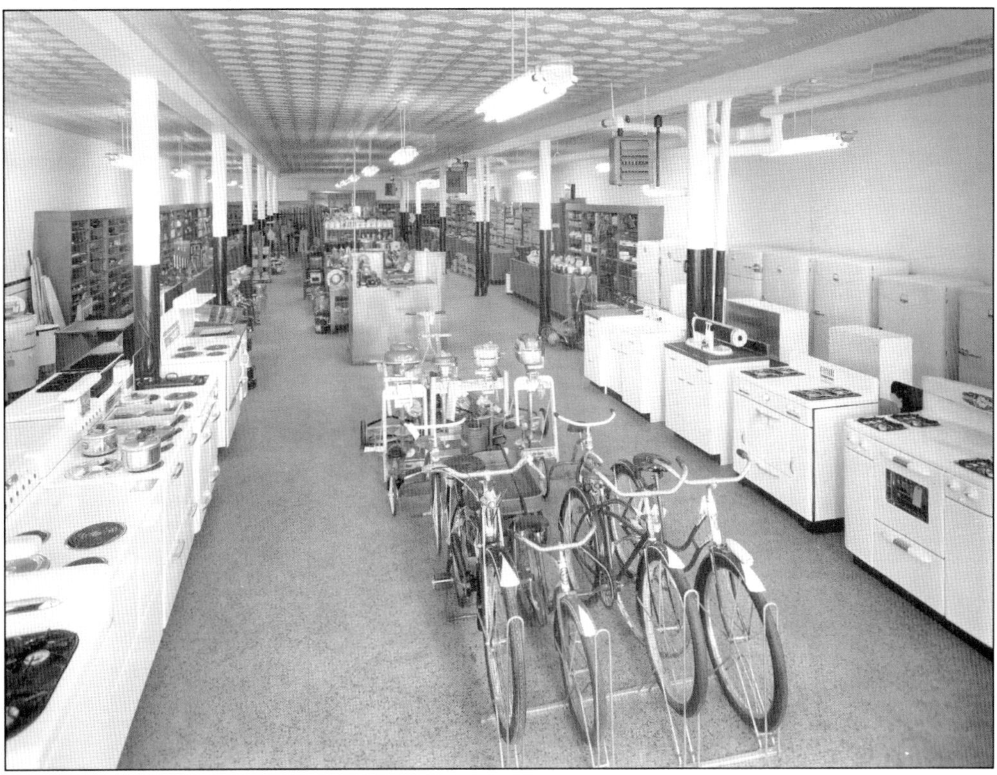

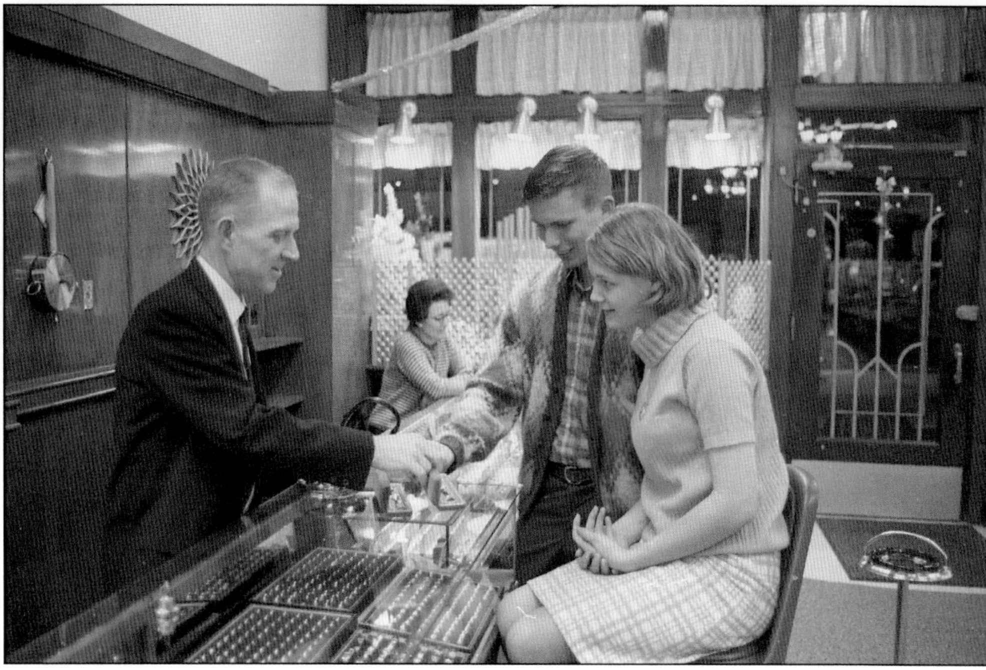

William Hodges waits on an unidentified young couple in Hodges Jewelers in 1967, after the store moved to 422 Main Street. Hodges ran the store from 1948 until his death in 1972; his widow, Jean (now Atchinson), ran the store until it closed in 1978. (Courtesy of *Madison Courier.*)

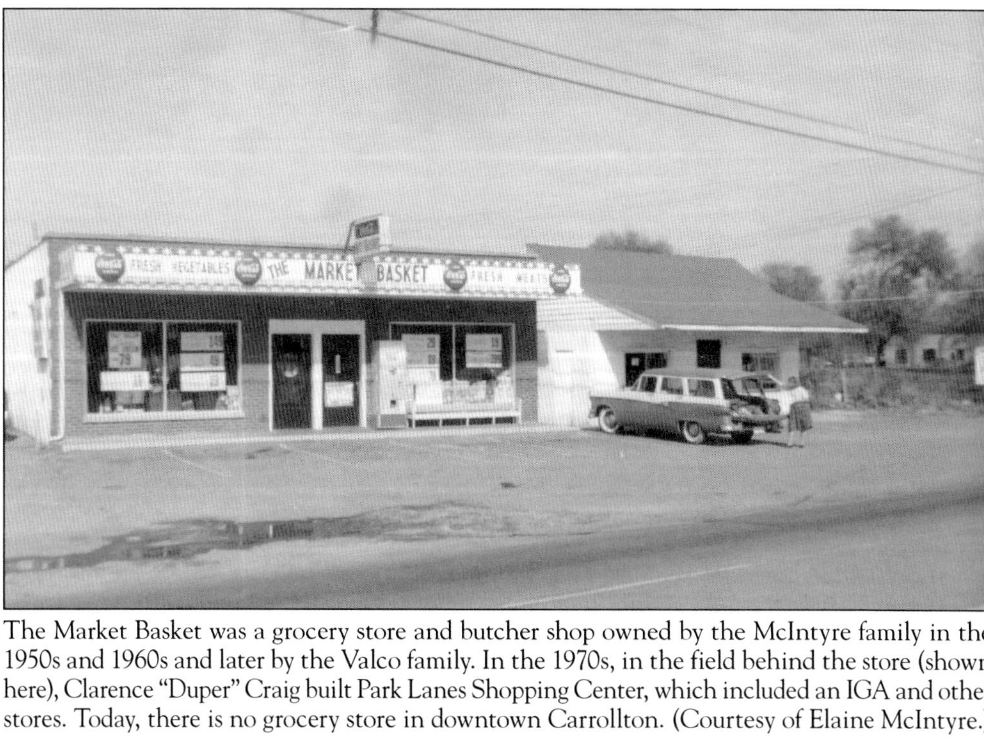

The Market Basket was a grocery store and butcher shop owned by the McIntyre family in the 1950s and 1960s and later by the Valco family. In the 1970s, in the field behind the store (shown here), Clarence "Duper" Craig built Park Lanes Shopping Center, which included an IGA and other stores. Today, there is no grocery store in downtown Carrollton. (Courtesy of Elaine McIntyre.)

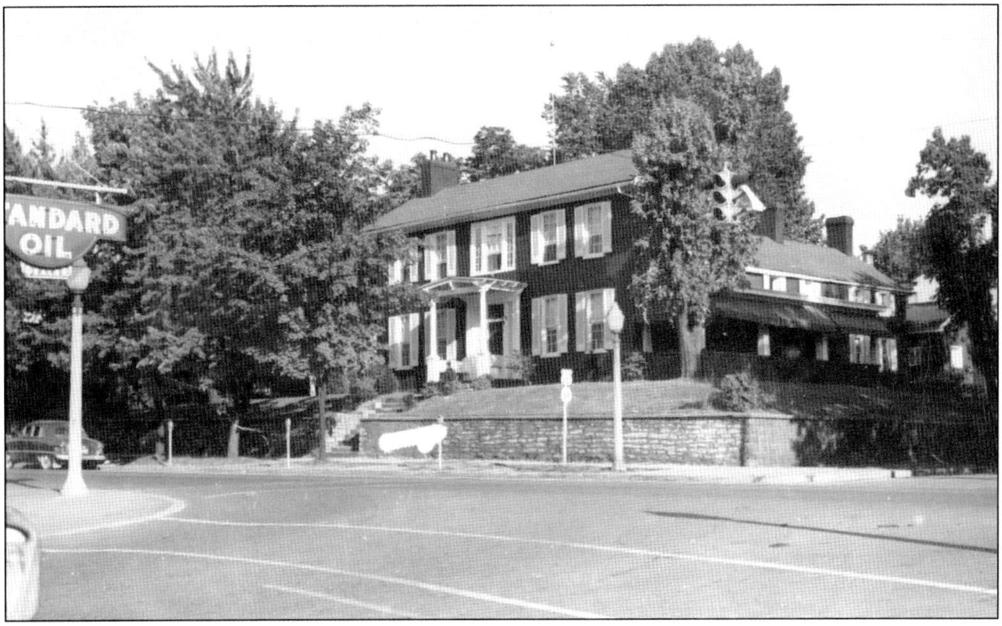

Many of downtown Carrollton's stately homes were razed to make room for businesses. Among them was this house at the corner of Fifth Street and Highland Avenue, owned by a Dr. Ryan, whose medical office was on Main Street. Today, the lot is level with Highland Avenue and is the location of a Speedway gas station and convenience store. (Courtesy of Gary Ford.)

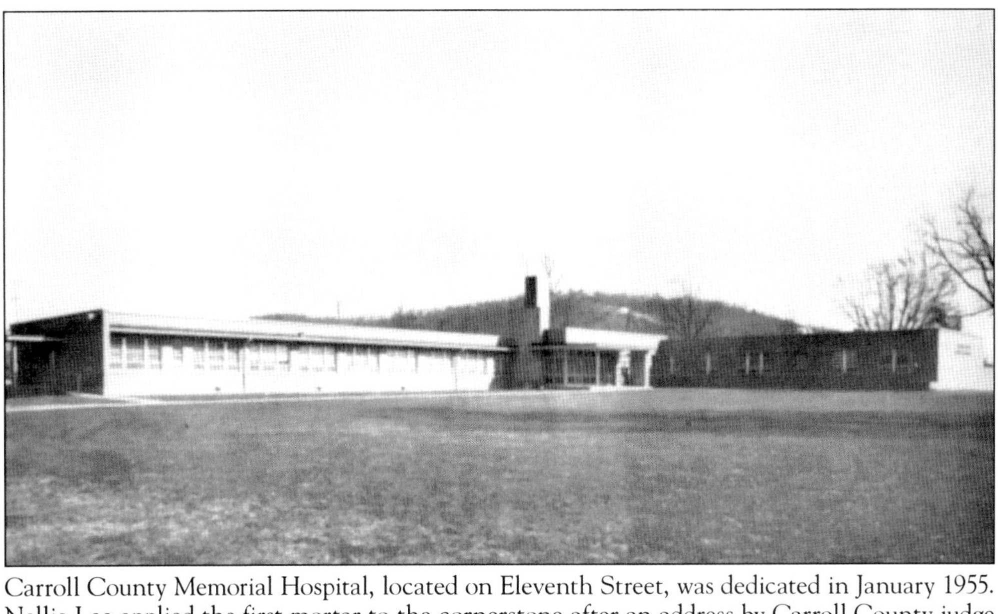

Carroll County Memorial Hospital, located on Eleventh Street, was dedicated in January 1955. Nellie Lee applied the first mortar to the cornerstone after an address by Carroll County judge Luther Fothergill. Stanley Grobmyer was the master of ceremonies for the event, which was attended by about 500 people. (Courtesy of Kathryn Salyers Archives.)

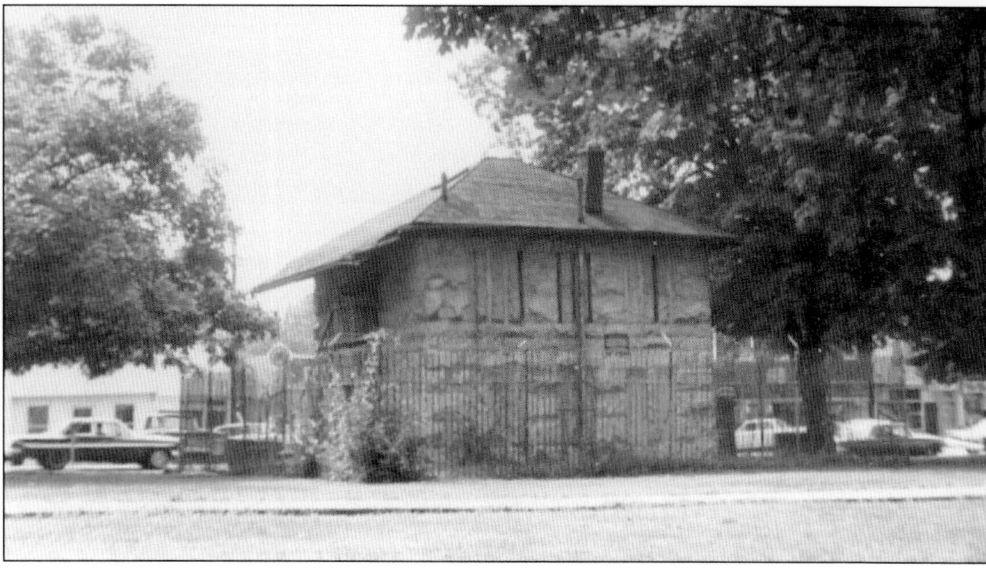

Facing Court Street, the Old Stone Jail was built in 1880 and replaced the first jail, which had been constructed in 1799 near what is now Point Park. Deemed the "best prison in northern Kentucky," the two-story limestone building was used until 1969, when it no longer met state standards. Today, it houses Carrollton's Main Street Program office and is open to tourists. (Courtesy of Amy Baglan.)

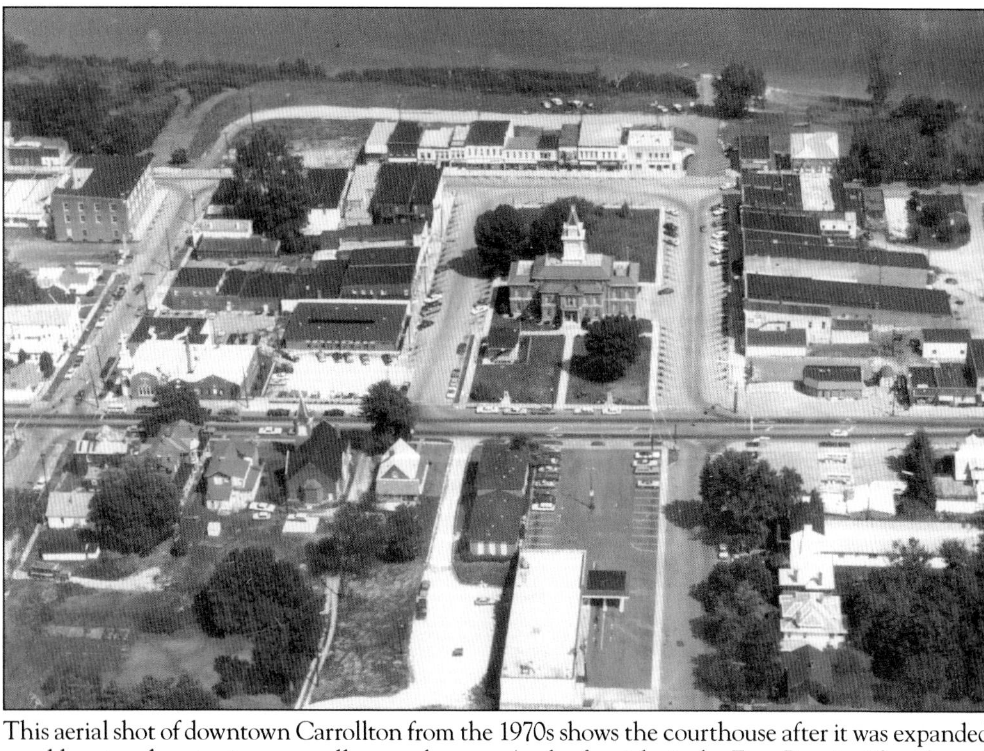

This aerial shot of downtown Carrollton from the 1970s shows the courthouse after it was expanded to add east and west wings, as well as an elevator. At the far right is the First Baptist Church, and next to that is the first permanent library, facing the Old Stone Jail. The library was renovated and expanded in 2006. (Courtesy of Carroll County Public Library.)

Two

OUT IN THE COUNTY

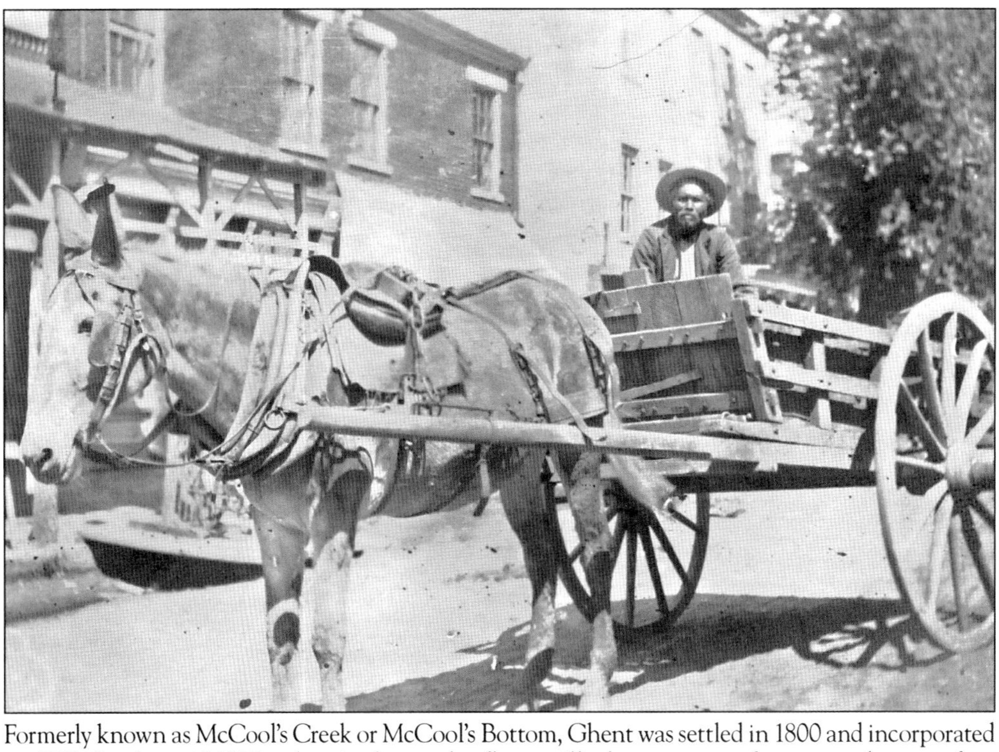

Formerly known as McCool's Creek or McCool's Bottom, Ghent was settled in 1800 and incorporated in 1852. In the mid-1870s, the city boasted a flour mill, three grocers, four general stores, four physicians, a druggist, and a population of 400. Early transportation included wagons like this one, driven by Sim Dillard, a Ghent farmer who is said to have also delivered the *Louisville Courier*. Ghent remains the county's second-largest city and is home to several industries. (Courtesy of City of Ghent, James Bond Collection.)

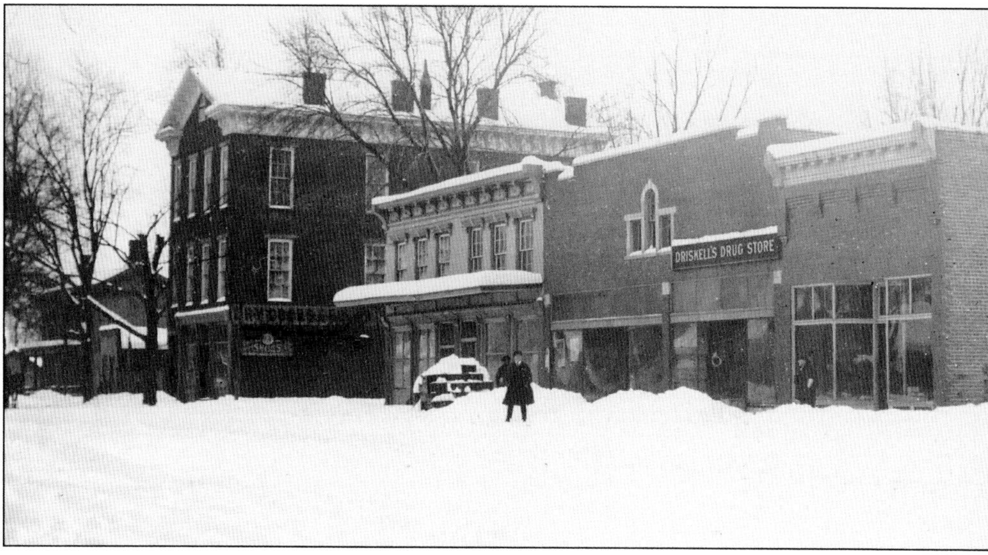

While Ghent thrived as a city in the late 1800s and early 1900s, it later was ravaged by fires that destroyed many of the buildings that lined Main Cross Street, shown above. Several of the buildings in this photograph (taken after a heavy snowstorm) were destroyed in a 1915 fire. The building below, which belonged to the Independent Order of Odd Fellows, was not damaged by the fire. It was, however, weakened by the loss of structures next to it, and collapsed shortly after the blaze. The Odd Fellows was one of a number of fraternal organizations with lodges in Ghent, which also included the Knights of Pythias and the Improved Order of Red Men. (Above, courtesy of Darrell Maines; below, courtesy of City of Ghent, James Bond Collection.)

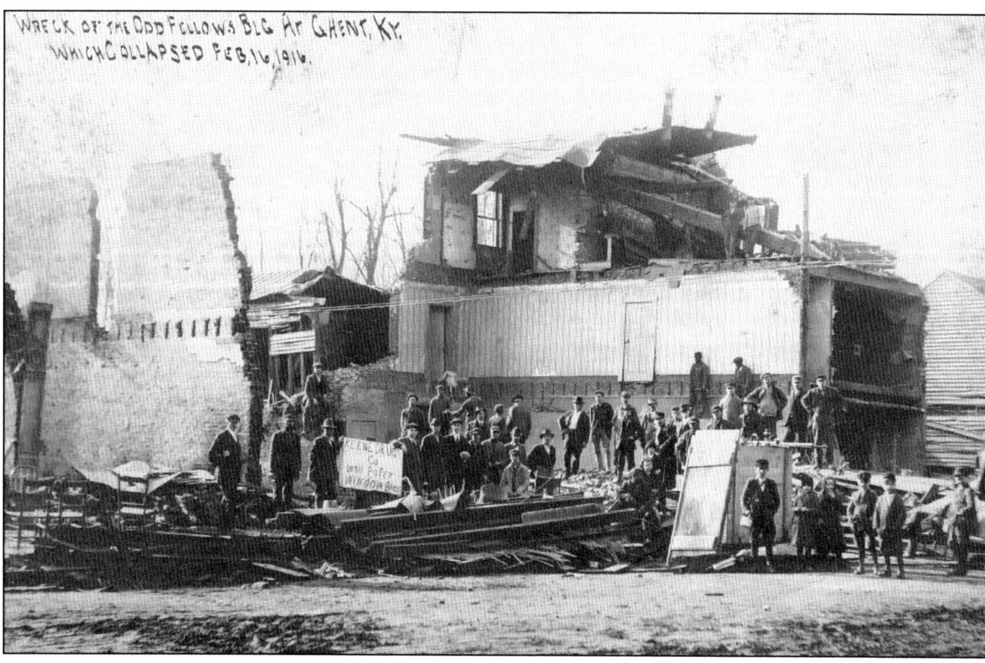

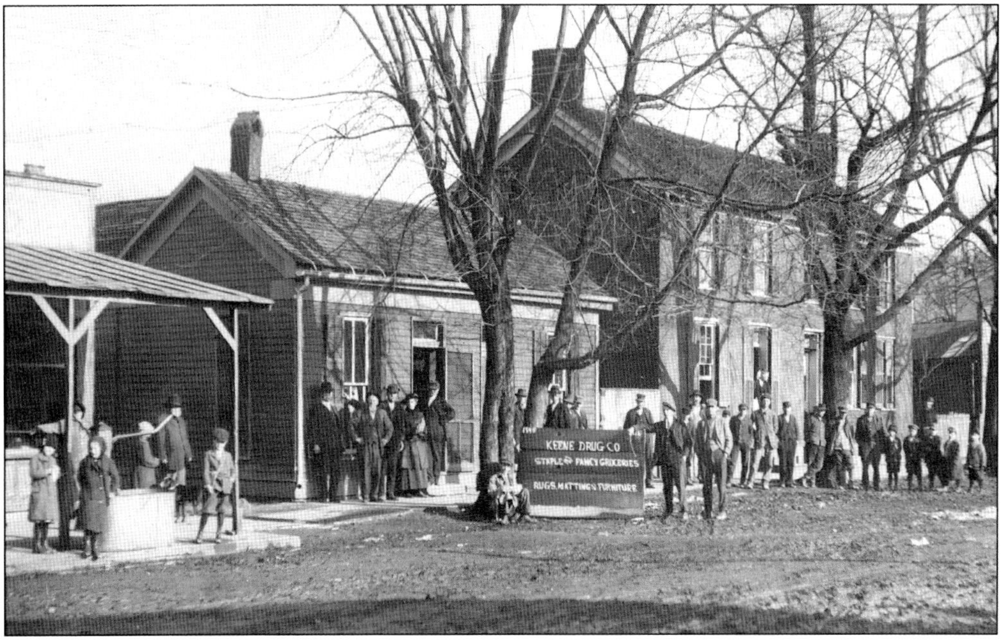

Established in 1895, the Keene Drug Company also was damaged in the fire of 1915. Above, townsfolk gather at another location on Main Street, where Keene had relocated in 1916. The sign advertises that Keene also sells "staple and fancy groceries" and "rugs, matting and furniture." At left, a little girl stands in front of the town pump and a trough used to water horses. Below, the interior of what probably was the original Keene store is shown, with one of its proprietors, Joshua Morris "Dot" Craig (far left), standing with, from left to right, Dr. N.C. Brown; Lucian Gex Keene, druggist and the other proprietor; and Dr. J. Samuel Brown. (Above, courtesy of City of Ghent, James Bond Collection; below, courtesy of Darrell Maines.)

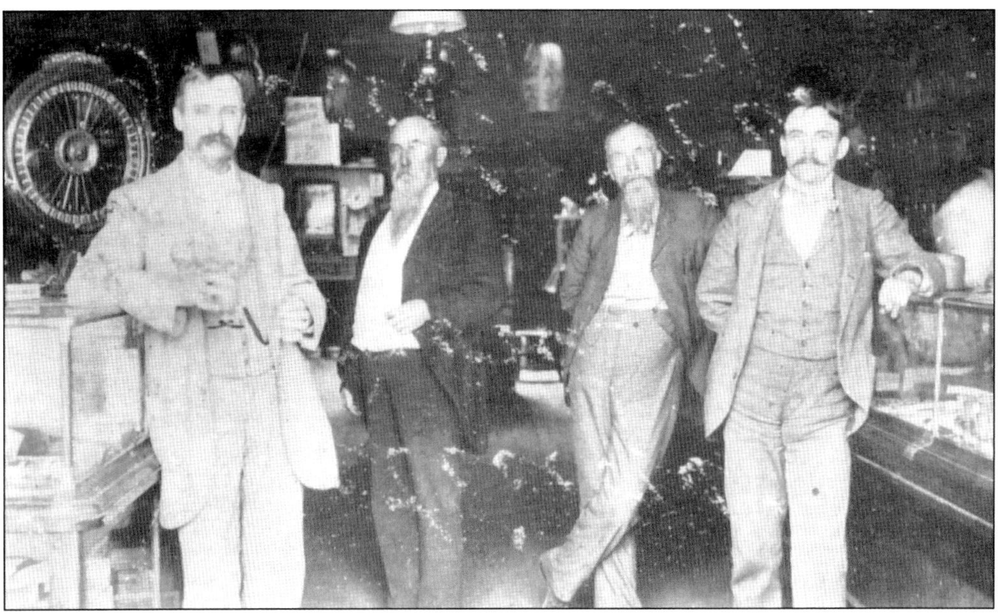

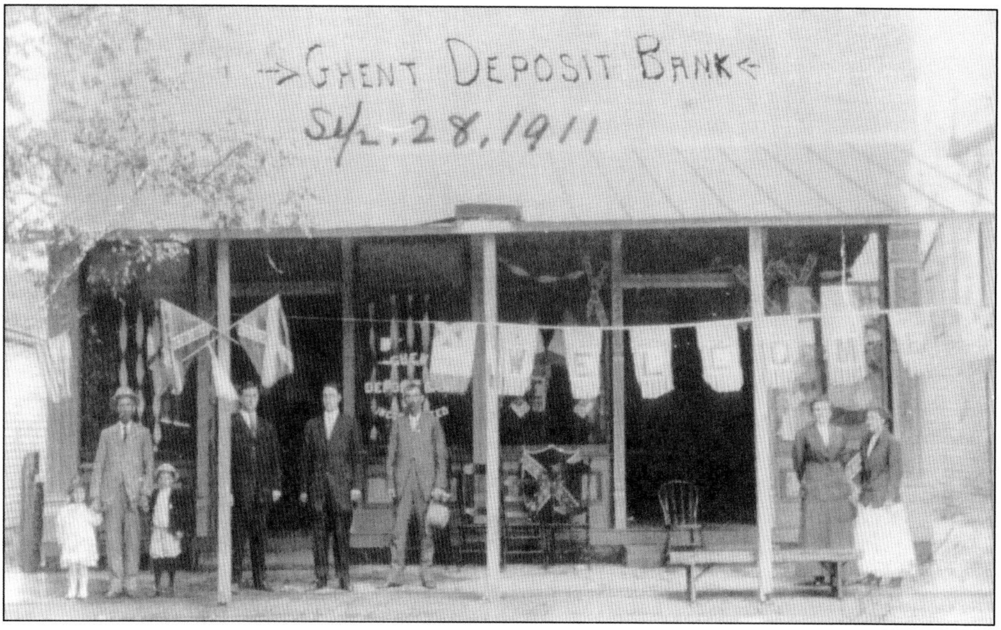

The Ghent Deposit Bank, shown here in a photograph dated September 28, 1911, was established in 1887. The bank enjoyed 50 years of success until losses from loans and frozen assets forced it to close at 11:20 a.m. on Saturday, June 26, 1937. (Courtesy of Kathryn Salyers Archives.)

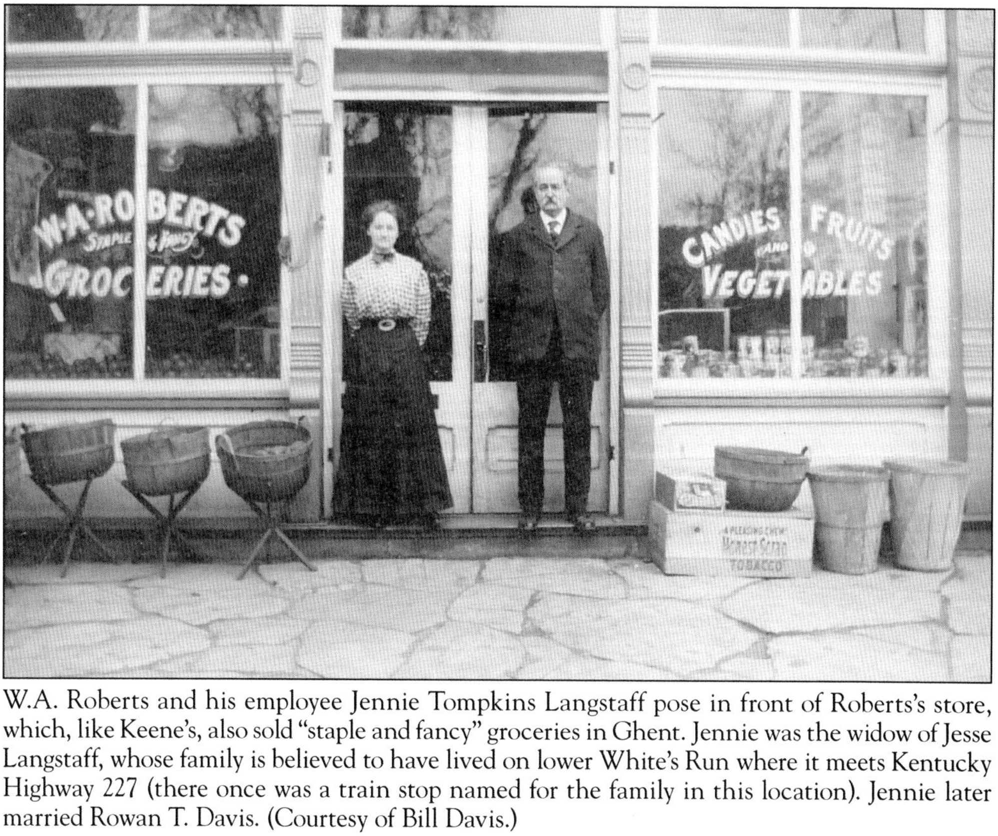

W.A. Roberts and his employee Jennie Tompkins Langstaff pose in front of Roberts's store, which, like Keene's, also sold "staple and fancy" groceries in Ghent. Jennie was the widow of Jesse Langstaff, whose family is believed to have lived on lower White's Run where it meets Kentucky Highway 227 (there once was a train stop named for the family in this location). Jennie later married Rowan T. Davis. (Courtesy of Bill Davis.)

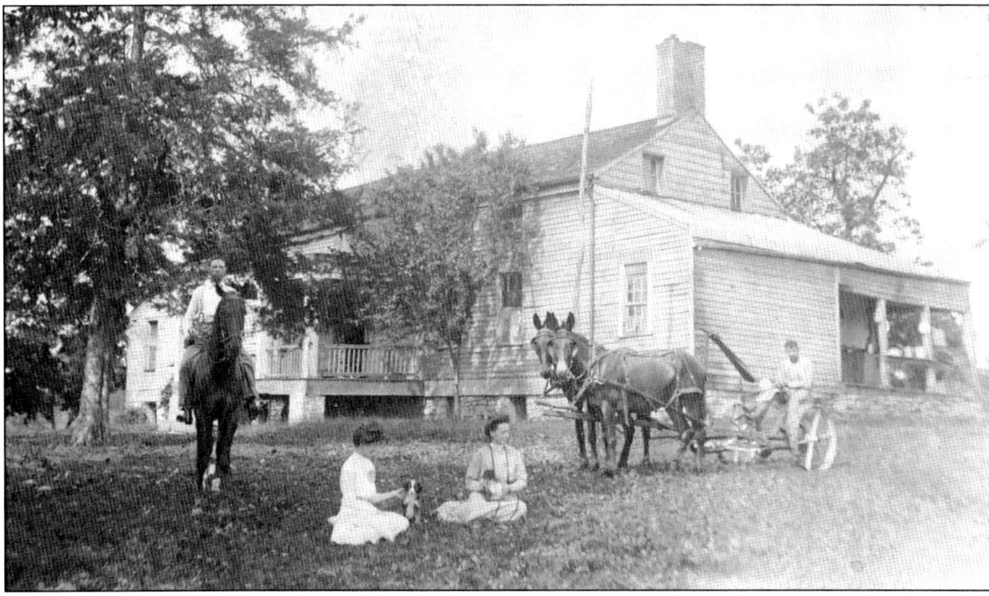

Grass Hills on Ghent-Eagle South Road was built by Lewis Sanders, a brother of Samuel Sanders, who founded Ghent. The one-and-a-half-story log cabin home still stands today, having been renovated in 2006. It is unknown which family is featured in this photograph. Lewis Sanders was a member of the Traveling Church that came from Virginia. He was the first to import purebred cattle from England and was influential in national politics. His friend US senator Henry Clay of Kentucky, is said to have visited Sanders often at Grass Hills. (Courtesy of Rhetta Lykins.)

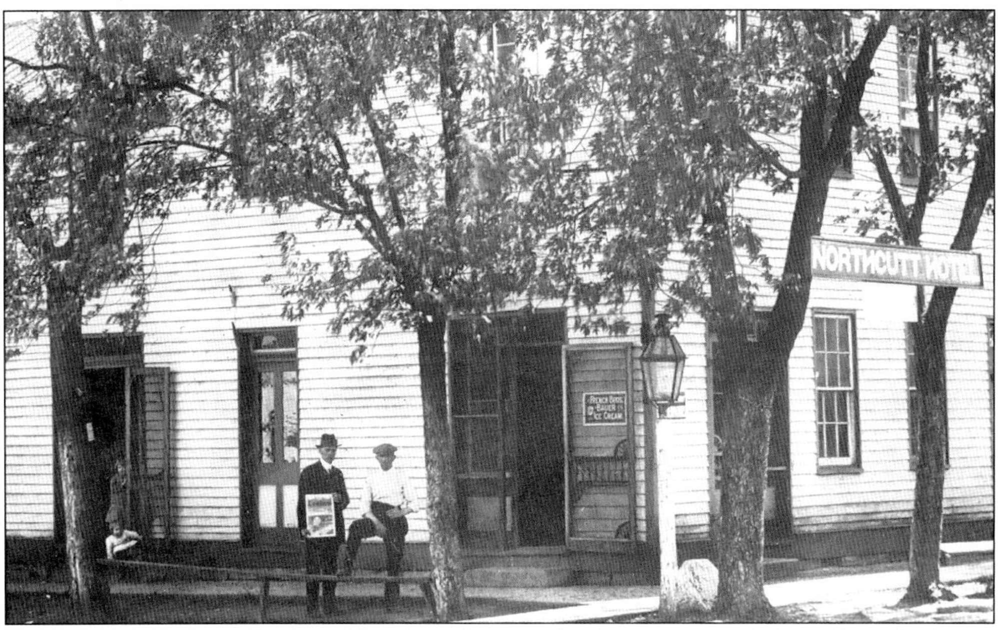

In 1876, Liberty Station (renamed Sanders a few years later) was a town of about 300—the largest town in the Eagle Valley, according to the *Kentucky State Gazetteer.* With the advent of the Louisville & Nashville Railroad, both Sanders and Worthville, its neighbor to the west, thrived well into the 1900s. In 1916, the Northcutt Hotel, above, was just one of several hotels in Sanders, including the Blue Lick Springs Hotel and the Howard House. (Courtesy of Darrell Maines.)

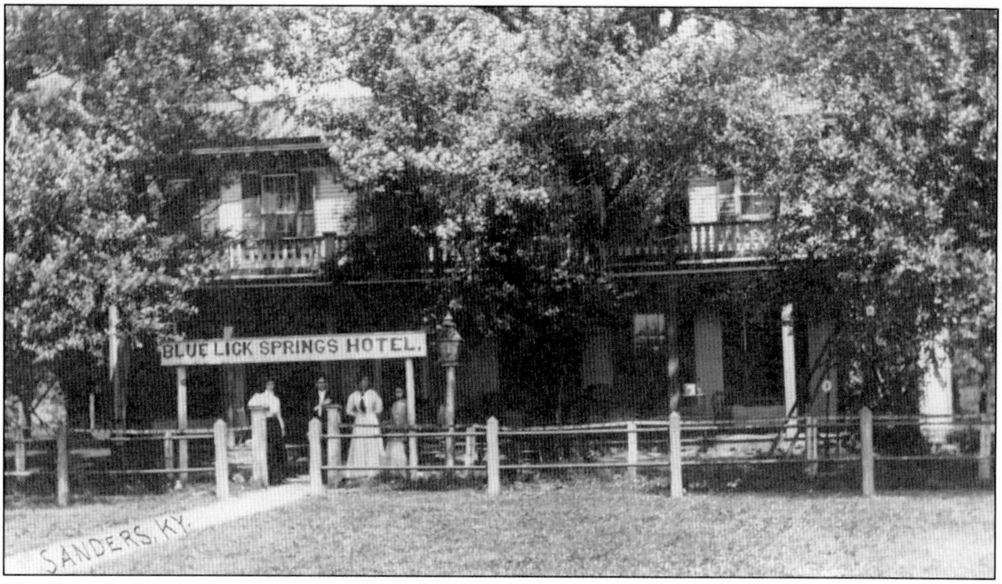

The Blue Lick Springs Hotel in Sanders was established by J. Frank Jacobs, a longtime agent for the Louisville & Nashville Railroad and the Adams Express Company. He moved to Sanders in 1876 and served four years as the town's postmaster. In 1880, he leased the hotel, and he bought it in 1884. Jacobs and his wife, the former Ella Cannon of Ironton, Ohio, had 10 children. (Courtesy of Darrell Maines.)

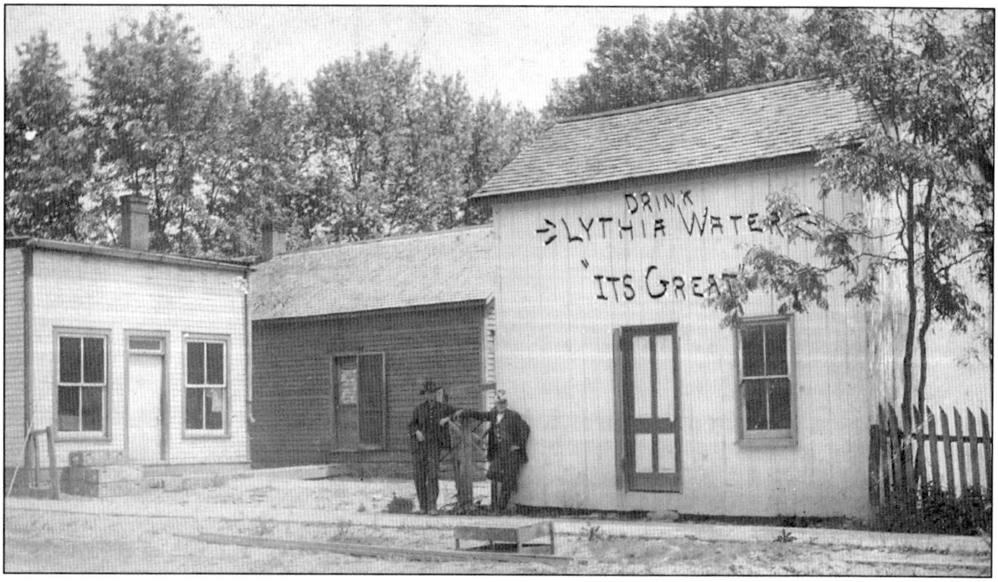

Though named as Lythia Water on this 1916 postcard, the water from this Sanders lithia spring contained lithium salts and was popular with tourists for its healing powers. Doctors of the day believed it could relieve arthritis, gout, Bright's disease, eczema, acne, and other ailments. Studies in the 1990s found that trace amounts of lithium in the mineral springs are shown to improve mood and cognitive function. (Courtesy of Darrell Maines.)

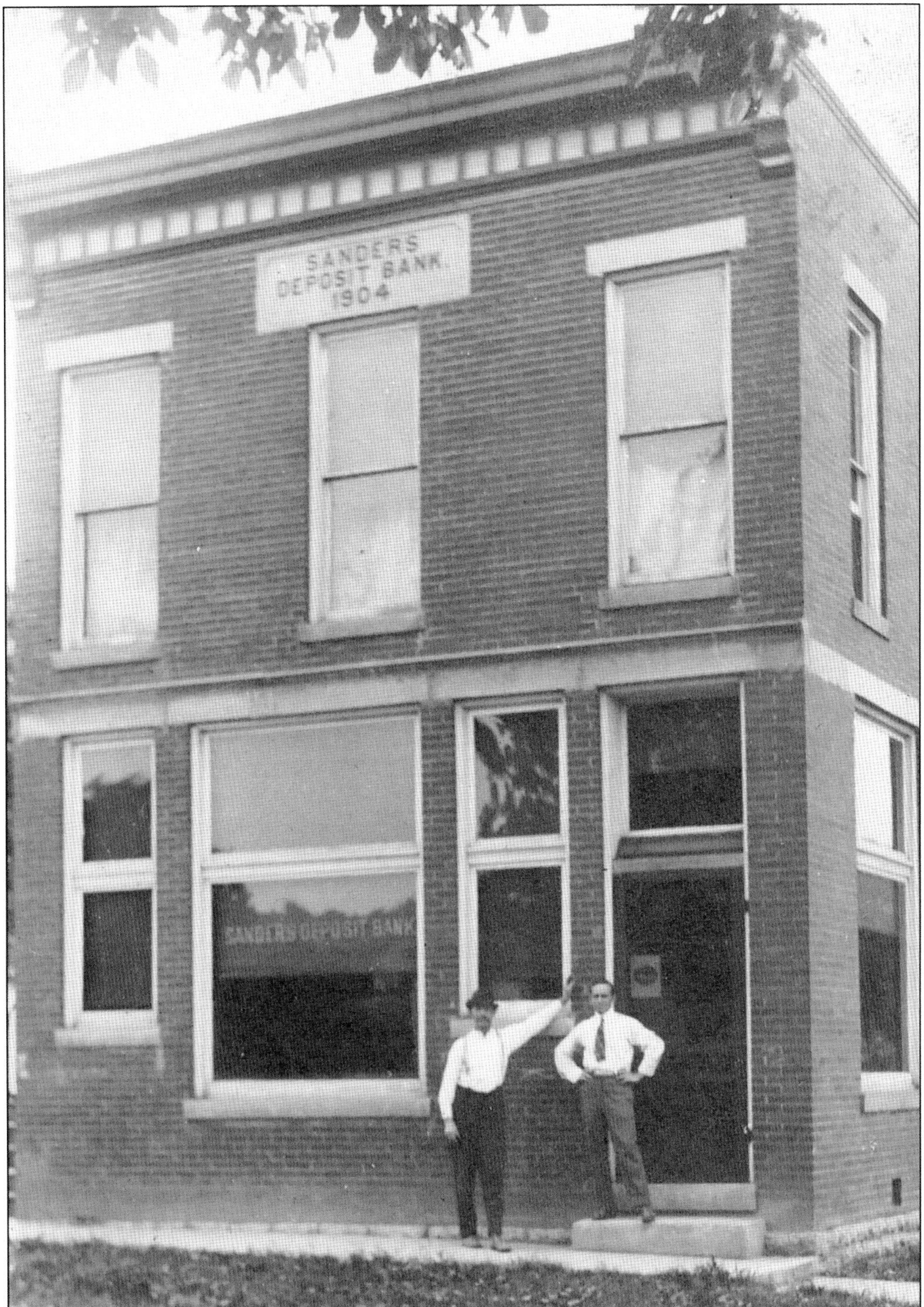

Sanders Deposit Bank opened October 27, 1904, with Charles Wesley Powell as its first cashier and George W. Deatherage as its first president. According to the *Warsaw Independent*, the first day's deposits totaled $16,169. The bank survived the Great Depression, eventually merging with the Sparta Bank in 1935 to become the Sparta-Sanders Bank. (Courtesy of Darrell Maines.)

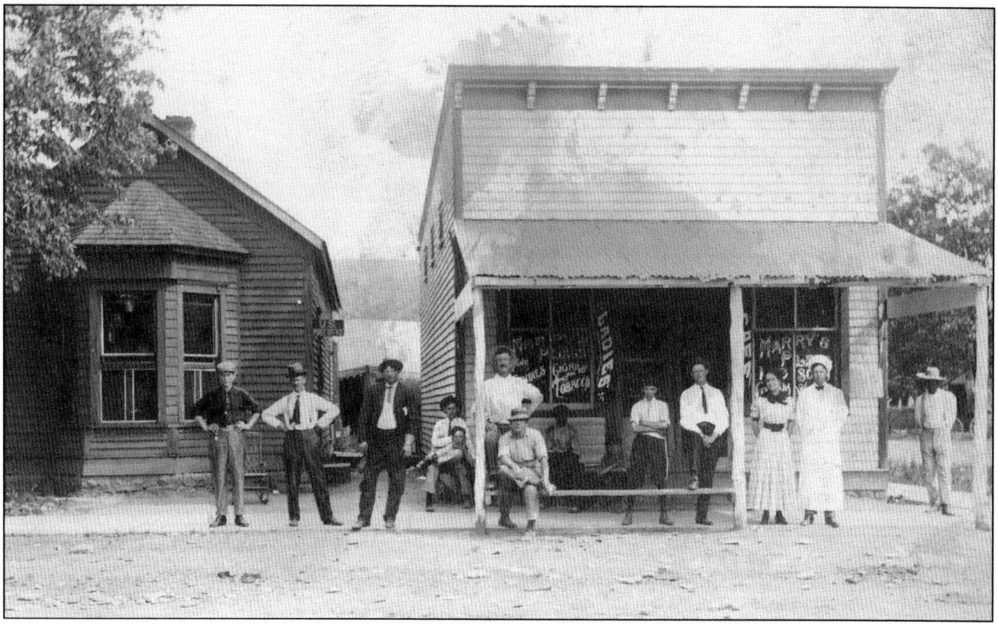

Above, Harry's Place was located next door to the Sanders Post Office, shown on the left. Advertising on the windows boasts Harry's deals in fine candies, cigars, tobacco, as well as ice cream. Below, in a c. 1916 postcard, is the Godman's Confectionery—another thriving business, which proudly served ice-cold Coca-Cola. (Both, courtesy of Darrell Maines.)

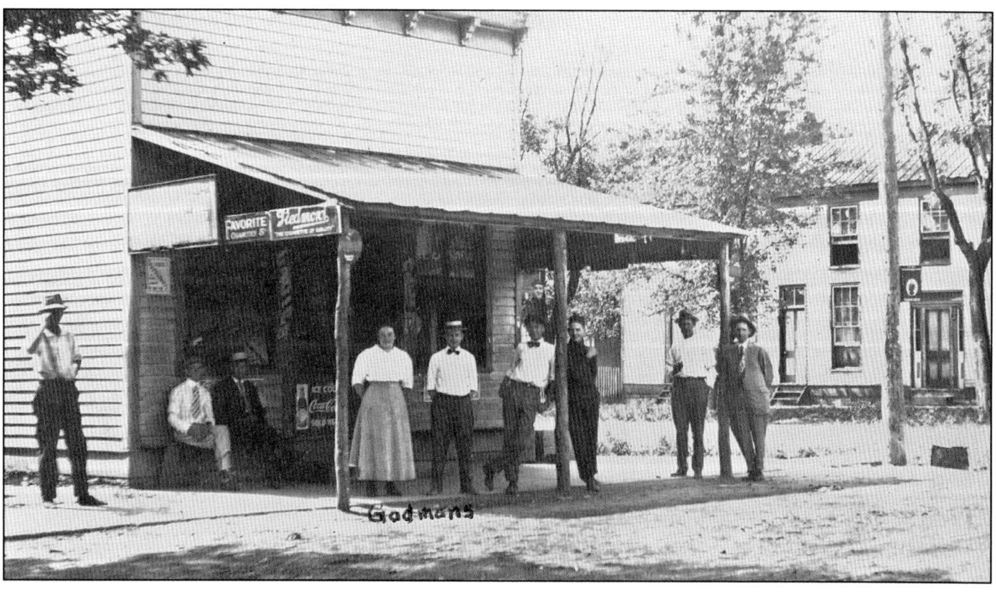

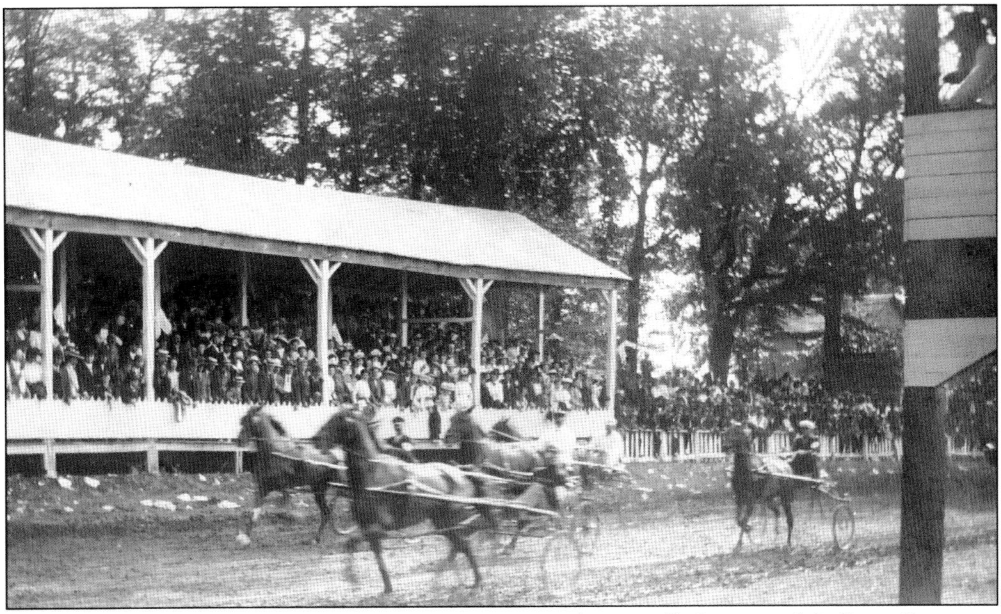

Sanders played host to the first Tri-County Fair in 1907 for Carroll, Owen, and Gallatin Counties, with a brand-new grandstand and harness-racing track. The grandstand, built by Perry Dufour of Ghent under the supervision of association president G.W. Shirley, seated 3,500 people. (Courtesy of Darrell Maines.)

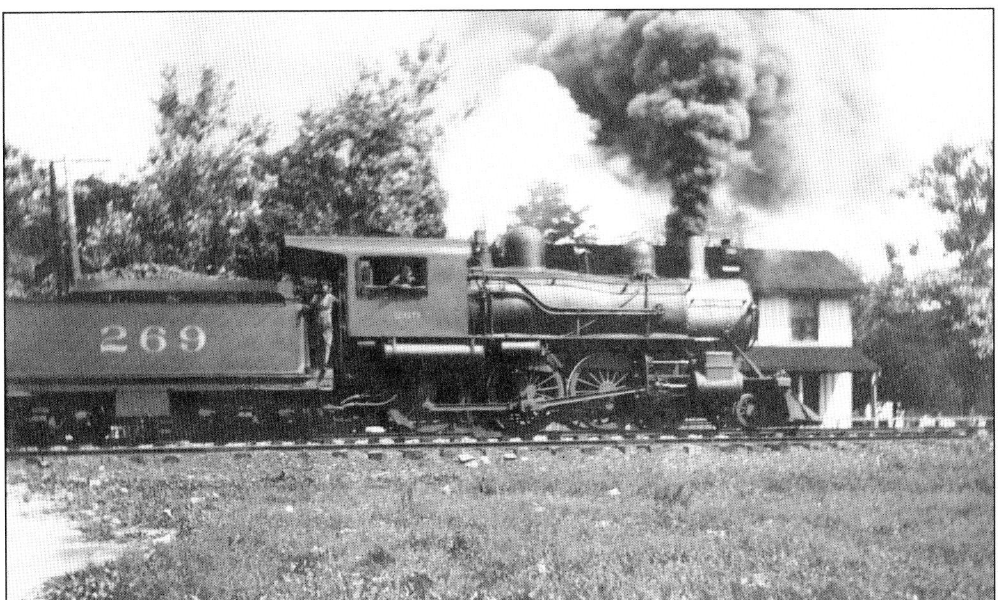

A steam engine on the Louisville & Nashville Railroad line leaves Sanders, headed west to Worthville. In 1867, L&N had proposed running the short line between La Grange and Covington through Carrollton, but the idea of such a change was rejected by the city's residents. Worthville and Sanders benefited instead, becoming bustling cities on the rail line in the late 1800s and early 1900s, with hotels, grocers, dry goods stores, and other businesses. (Courtesy of Darrell Maines.)

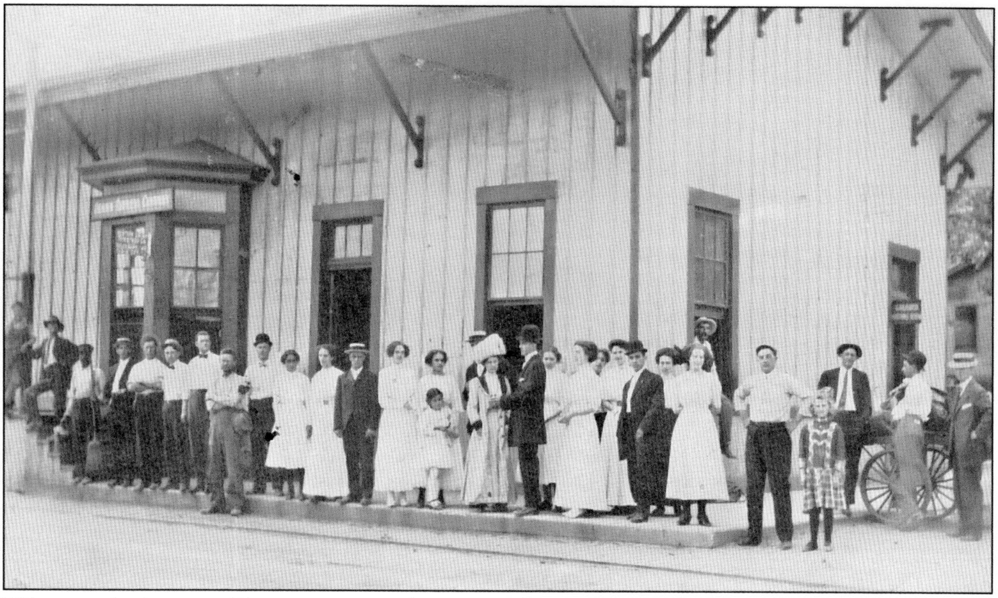

What might be a wedding party stands waiting for a train at the Worthville station. In the background, on the right, is a sign that reads "Colored Waiting Room." One version of this postcard (postmarked in 1913) shows a man named Earl, who indicated with an X that he is the fifth person from the right in this photograph. (Courtesy of Darrell Maines.)

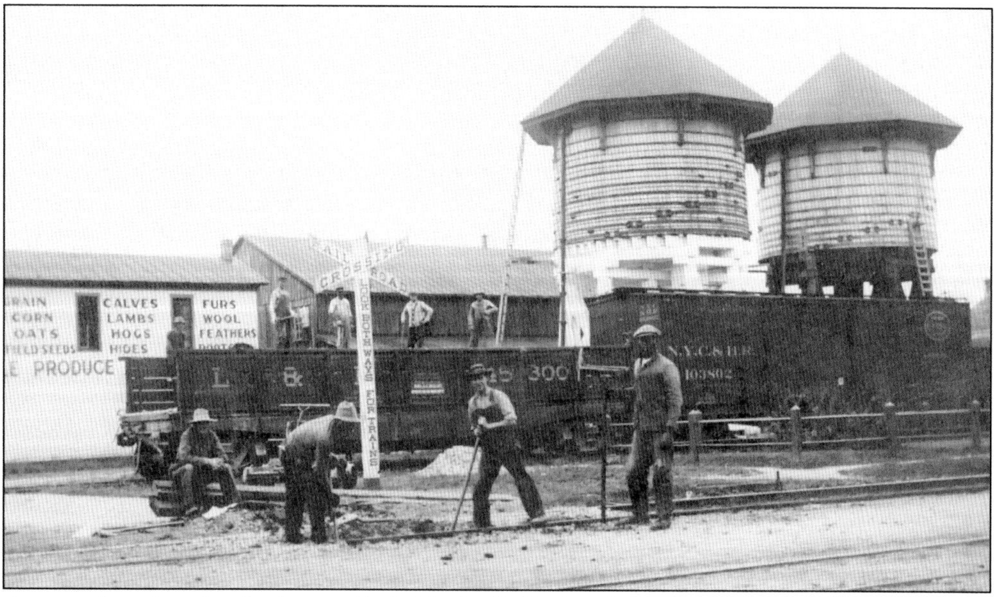

A crew of workers for the Louisville & Nashville Railroad, which is now owned and operated by CSX, poses in Worthville. The train is stopped in front of two towers that provided water for steam engines. (Courtesy of Darrell Maines.)

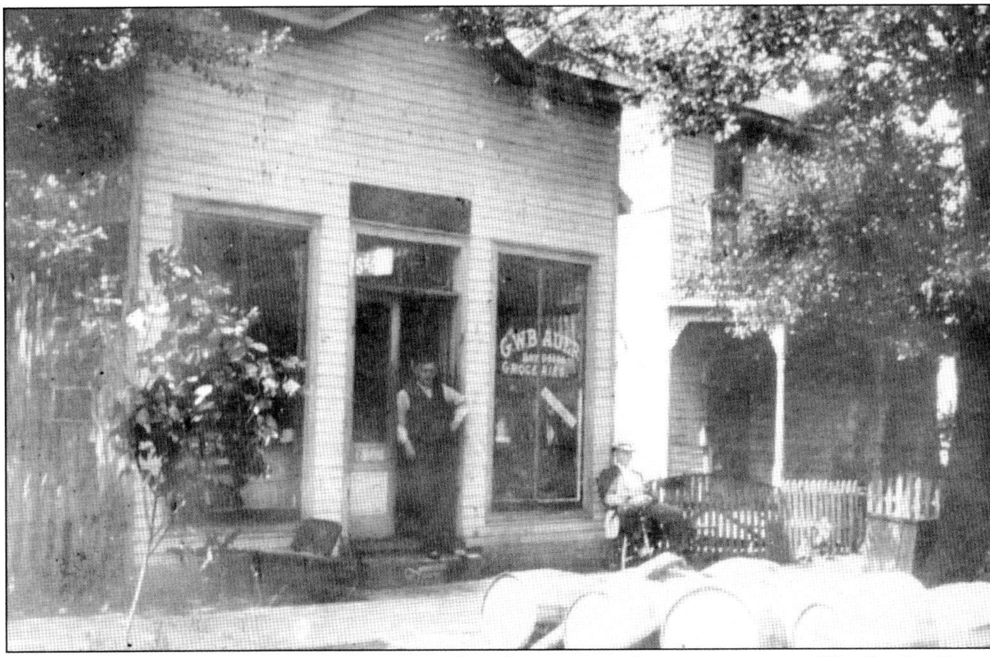

George Washington Bauer poses in front of his dry goods and grocery store in Worthville. Bauer worked as a merchant for 38 years until his retirement in 1945. Like Sanders, Worthville—originally named Coonskin but renamed for Gen. William Jenkins Worth, a Mexican War hero—flourished from the mid-1800s into the 1900s, with banks, barbershops, hotels, and other businesses. (Courtesy of Darrell Maines.)

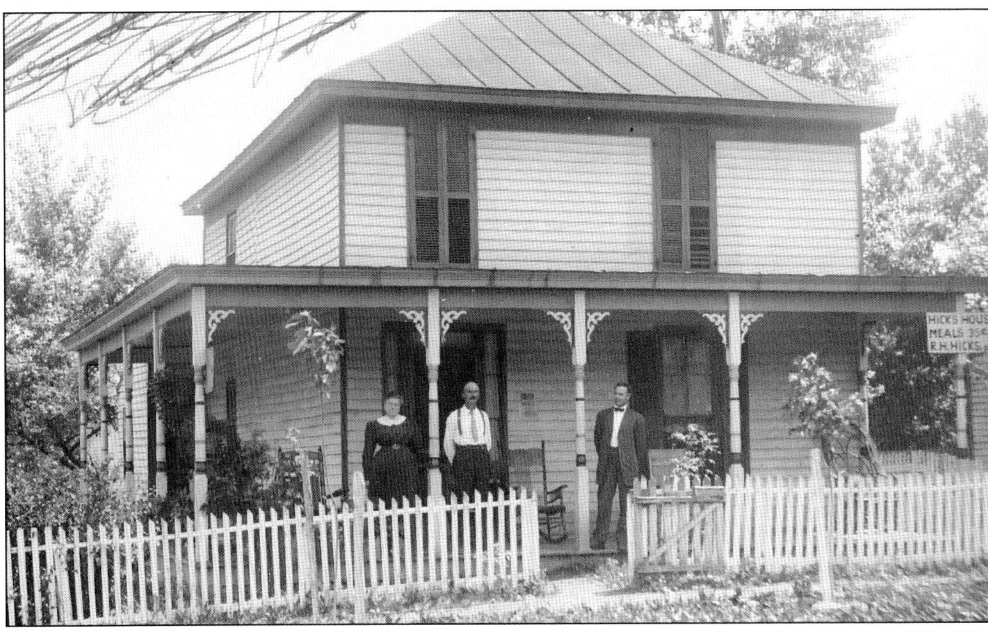

This is Hicks House in Worthville, where, at the time of this postcard, meals were served for 35¢. R.H. Hicks is named as the proprietor. Hicks also served as a town marshal and tax collector. He was killed in 1943 while attempting to cross the tracks ahead of an L&N freight train. (Courtesy of Darrell Maines.)

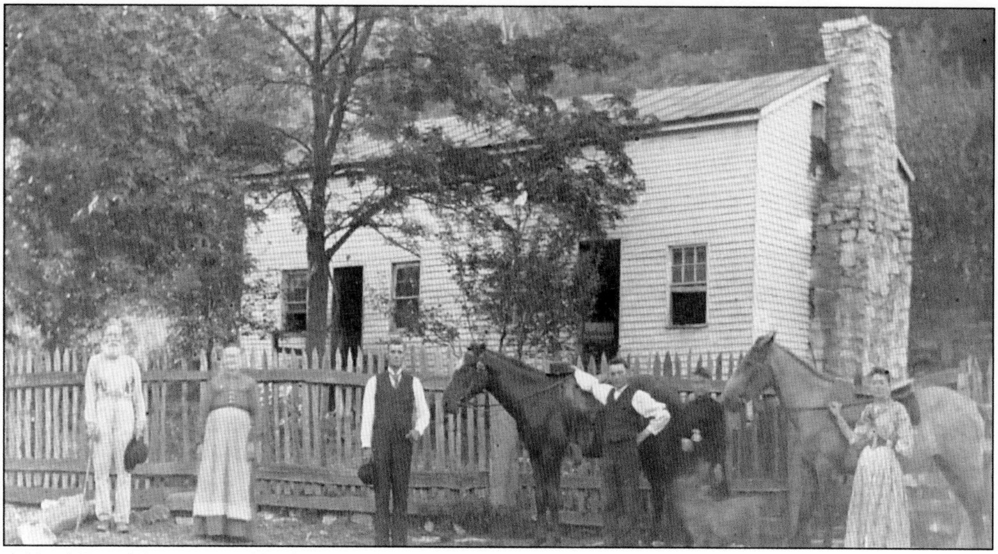

Alfred Franklin Dunn (far left) and his wife, Susan Lydia May Dunn (second from left), pose with their family for a portrait at their home on Carlisle Road outside of Prestonville, about 1890. Their son, Alvin Meade Dunn, and daughter, Effie Goodloe Dunn, stand at the right with the two horses. The man in the center is unidentified. (Courtesy of Jean Dunn Yager.)

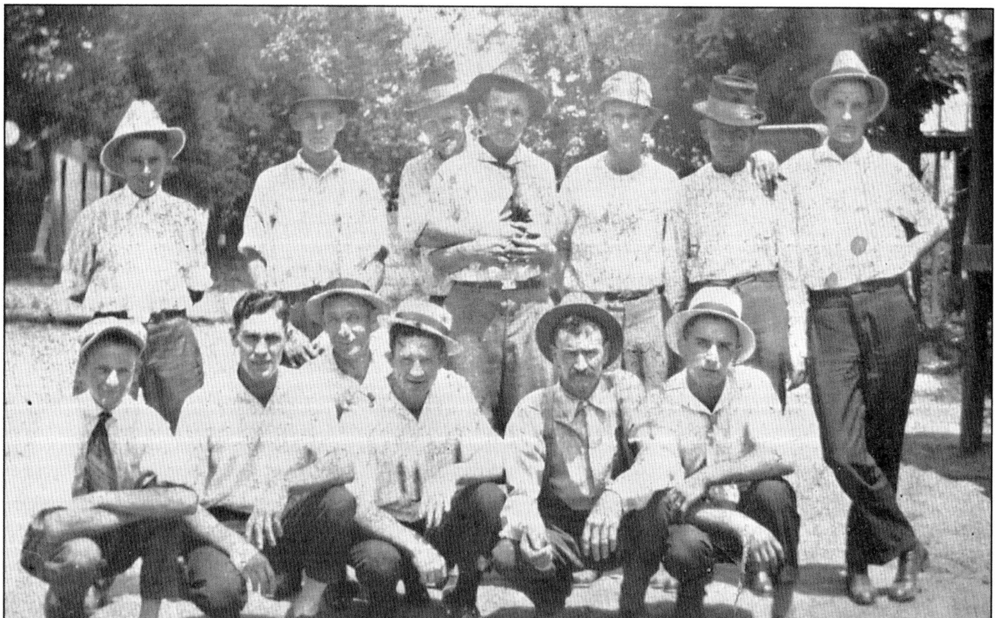

Arthur Prentice "Yak" Dunn stands second from the left with a group of Prestonville men, possibly employees of the Prestonville distillery. The distillery was established by Andrew W. Darling, who created the still-famous Old Darling brand. Darling was a Scotsman, whose brothers, Thomas and Adam, built Cedar Lock (or Lock Three) on the Kentucky River. (Courtesy of Jean Dunn Yager.)

Three

People

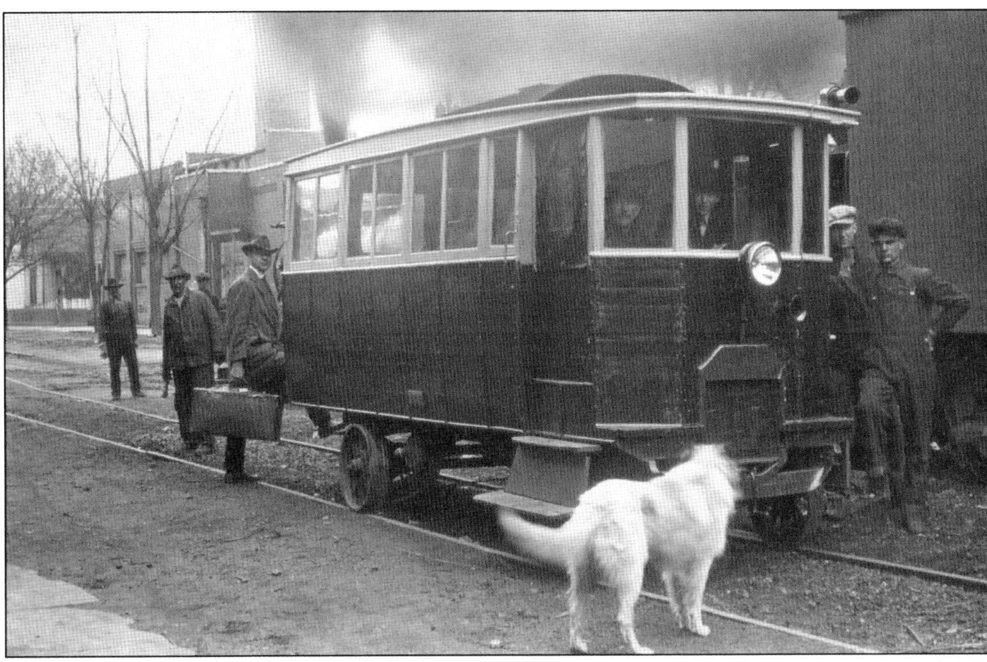

Travelers and workers board one of the many jitneys on the L&N rail line that linked Worthville to Carrollton, which was completed in 1905 and transported commuters and mail until 1926. (Courtesy of Darrell Maines.)

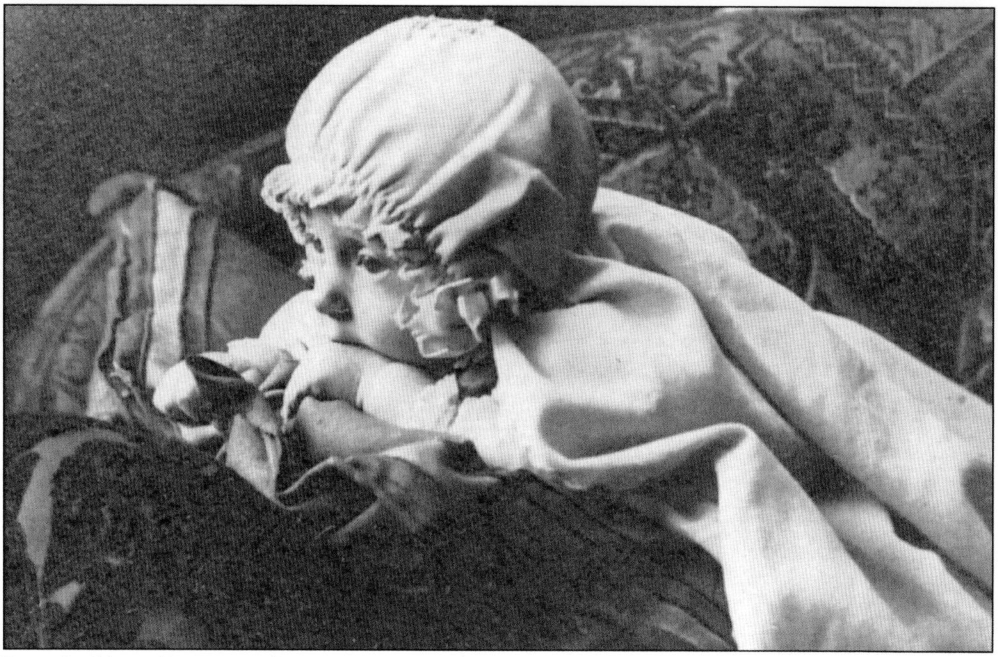

Beverly Oliver Dunn was born in 1912 to Clarence Bosworth and Lelia Oliver Dunn in Lamb, Indiana. By 1920, the family lived in Carroll County. Beverly and his wife, Lula Frances Davis Dunn, were parents of James Beverly "Jimmy" Dunn, who served as Carroll County coroner from 1980 until his death in 2008. (Courtesy of Jean Dunn Yager.)

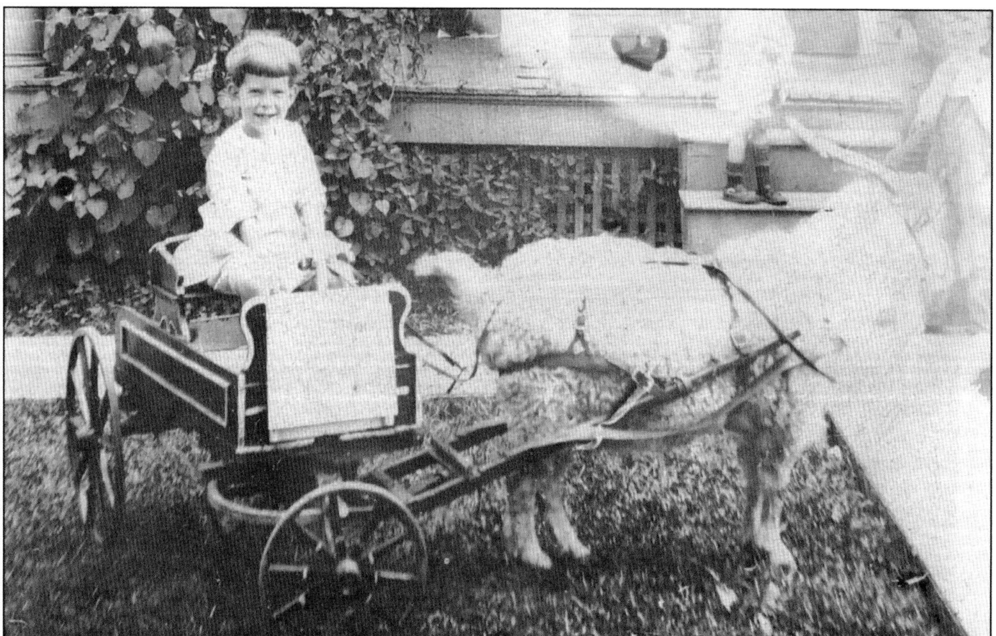

Jean Dunn, age four, is posed in a goat cart on the front lawn of a house on Fifth Street in Carrollton. The traveling photographer would bring the goat or a pony and go house to house to sell portraits of children in the cart. Standing to the right are Arthur Baker and Loretta Baker and J. Pickett on the steps. (Courtesy of Jean Dunn Yager.)

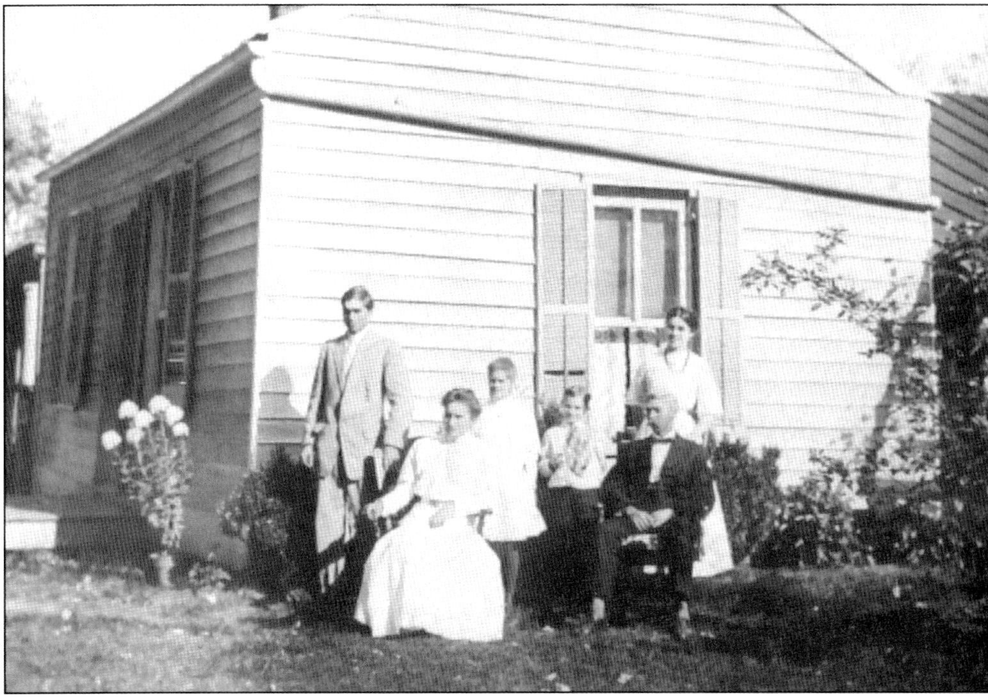

This postcard is believed to depict the Daniel and Celeste Hanlon family on Union Street in Ghent. The 1920 census shows Daniel to be the proprietor of a livery stable and their daughter Elizabeth to be a teacher at the grade school. (Courtesy of City of Ghent, James Bond Collection.)

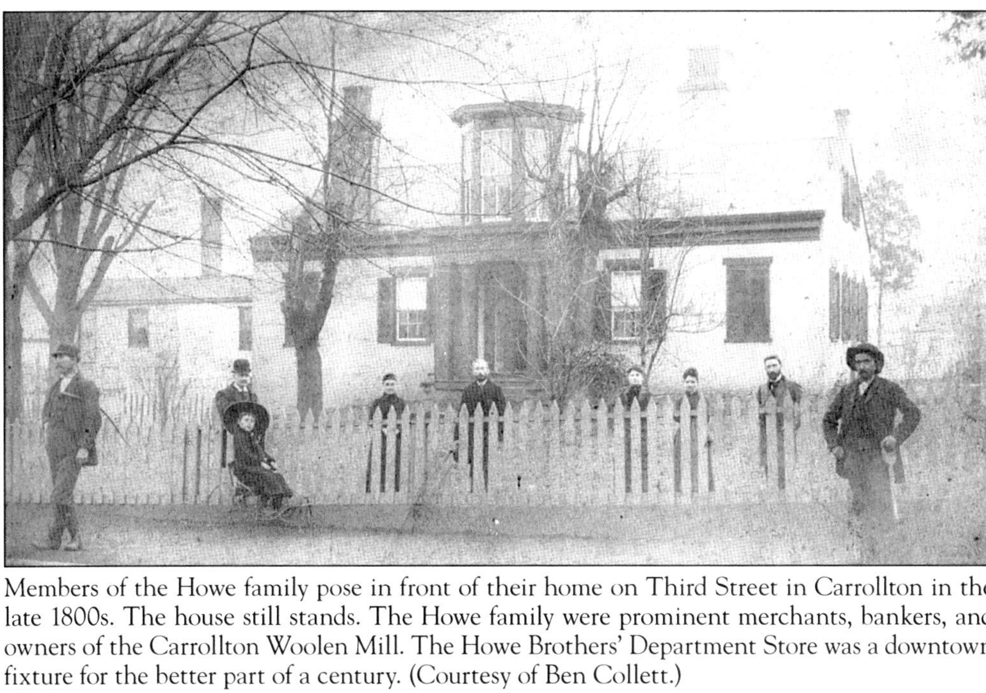

Members of the Howe family pose in front of their home on Third Street in Carrollton in the late 1800s. The house still stands. The Howe family were prominent merchants, bankers, and owners of the Carrollton Woolen Mill. The Howe Brothers' Department Store was a downtown fixture for the better part of a century. (Courtesy of Ben Collett.)

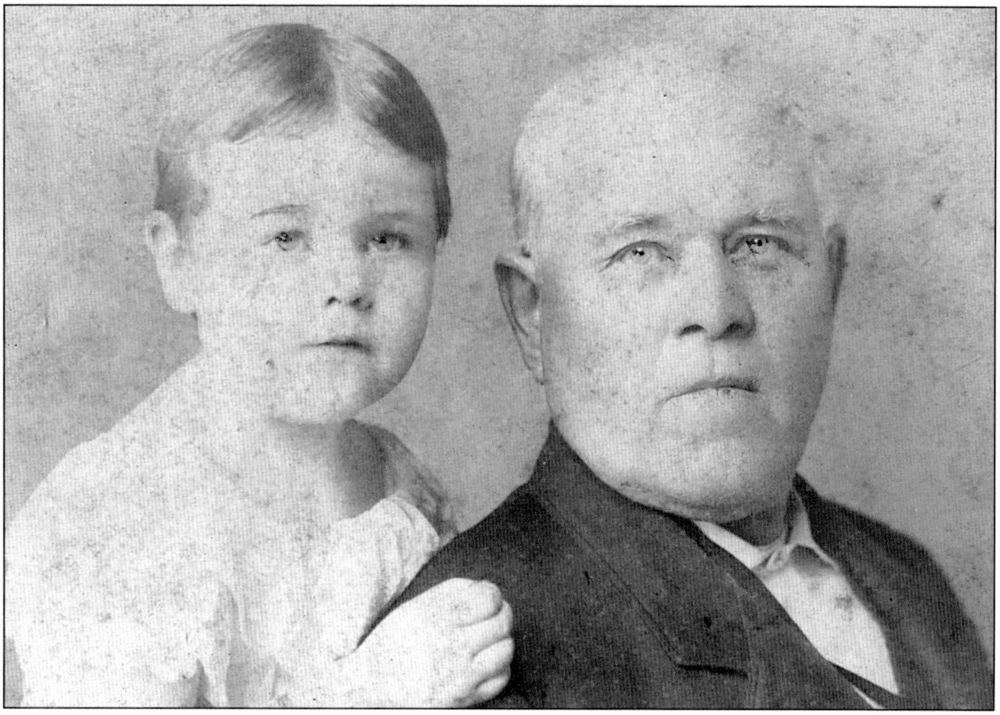

William Buford Lindsay poses with his granddaughter Willie Grigron. Lindsay, who married Margaret Sanders (daughter of Lewis Sanders), played a key role in the formation of Ghent Deposit Bank, which was in business from 1887 to 1937. (Courtesy of Port William Historical Society.)

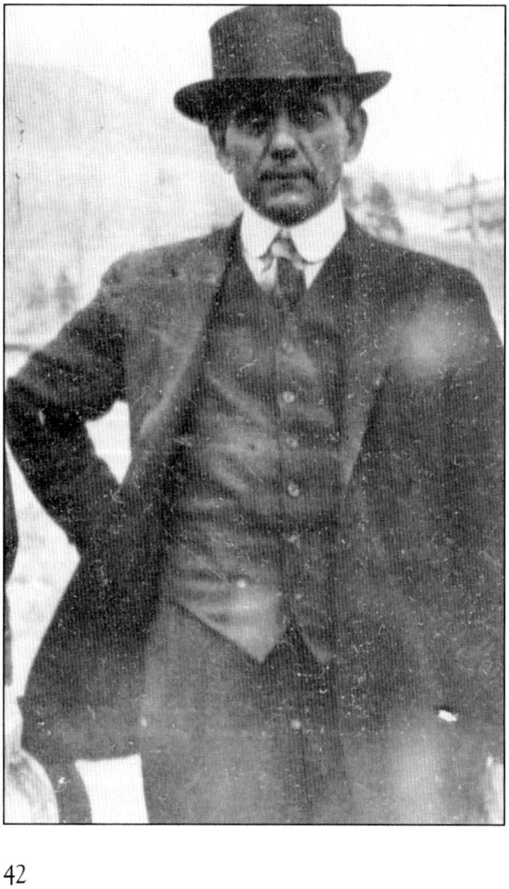

George Washington Bauer poses near Worthville, Kentucky, where he owned and operated a general store. He married Dora Belle Spenneberg. Their daughter Marjorie Stafford was a teacher in the Carroll County School system. (Courtesy of Port William Historical Society.)

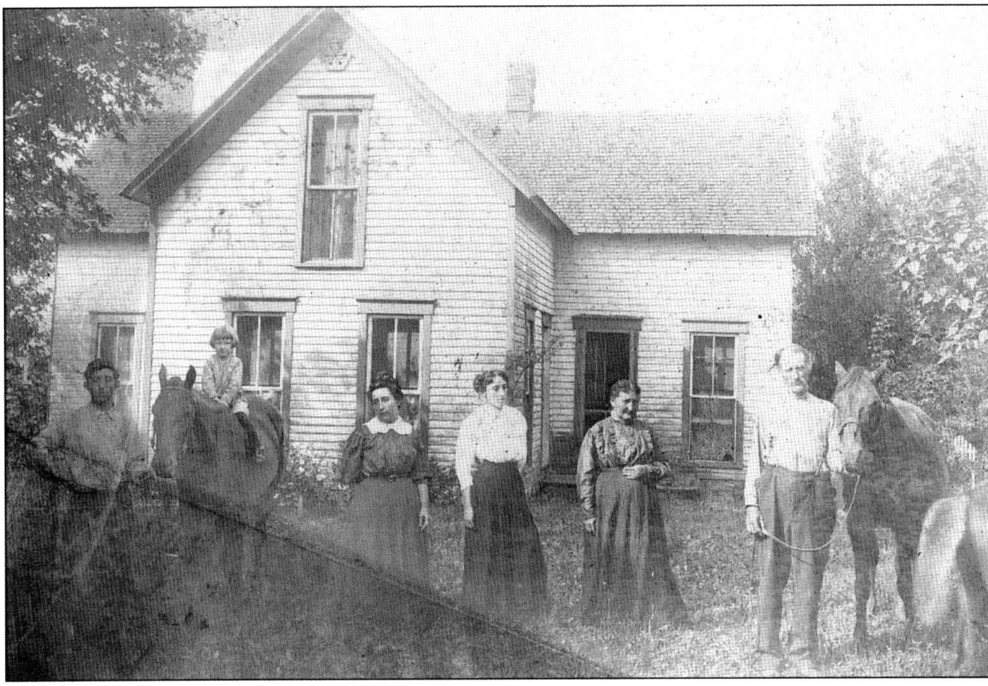

The Ford family of Mound Hill pose at their homestead about 1903. They are, from left to right, Ira Ford, Dewitt Wallace (on horse), Clara Ford, Rosa Ford Wallace, Mary Ellen Wyatt Ford, and Ulysses Ford. (Courtesy of Gary Ford.)

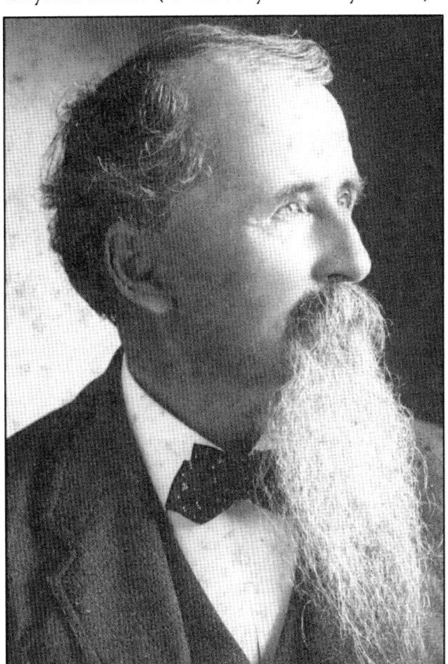

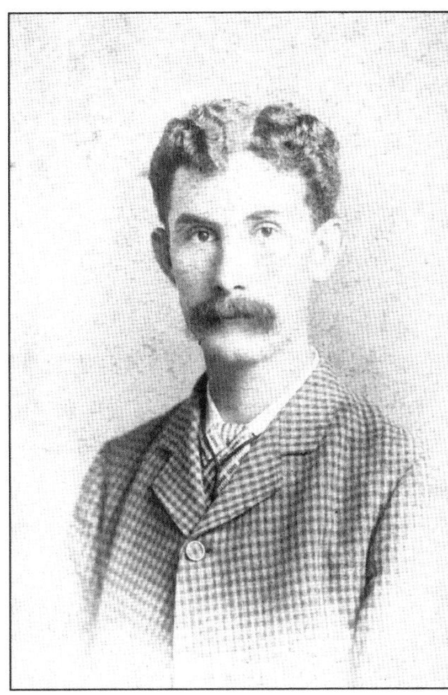

Dr. Solomon Ernest Hampton (left) was a prominent physician and farmer in Hunters Bottom in western Carroll County. He was a Civil War veteran who fought for the Union in the 4th Indiana Cavalry and the 137th Indiana Infantry. Edward Clarence Masterson (right), grandson of Richard and Sarah, lived in Prestonville with his wife, Nettie, and worked as a bookkeeper in a dry goods store. (Both, courtesy of Port William Historical Society.)

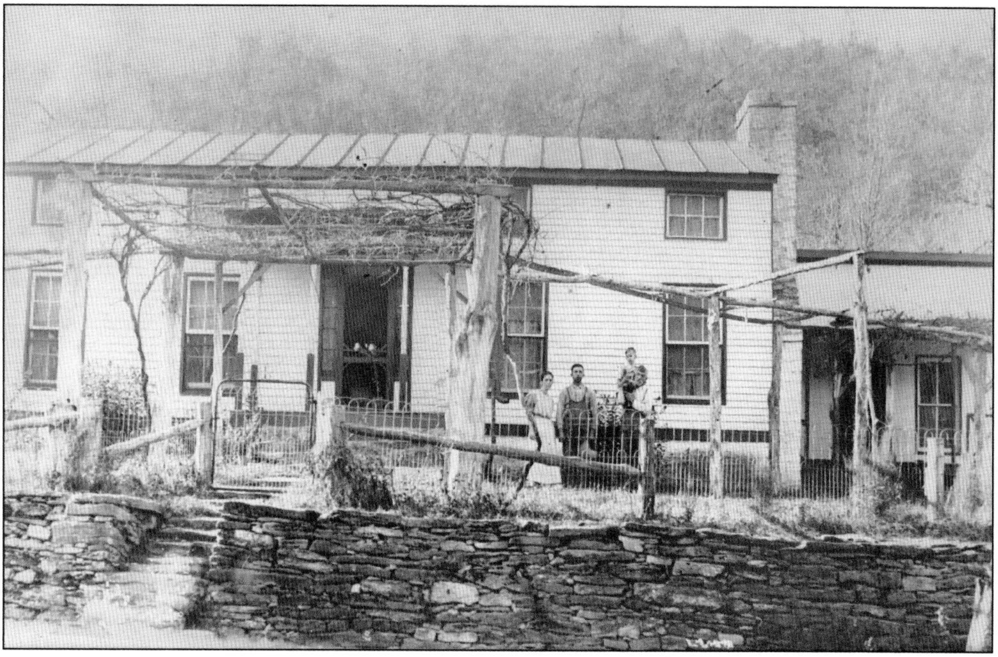

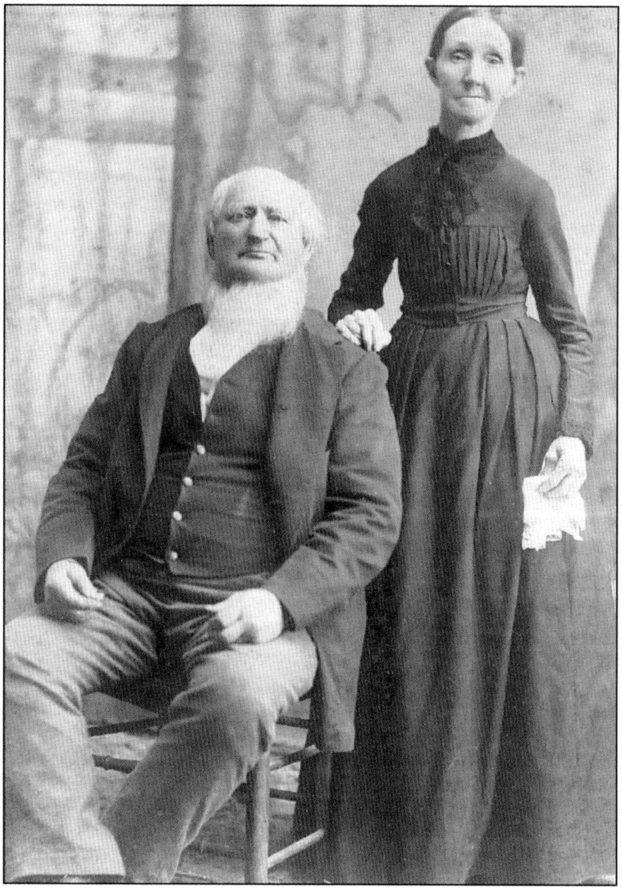

This home is believed to have been near Worthville and shows a particular kind of architecture popular among the oldest homes in the area. (Courtesy of Port William Historical Society.)

In 1948, Adam Crosswhite, a slave, escaped the Hunters Bottom area of Carroll County with his family, traveling to Michigan via the Underground Railroad. David Giltner (pictured), son of the Crosswhites' owner, led a posse to Marshall, Michigan, and attempted to reclaim the family as property. There, the townspeople rallied around the Crosswhites and convinced the local sheriff to arrest Giltner and his men, who later stood trial for attempted kidnapping. The case is believed to have contributed to Henry Clay's revisions to the Fugitive Slave Act in 1850, which made reclamation easier for slave owners. (Courtesy of Port William Historical Society.)

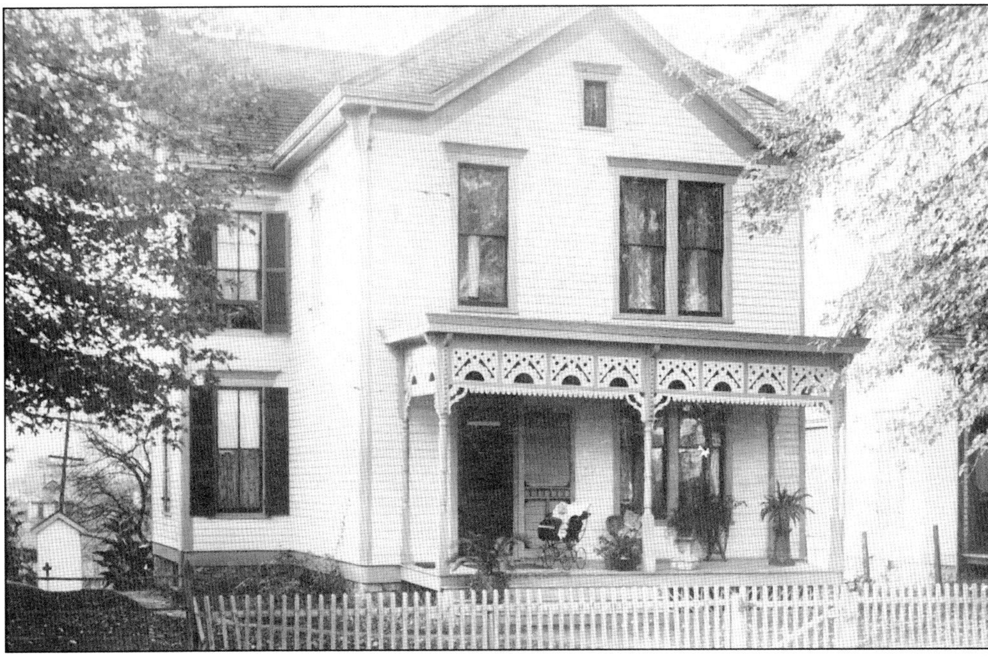

At the time of this photograph, this was the John Glauber family home. The house still stands among many other historic and grand homes on Highland Avenue (originally known as High Street) in Carrollton. (Courtesy of John and Carolyn Glauber.)

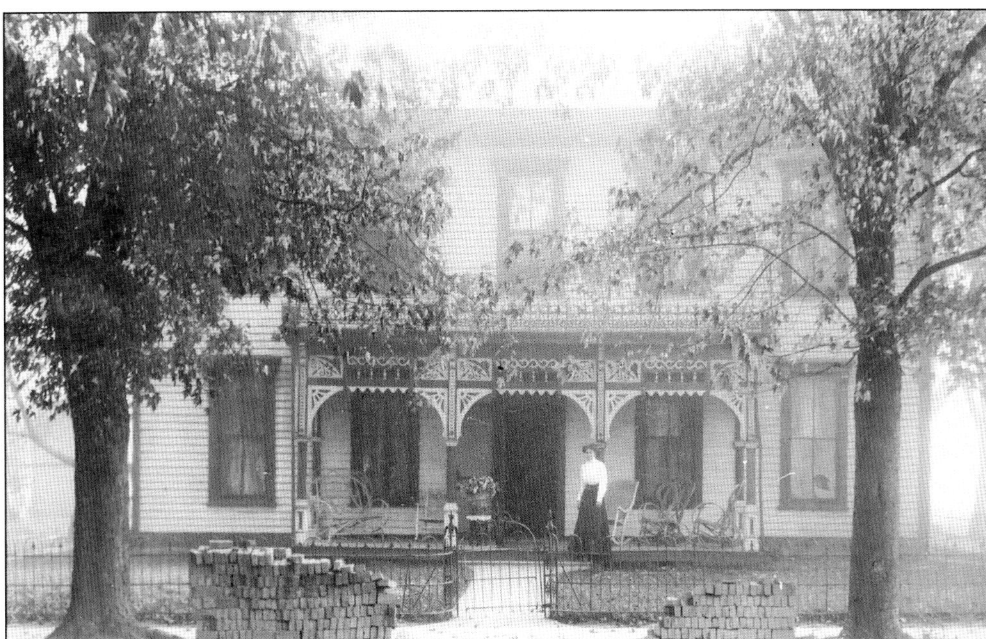

The Grobmyer home is still one of the grand homes on Fifth Street in Carrollton. H.C. Grobmyer was town clerk in the late 1800s and also was a member of the American Saddlehorse Breeders Association, which lists him and J.E. Grobmyer as owners of several mares—Ida G., Lizzie G., and Nanny Tandy. (Courtesy of John and Carolyn Glauber.)

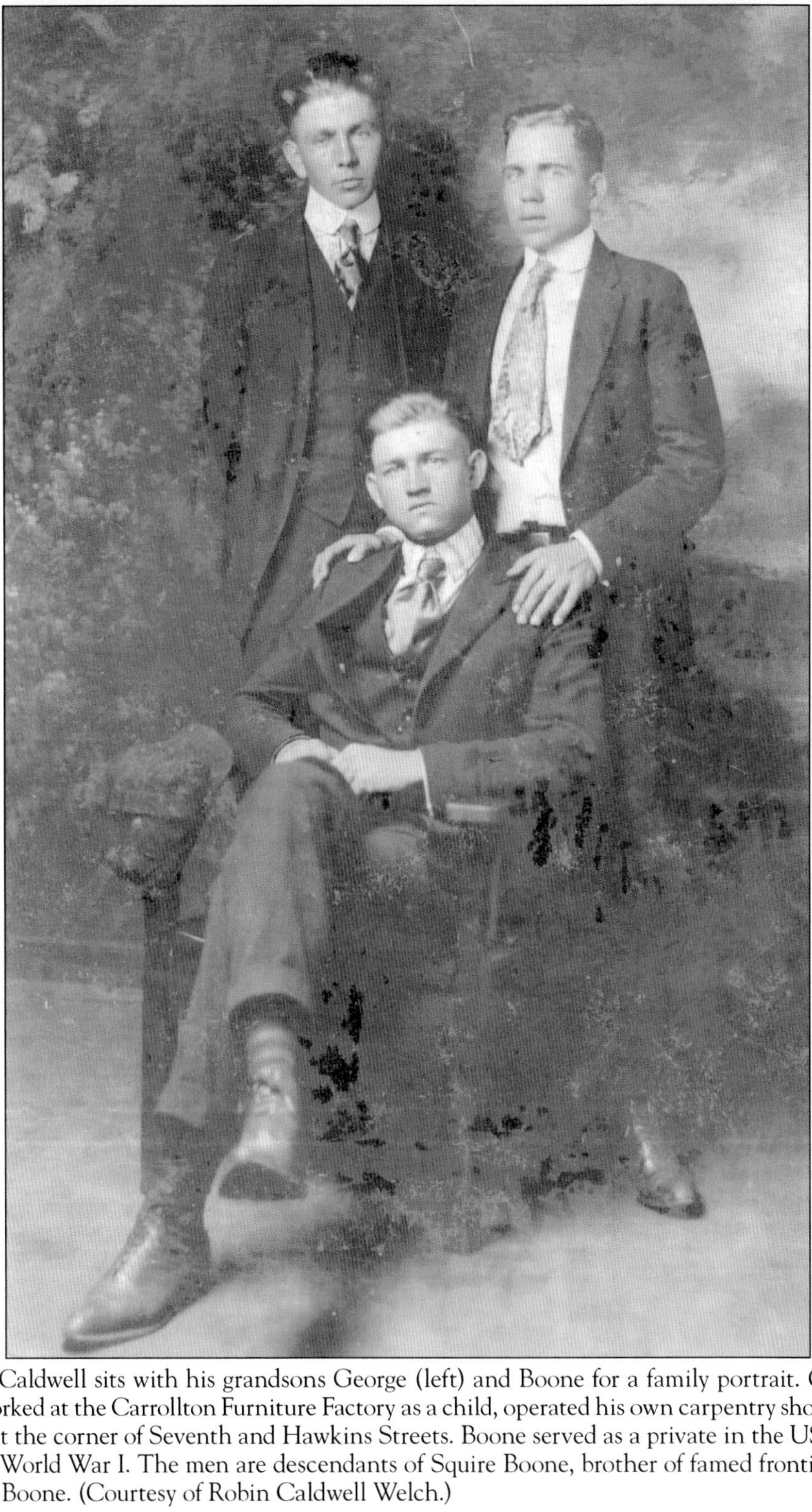

Henry Caldwell sits with his grandsons George (left) and Boone for a family portrait. George, who worked at the Carrollton Furniture Factory as a child, operated his own carpentry shop in his home at the corner of Seventh and Hawkins Streets. Boone served as a private in the US Army during World War I. The men are descendants of Squire Boone, brother of famed frontiersman Daniel Boone. (Courtesy of Robin Caldwell Welch.)

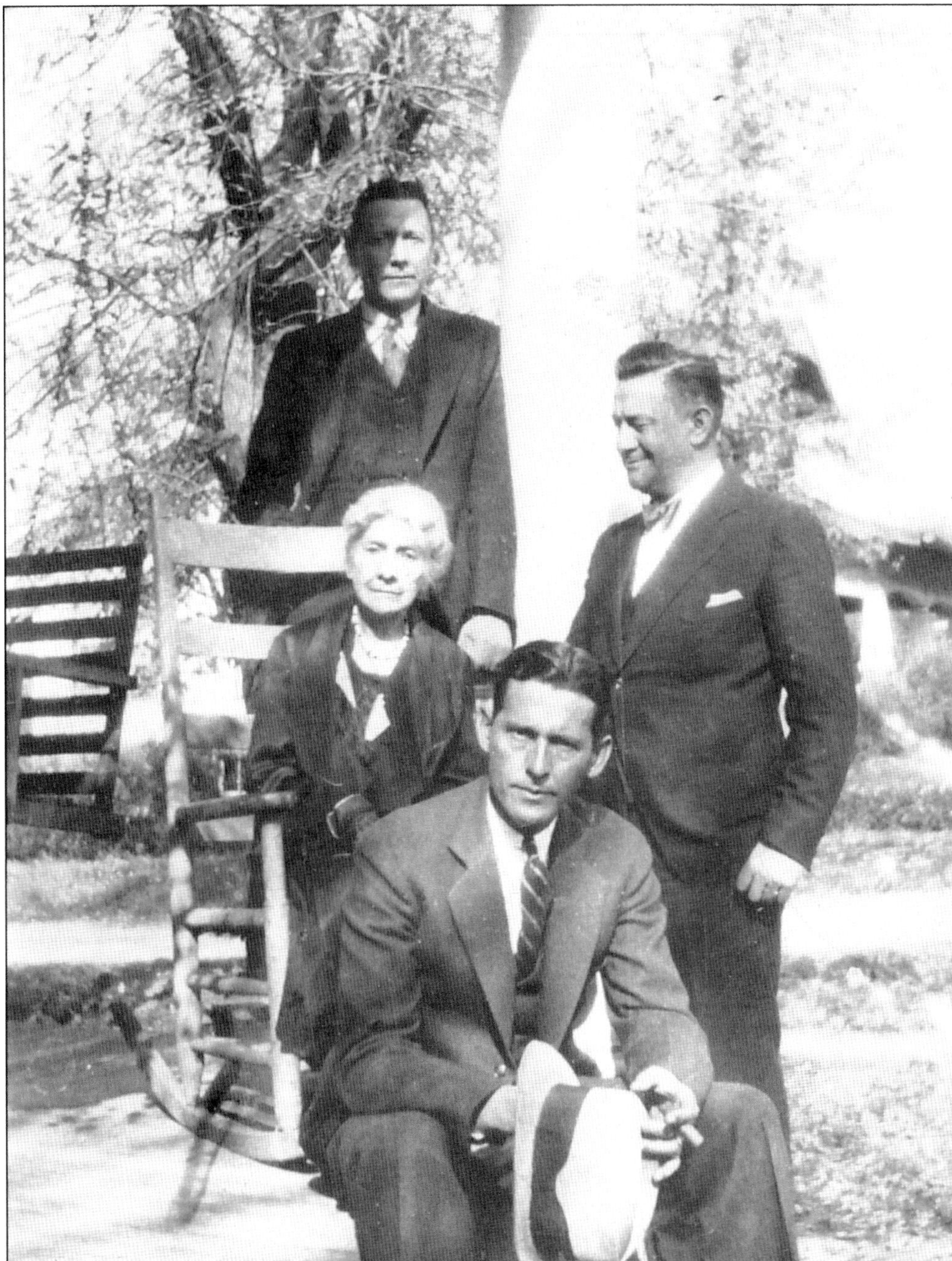

Known as "Miss Atha," Atha Hanks was born in Carroll County in 1844 and married Edmund Asbury Gullion in 1879. She was active in the Carrollton Christian Church and owned and operated a bookstore on Main Street. Edmund was editor of the *Carrollton Democrat* in the 1870s. Posing with her are her sons, from back to front, Allen, Carroll, and Walter. Allen and Walter were both graduates of West Point. In World War II, Allen rose to the rank of major general and served on Gen. Dwight D. Eisenhower's staff in Europe. Carroll and Walter both retired as colonels in the US Army. (Courtesy of Carrollton Christian Church.)

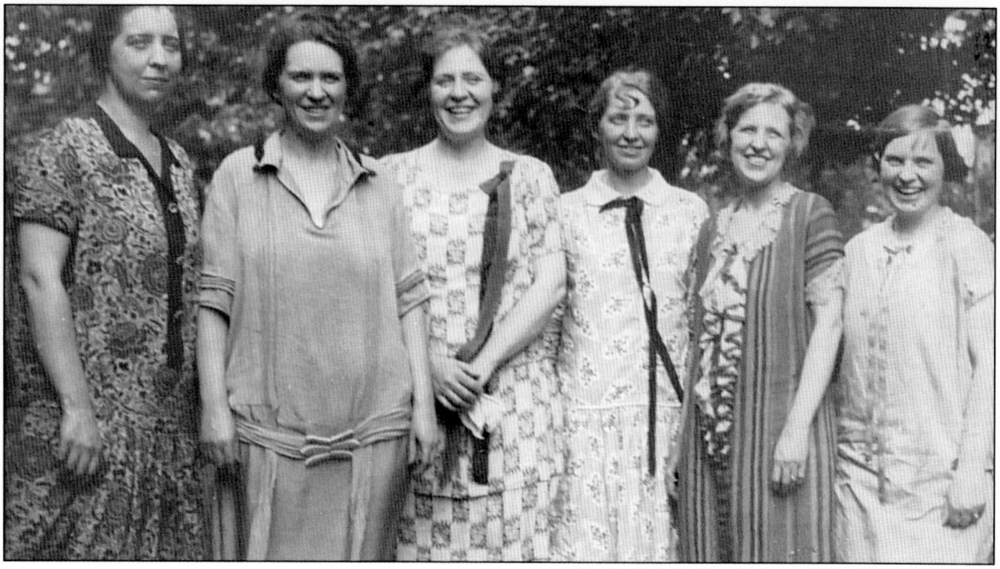

The Tandy sisters are, from left to right, Janette Tandy, Harriet Meng, Elizabeth Tandy, Julia Tandy, Mary Sutton, and Justine Campbell. (Courtesy of Port William Historical Society.)

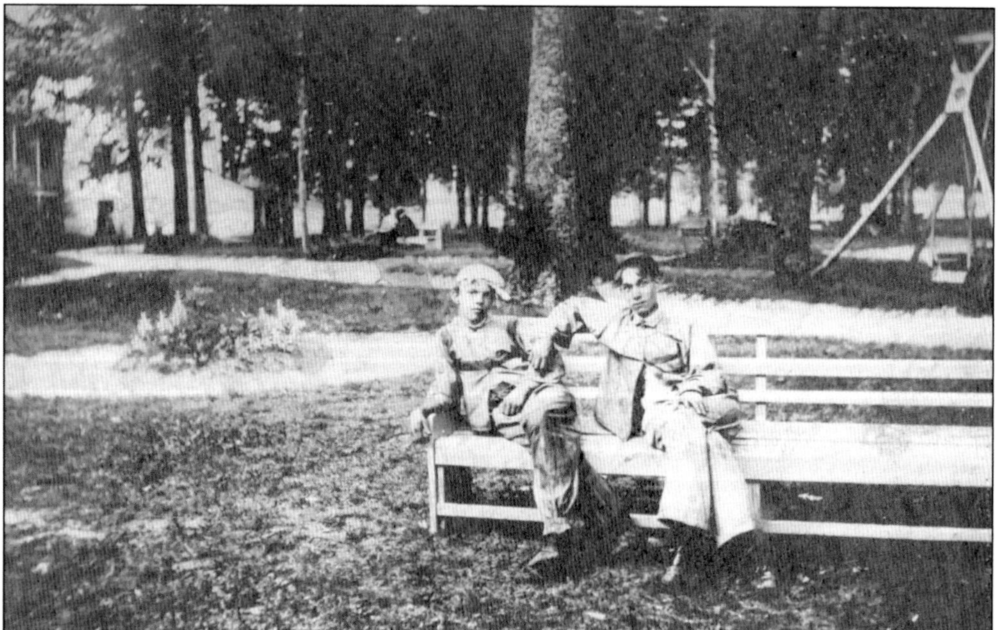

J. Lyter Donaldson (left), who later became a commissioner for the state highway department, lounges with friend Stanley Grobmyer on a bench near the river. Donaldson ran for governor of Kentucky in 1943. In 1911, Grobmyer became superintendent of the Carrollton Brick Company; he also was in the coal business. (Courtesy of Port William Historical Society.)

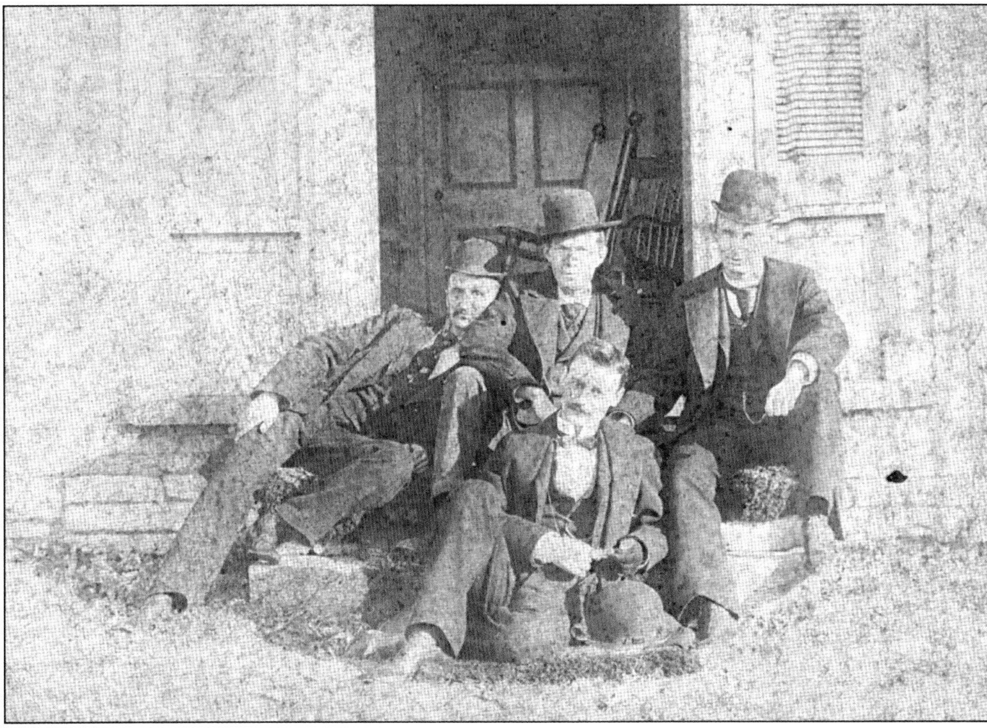

Taking time out for a portrait are (back row), from left to right, George B. Winslow, William Masterson, Columbus R. "Lum" Melcher, and (in front) a Mr. Hennesey. Winslow became a lawyer; Masterson became an American consul to Turkey; Melcher, of Vevay, Indiana, became a professor and later a dean at the University of Kentucky. (Courtesy of Port William Historical Society.)

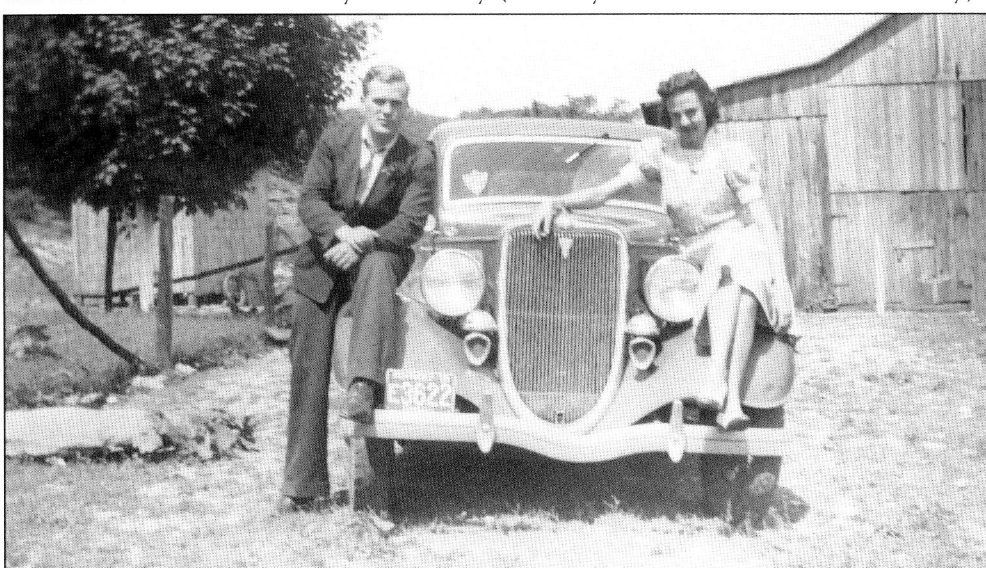

William P. and Margaret Ruth Jenkins Thompson pose in 1939, before William's departure to fight in World War II. He served as a captain in the 84th Infantry Division, known as the "Kentucky Rail Splitters," and was awarded several medals. He died shortly after returning home from the war. (Courtesy of *News-Democrat.*)

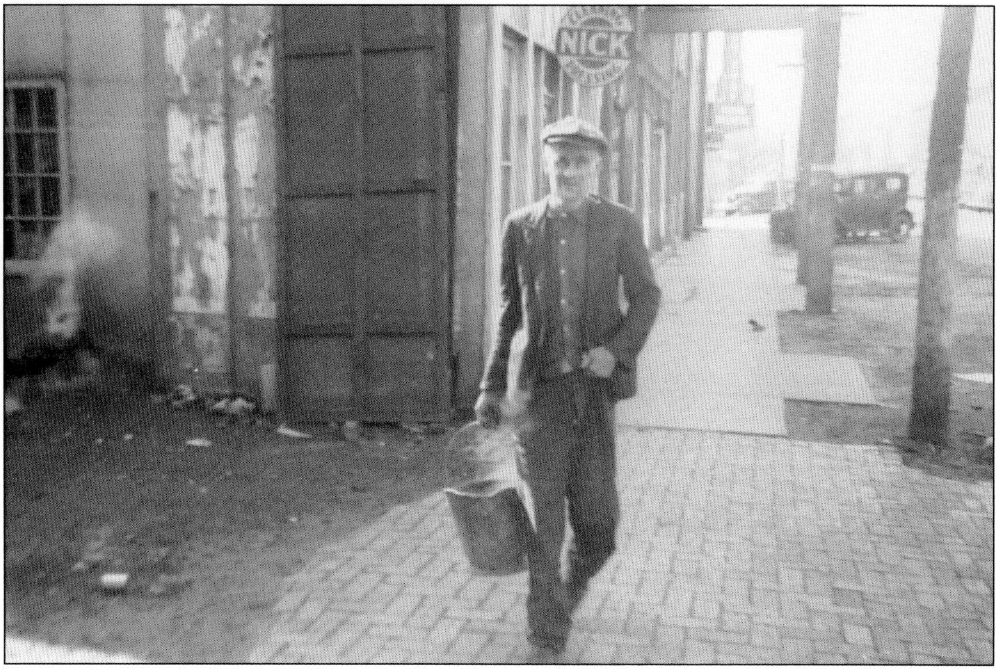

"Squirrelly" Carter, one of the city's more colorful characters, walks down Main Street in Carrollton. A resident of the county poorhouse (which used to stand where the county's Robert Westrick Park is located), he would sell squirrel meat to earn money. (Courtesy of Amy Baglan.)

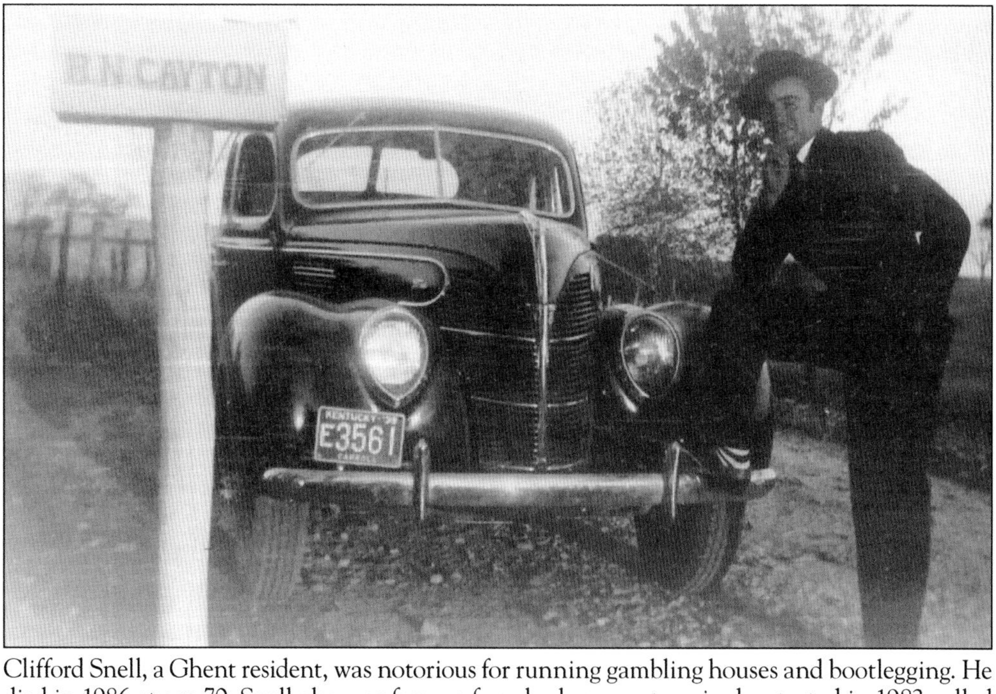

Clifford Snell, a Ghent resident, was notorious for running gambling houses and bootlegging. He died in 1986 at age 70. Snell also was famous for a barbecue enterprise he started in 1982 called Backwoods Pit. (Courtesy of Charles "Buck" Johnson.)

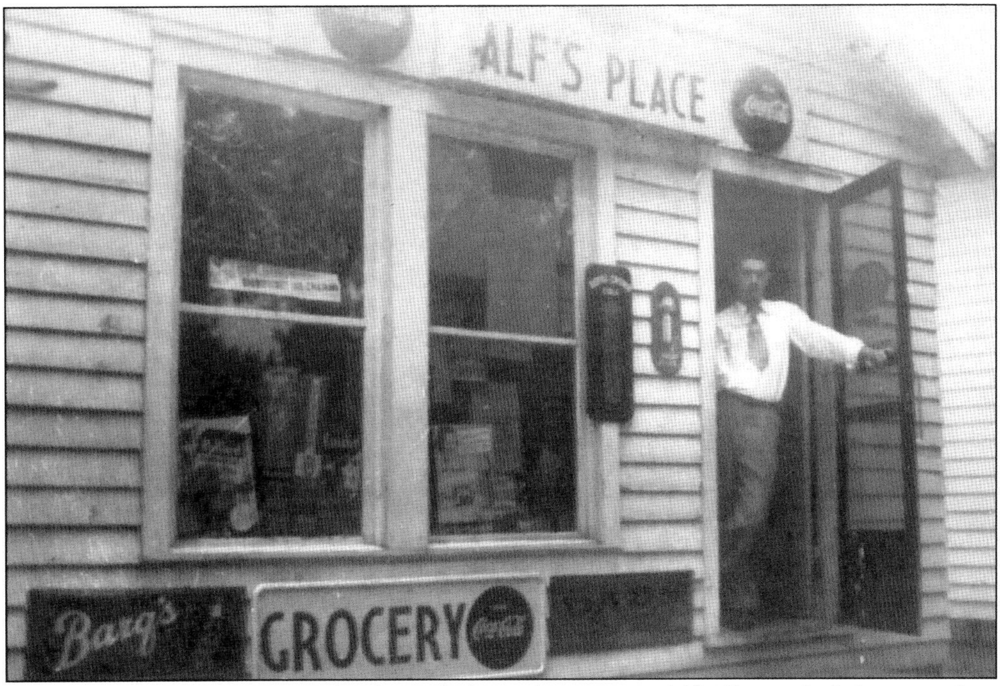

Alf Renschler poses in his Sunday dress clothes at his grocery, Alf's Place, which he opened on Sixth Street in Carrollton in 1948, a year after he graduated from Carrollton High School. His mother, Julia, operated the store while he served in the US Army from 1951 to 1953. He closed the store in 1955, and the building is now his home. (Courtesy of Betty's Collectibles.)

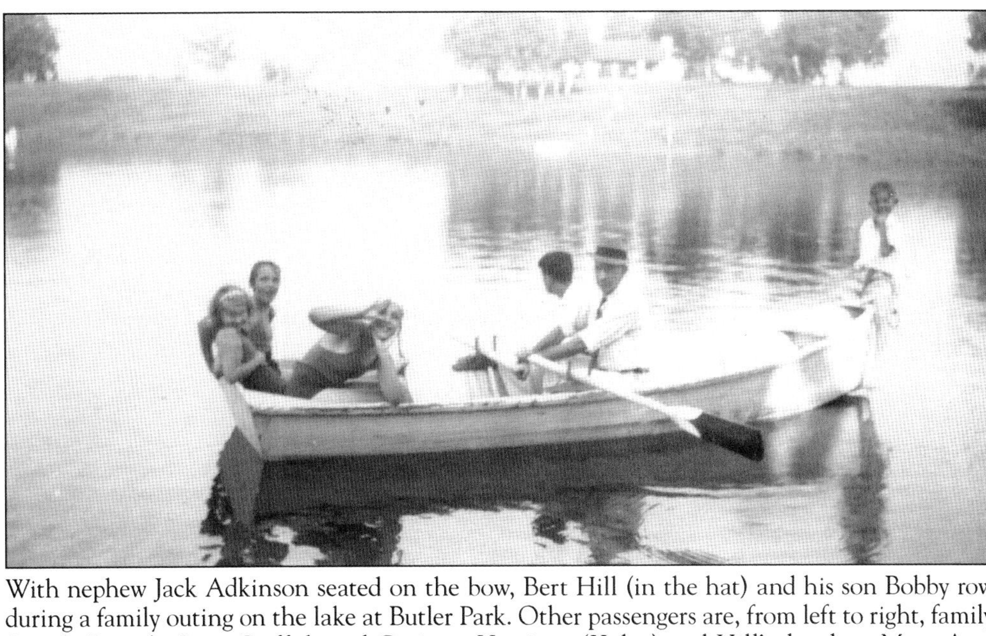

With nephew Jack Adkinson seated on the bow, Bert Hill (in the hat) and his son Bobby row during a family outing on the lake at Butler Park. Other passengers are, from left to right, family friends Dorothy Jean Griffith and Corinne Harrison (Kuhn) and Hill's daughter Mary Ann (Gentry). The photograph was taken about 1935. (Courtesy of Amy Baglan.).

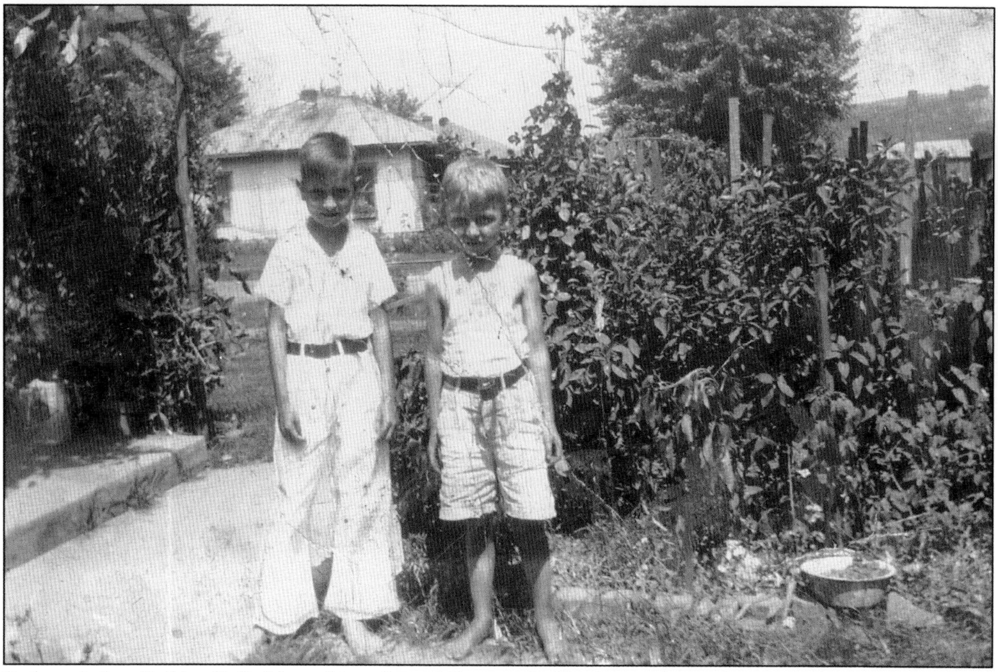

Robert John Caldwell (left) and his friend Everett Tilley have their photograph taken near the Caldwells' home on Seventh Street in Carrollton. Later nicknamed "Goose," Caldwell enlisted in the US Army and served in World War II. He later served in Vietnam as a member of the Kentucky National Guard unit based in Carrollton. (Courtesy of Robin Caldwell Welch.)

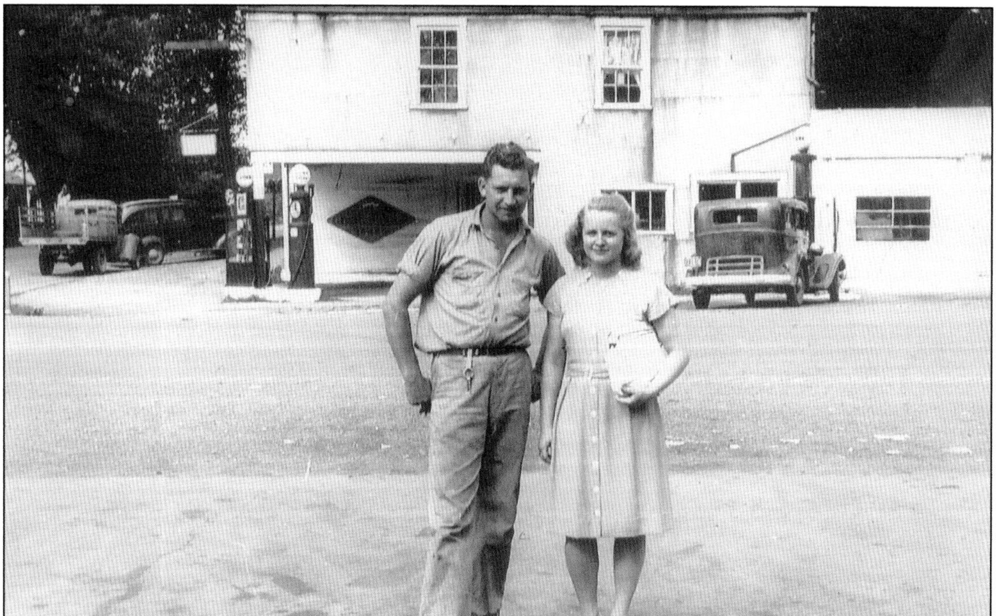

Jack William "J.W." Wheeler and Elizabeth Kring pose at the corner of Main and Main Cross Streets in Ghent, across from the station where he worked as an automobile mechanic. Wheeler served in the Aleutians and the Philippines in World War II, but was killed in 1949 when his truck struck a tree on US 42. (Courtesy of Charles "Buck" Johnson).

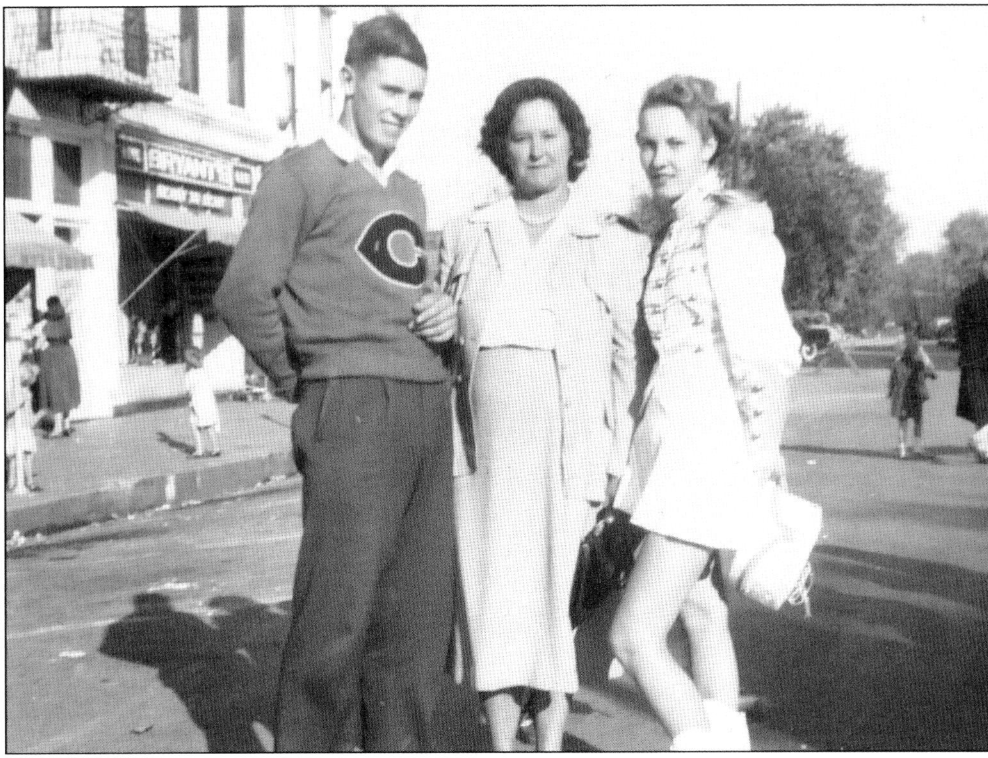

Charles "Buck" Johnson, wearing his freshman letterman's sweater from Carrollton High School, stands on Main Street with his mother, Susie, and his then girlfriend, majorette Jean Allen Willis, following the Tobacco Festival Parade in 1950. Johnson was the top high school basketball player in Kentucky in 1952. (Courtesy of Charles "Buck" Johnson.)

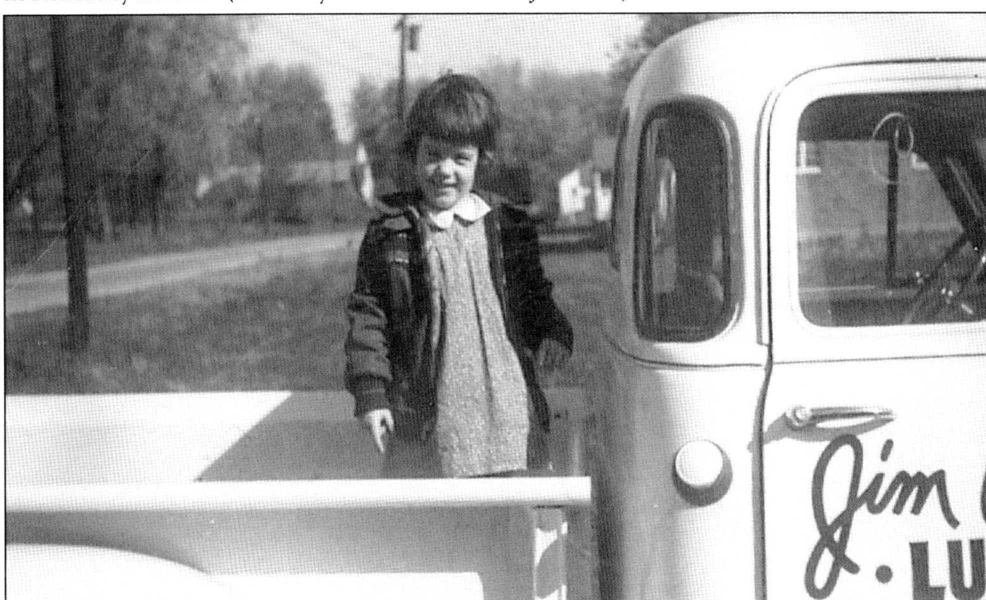

Margaret Brown stands in the back of her father's pickup truck, which he used for his Carrollton business, the Jim Brown Lumber Company. (Courtesy of Margaret Brown Walker.)

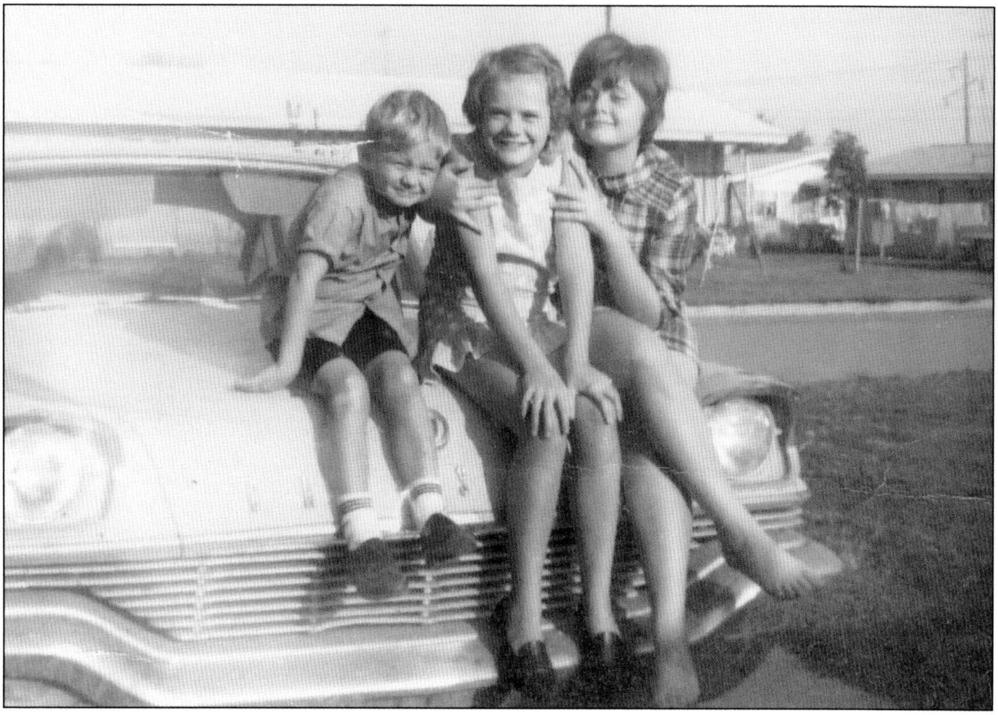

Siblings Lenny (left), Melanie (center), and Christie Eversole enjoy a warm late-summer evening at their home on Eighth Street in Carrollton in September 1968. (Courtesy of the Eversole and Harsin families.)

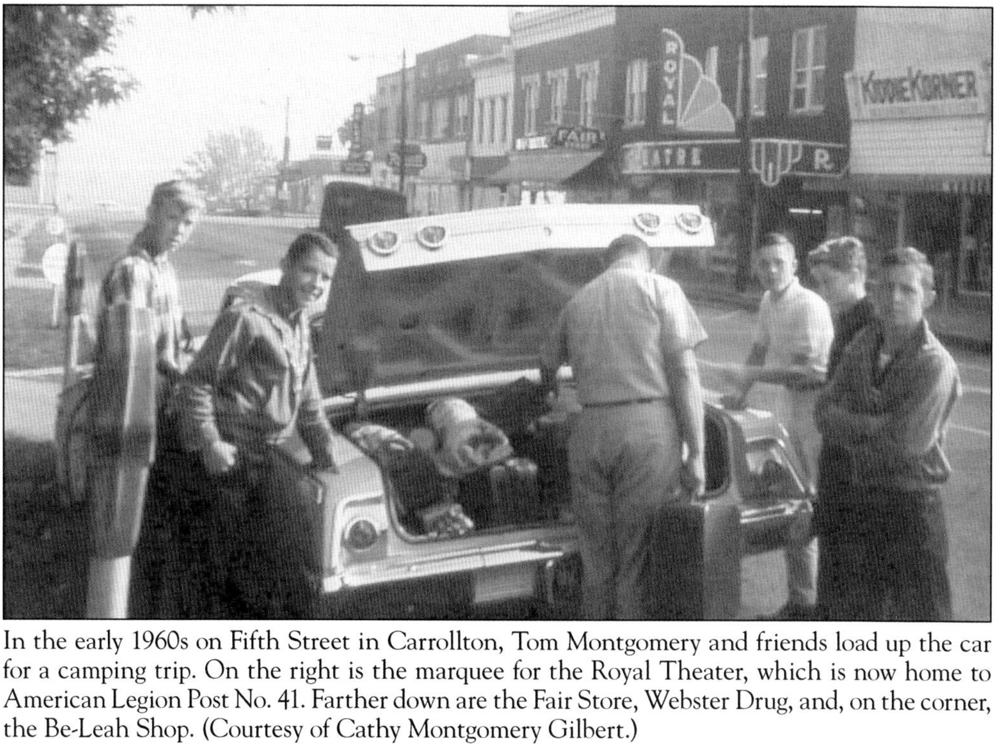

In the early 1960s on Fifth Street in Carrollton, Tom Montgomery and friends load up the car for a camping trip. On the right is the marquee for the Royal Theater, which is now home to American Legion Post No. 41. Farther down are the Fair Store, Webster Drug, and, on the corner, the Be-Leah Shop. (Courtesy of Cathy Montgomery Gilbert.)

Four

A Call to Serve

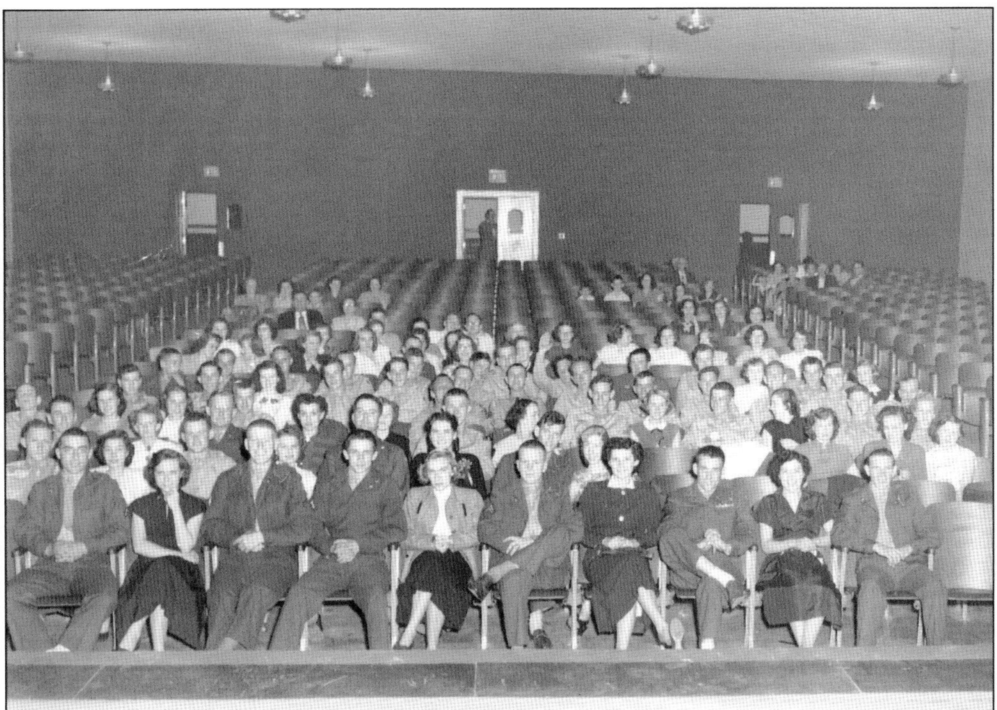

Families and friends gathered in the auditorium at Carrollton High School in 1951 to send off local men who were being sent to fight in the Korean War. (Courtesy of *News-Democrat*.)

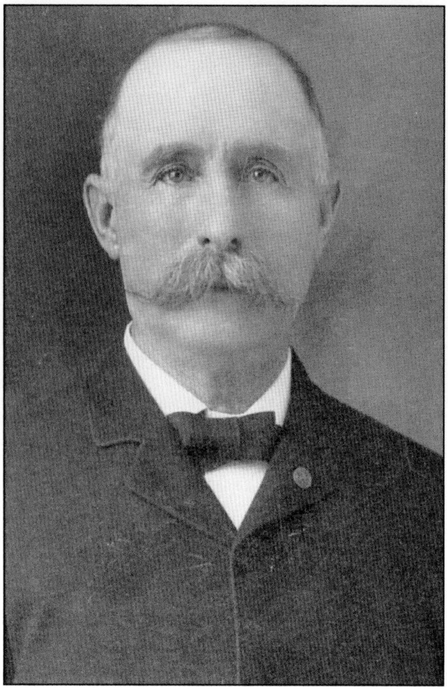

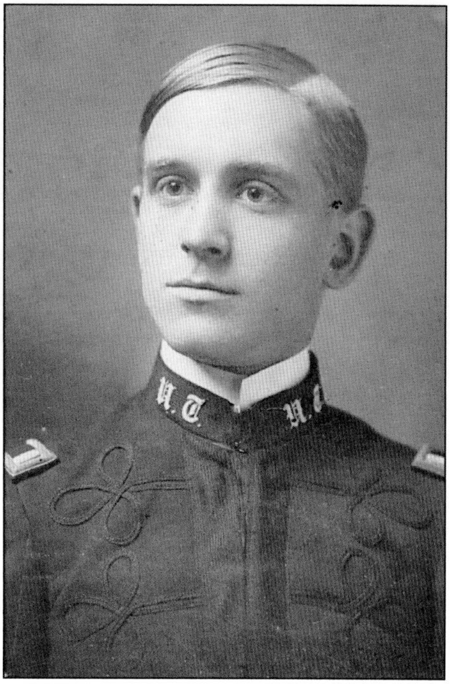

Albert Newton Jett (left) served in Company K of the Union's 13th Kentucky Infantry from February 1863 to January 1865. Entering as a second sergeant, he attained the rank of captain. Beverly Winslow Howe (right) served in World War I and later became an accomplished Chicago lawyer and student of Abraham Lincoln. (Left, courtesy of Jim Fothergill; right, courtesy of Ben Collett.)

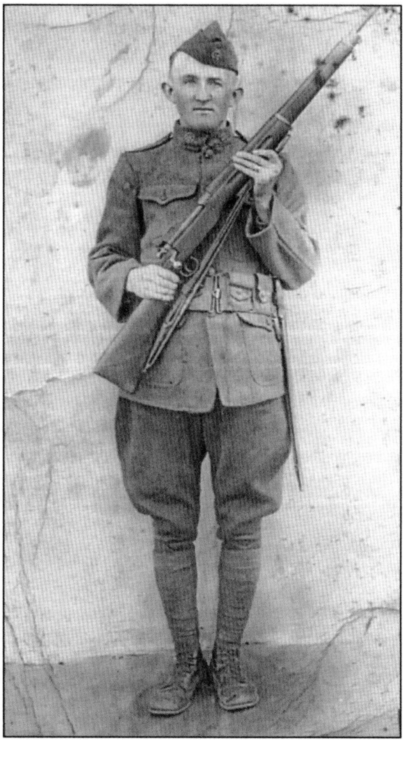

In World War I, Kirbie F. House, son of Willis and Ida House, served as a private in 9th Company, 154th Depot Brigade, in Camp Meade, Maryland. The brigade trained more than 103,000 men during the war and included a remount station that cared for horses later sent to camps in the United States and Europe. House married Cora Scudder, daughter of Frank and Martha Scudder of Prestonville. (Courtesy of Gary Ford.)

Herbert A. Morgan was a private in the US Army during World War I. He married Florence Wood, who is pictured on the cover with her friends at the dam on the Kentucky River. Born in Prestonville, he was a farmer in Campbellsburg until his death in 1972. (Courtesy of Rebecca Morgan Tull.)

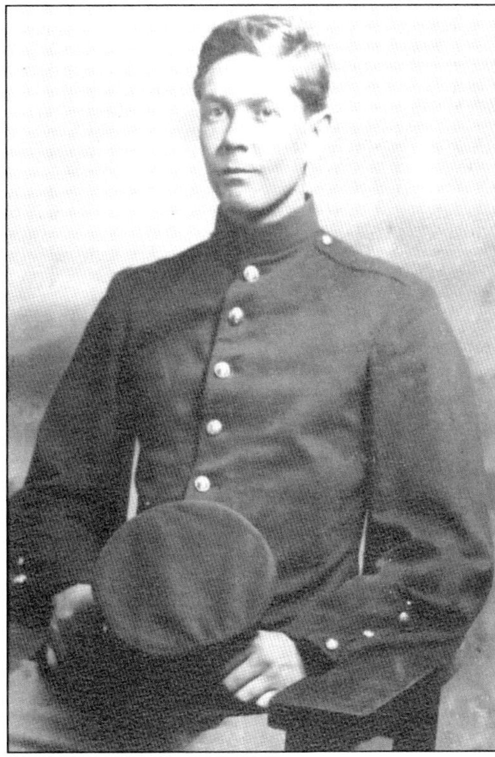

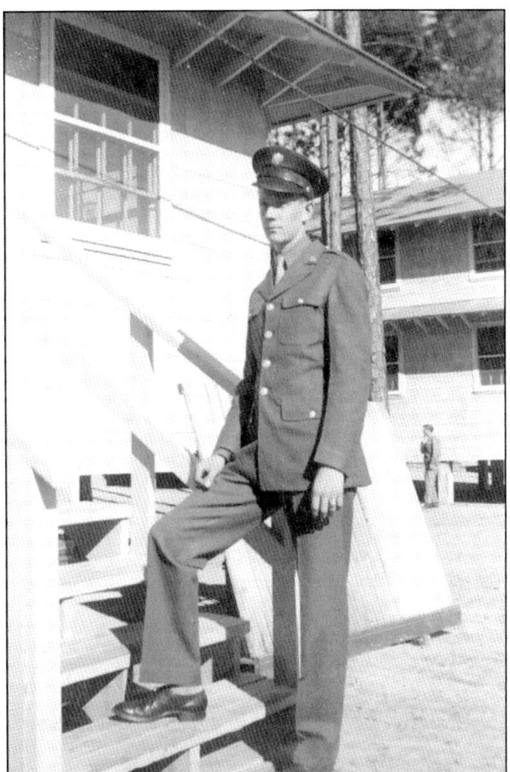

Roger William Morgan followed in his father Herbert's footsteps when he was drafted to serve in the 82nd Airborne Division of the US Army Air Corps. He died during a bombing mission on June 8, 1944, when his plane crashed near Dover, England. (Courtesy of Rebecca Morgan Tull.)

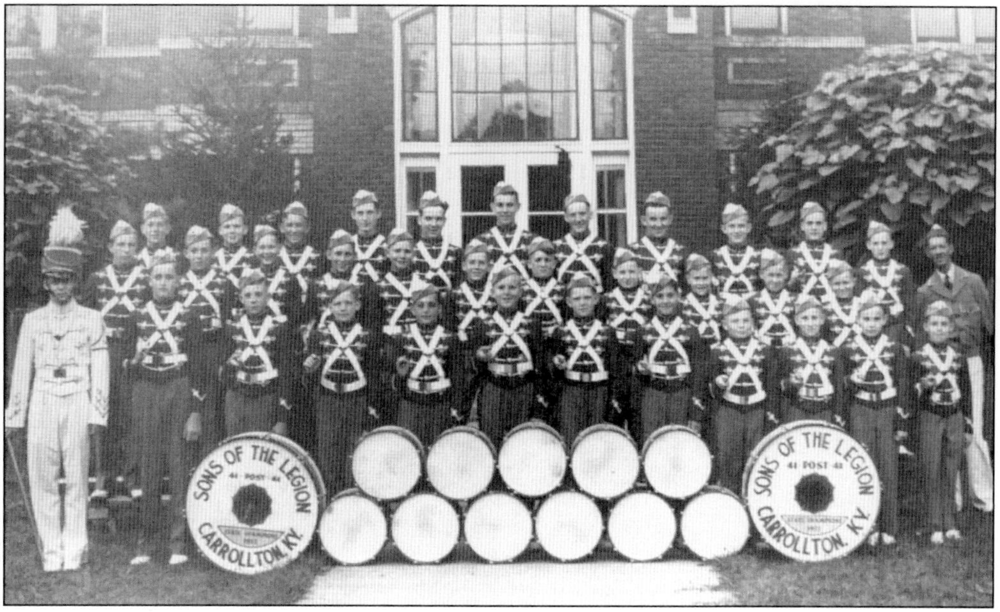

For at least four years straight, 1937 to 1940, the Drum and Bugle Corps of the Carrollton Post's Sons of the American Legion was champion of the annual competition held during the state American Legion conference. In this photograph, drum major J.W. Fisher stands with the rest of the boys, ages 8 to 20, who all were sons of members of Post 41 in Carrollton. (Courtesy of *News-Democrat*.)

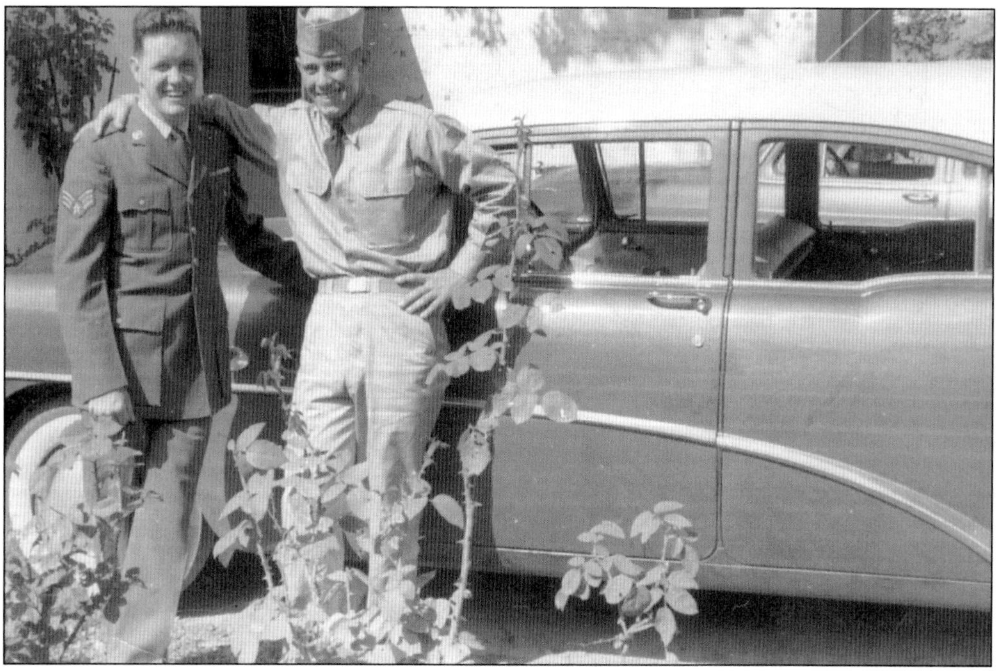

Charles "Buck" Johnson (right) leans on his pal, Ted Terry, as both pose in their military uniforms. Johnson served during the Vietnam War at Fort Knox, Kentucky. During his time at Carrollton High School, particularly in his senior year in 1952, Johnson was one of the top basketball players in the state. (Courtesy of Charles "Buck" Johnson.)

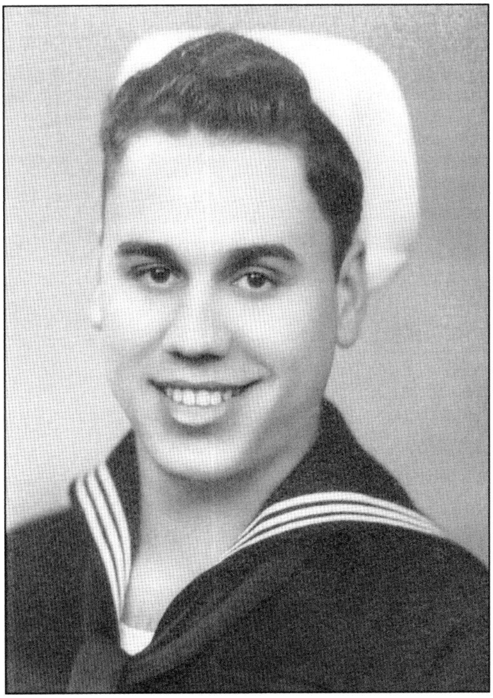 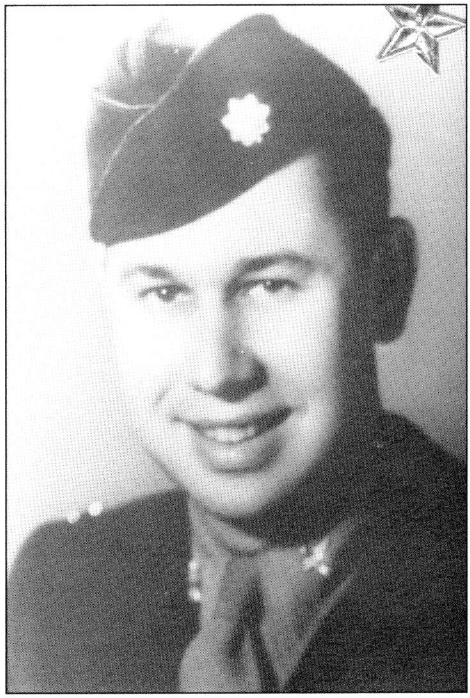

Robert A. Grobmyer (left) and his brother Jack (right) both served in the military during World War II. Jack died in the war. Below, US Army officials deliver Jack's posthumous medals to his parents, Stanley and Hester Bruce Grobmyer in 1945. Robert died in an accident in 1957, leaving his wife, the former Nancy Jo Ellis, to raise their four children. She is a well-known voice and piano teacher and retired after serving 32 years on Carrollton City Council. (All, courtesy of Nancy Jo Grobmyer.)

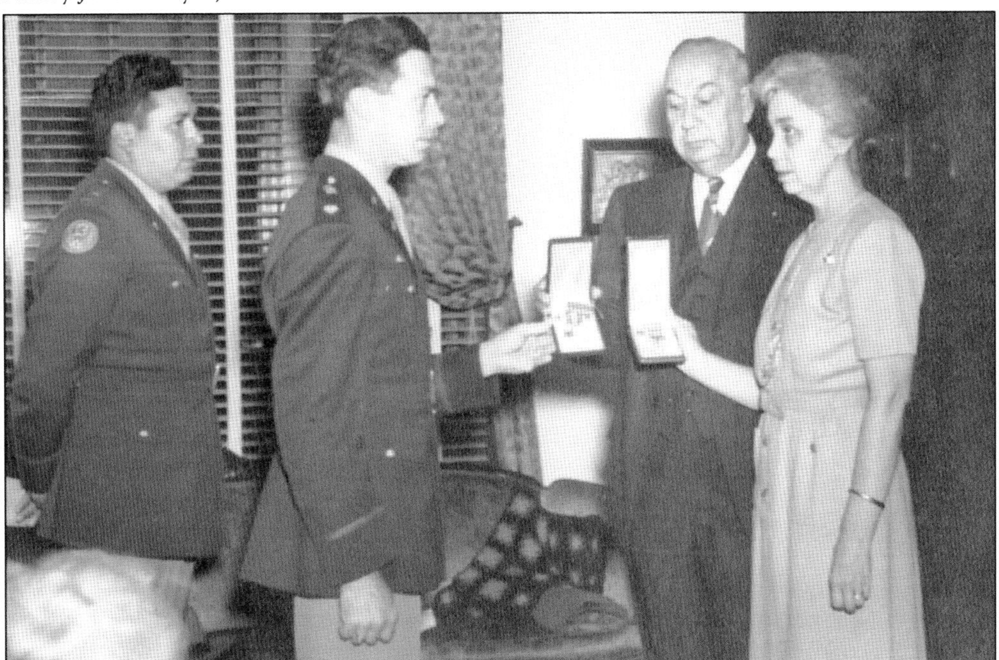

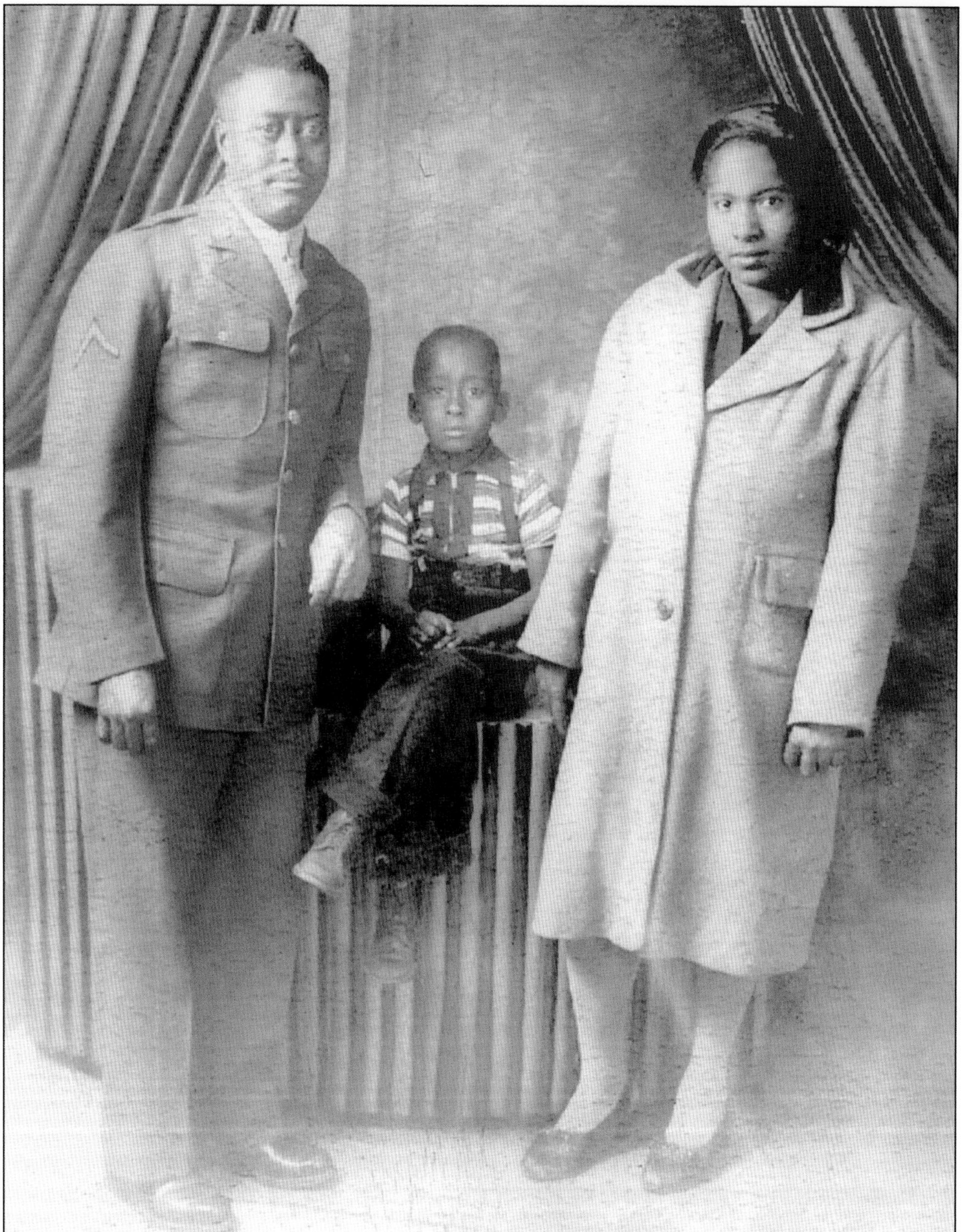

A young William Mumphrey poses in a Carrollton photography studio with his father, Lawrence Purdue (who served in the US Army Air Force in World War II), and his mother, Pearl Mumphrey. William went on to serve in the US Army during the Vietnam era. In 2006, he was the first African American elected mayor of Ghent, a position he holds today. (Courtesy of William Mumphrey.)

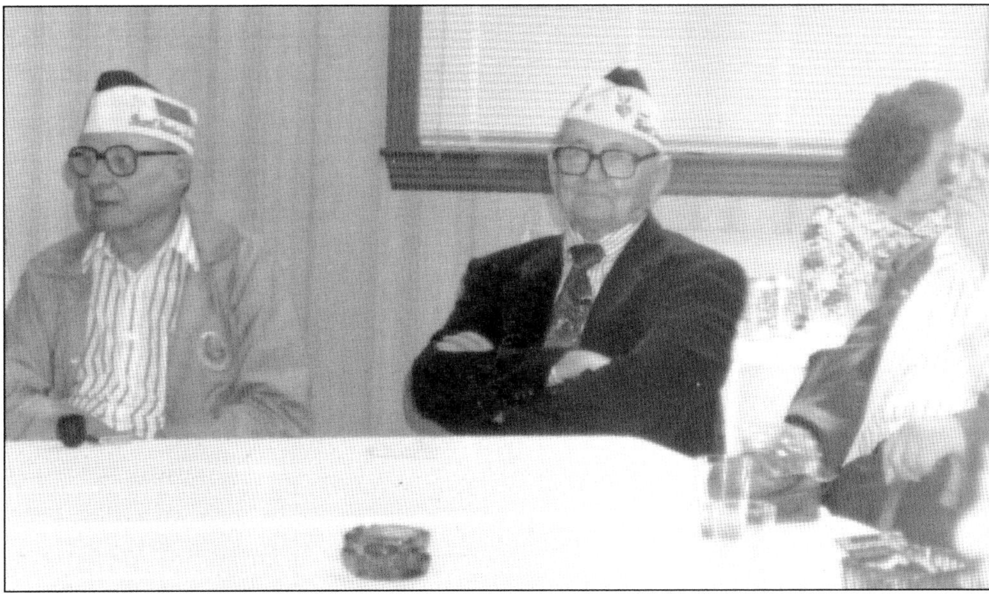

An event was held to honor Carroll County veterans who served at Pearl Harbor on December 7, 1941. (Courtesy of *News-Democrat*.)

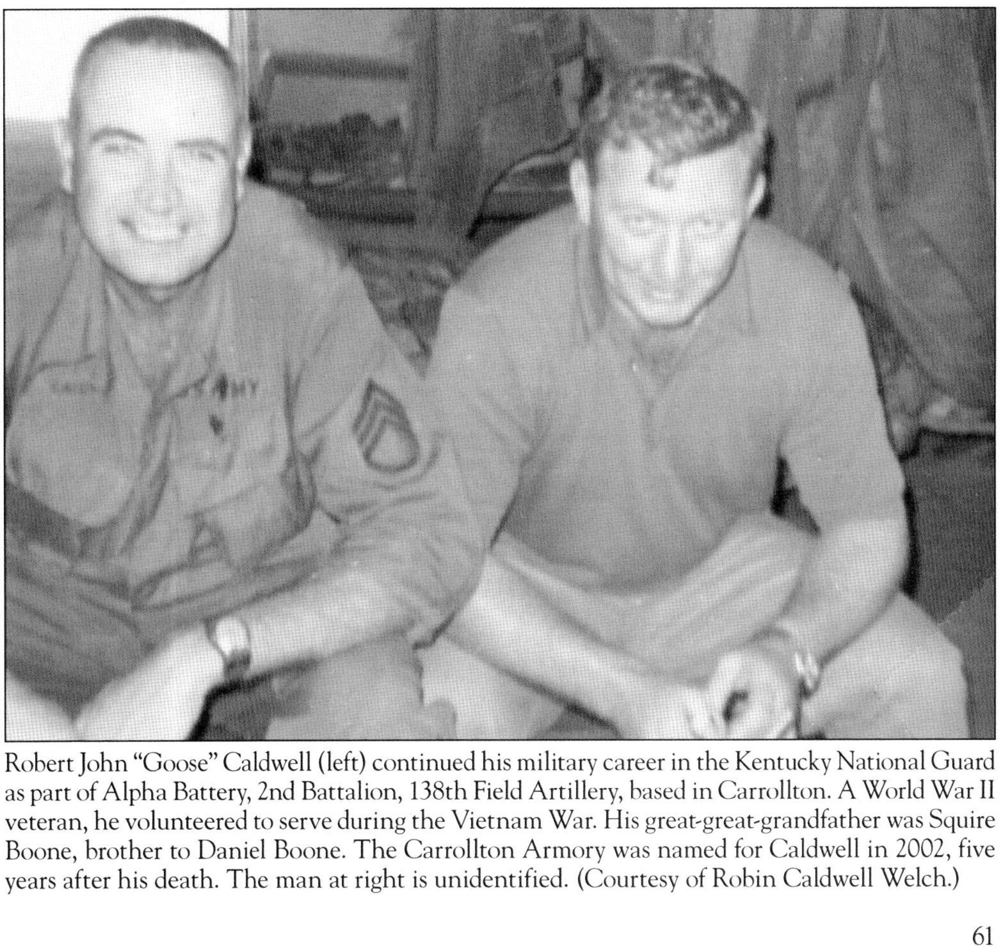

Robert John "Goose" Caldwell (left) continued his military career in the Kentucky National Guard as part of Alpha Battery, 2nd Battalion, 138th Field Artillery, based in Carrollton. A World War II veteran, he volunteered to serve during the Vietnam War. His great-great-grandfather was Squire Boone, brother to Daniel Boone. The Carrollton Armory was named for Caldwell in 2002, five years after his death. The man at right is unidentified. (Courtesy of Robin Caldwell Welch.)

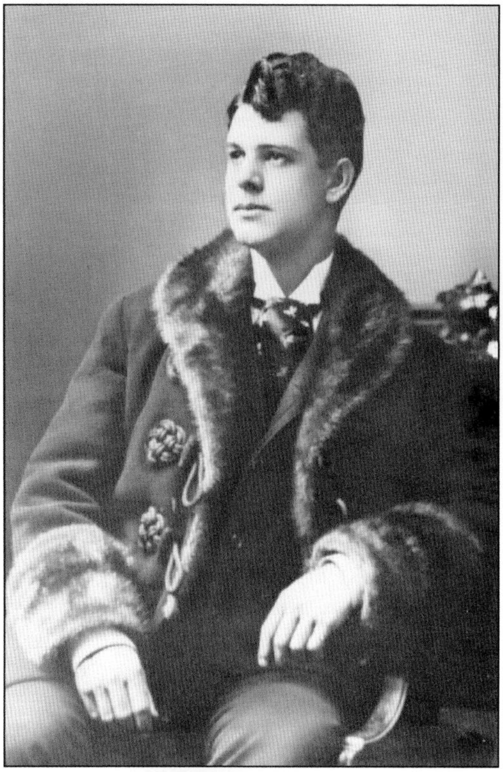

Famed Ghent resident James Tandy Ellis, left, well-known for his books of prose and poetry, as well as for his columns published by the *News-Democrat* and the *Louisville Courier*, served as adjutant general of the Kentucky National Guard from 1914 to 1919. Below right, Jesse Lindsay, of Ghent, served that same office from 1951 to 1955. He also had been a Carroll County judge from 1937 until his appointment. Kentucky's first adjutant general was Carroll Countian Percival Pierce Butler, below left, who served from 1793 to 1817. His father, Percival Richard, served at Valley Forge with Gen. George Washington. Butler's brothers also were military heroes: Maj. Thomas Butler was an aide to Gen. Andrew Jackson, and Maj. Gen. William Orlando Butler, namesake of General Butler State Resort Park, was commander of American forces during the Mexican War. (Left, courtesy of Nancy Jo Grobmyer; both below, courtesy of Kentucky National Guard.)

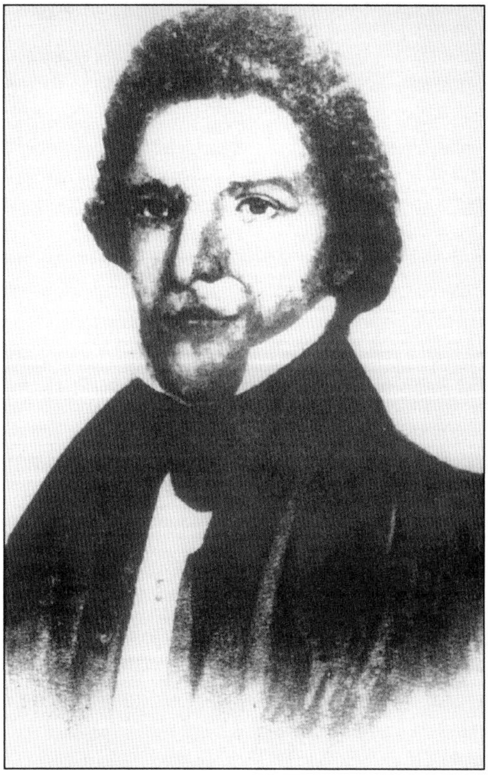

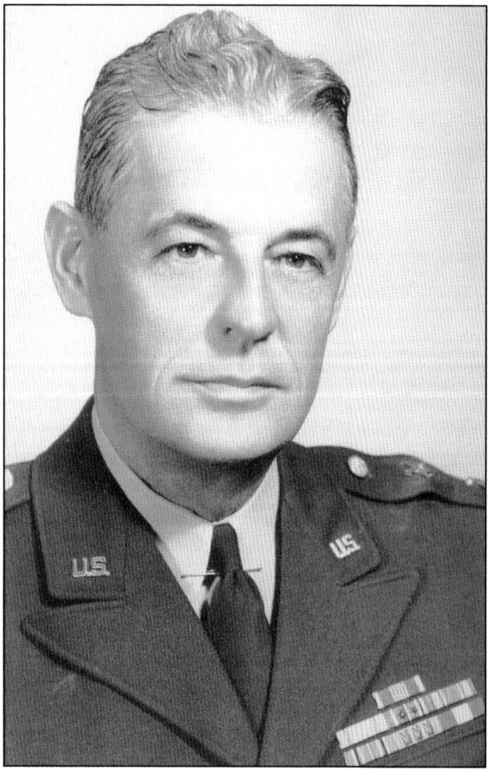

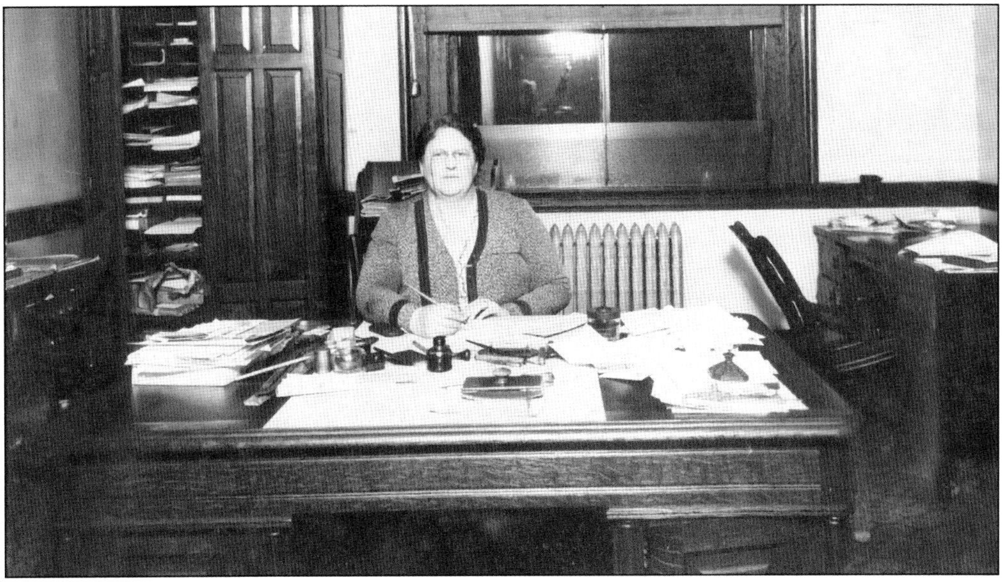

Mabel Jane Kirtley Kipping sits at her desk at the Carrollton Post Office, where she served as the state's first female postmaster from 1921 to 1932. Originally called the Customs House, the city's first permanent post office was built in 1902. Mabel was the wife of funeral home director Oscar Kipping. (Courtesy of Jane Graham Arnold.)

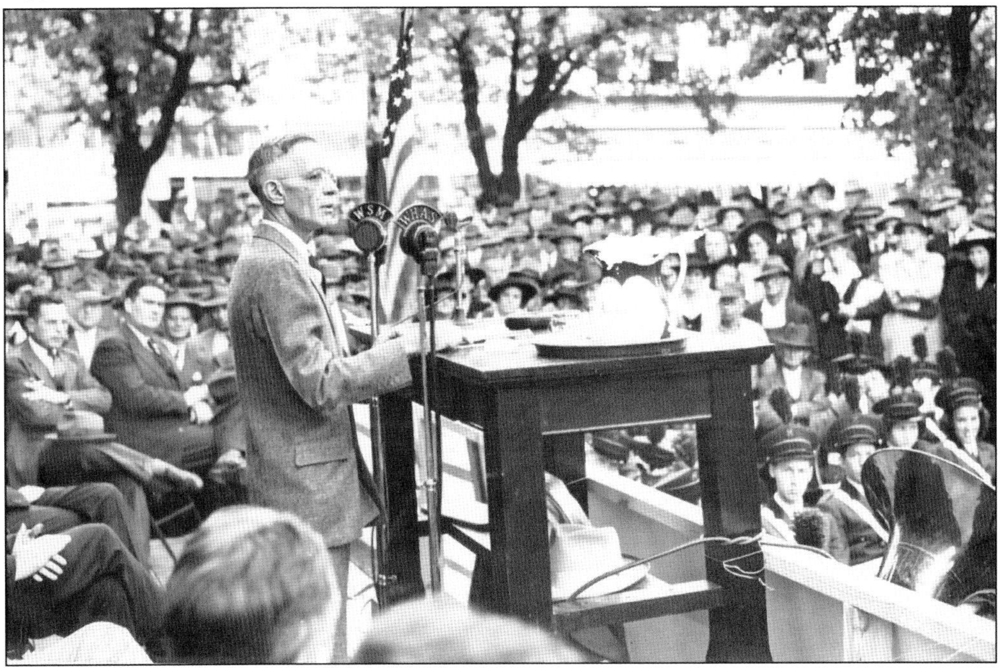

Joseph Lyter Donaldson, Carroll County attorney from 1921 to 1930, was an influential member and chairman of the Kentucky Highway Commission. Here, in 1943, he announces his candidacy for governor to a huge crowd outside the Carroll County Courthouse and to listeners of WHAS in Louisville and WSM in Nashville. Donaldson was instrumental in bringing Louisville-Cincinnati connector US 42 through Carroll County and bringing the Cincinnati airport to northern Kentucky. (Courtesy of *News-Democrat*.)

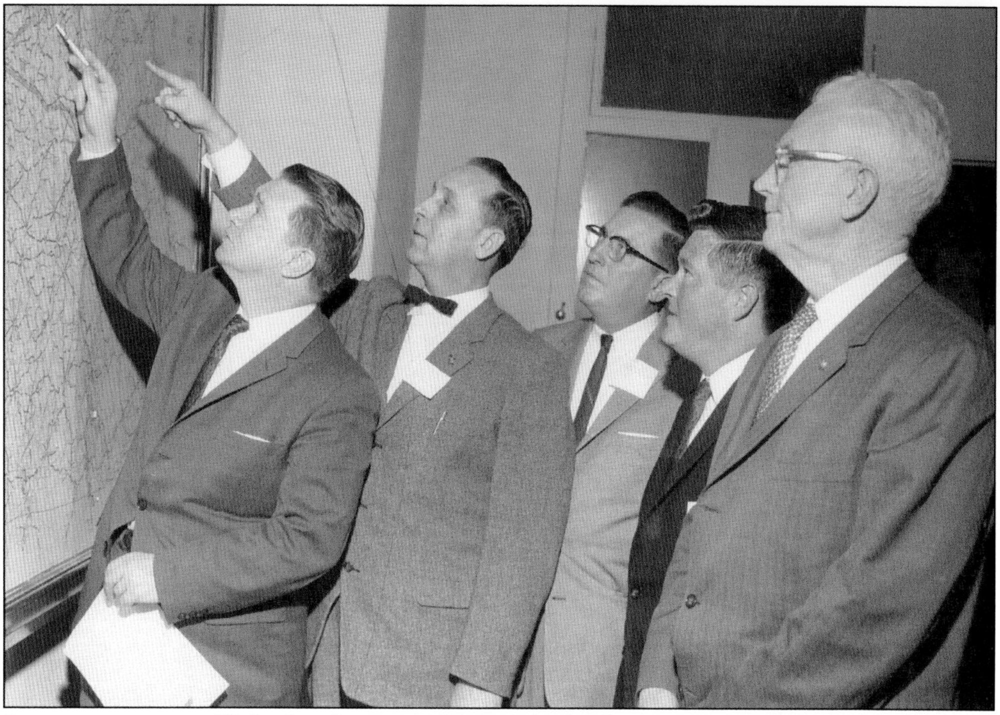

State representative W. Jay Louden, second from left, checks out a map with other state officials during the planning of the Markland Dam Bridge, one of his pet projects. He served the 59th District from 1968 to 1974. The bridge, in nearby Gallatin County, was completed in 1977. (Courtesy of Carol Louden Shelton.)

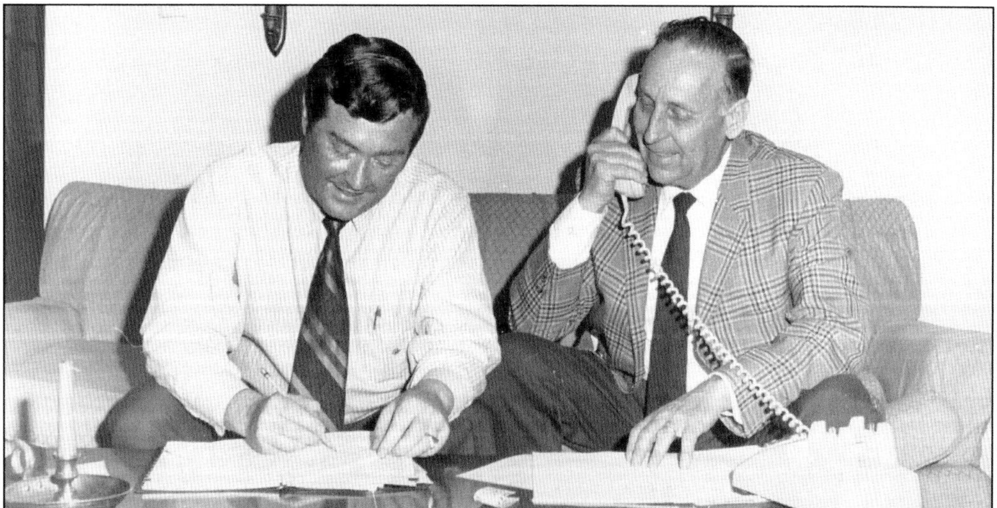

State representative W. Jay Louden, right, works with his friend Charlie Webster on Webster's 1970 campaign for Congress. Webster, who was Carrollton's mayor from 1962 to 1969 and again from 1979 to 1985, made an unsuccessful bid for the 4th District seat in the House of Representatives. He owned Webster Drug from 1956 until his death in 2012, was active at St. John Catholic Church, and was a longtime friend of former US senator Jim Bunning. (Courtesy of Carol Louden Shelton.)

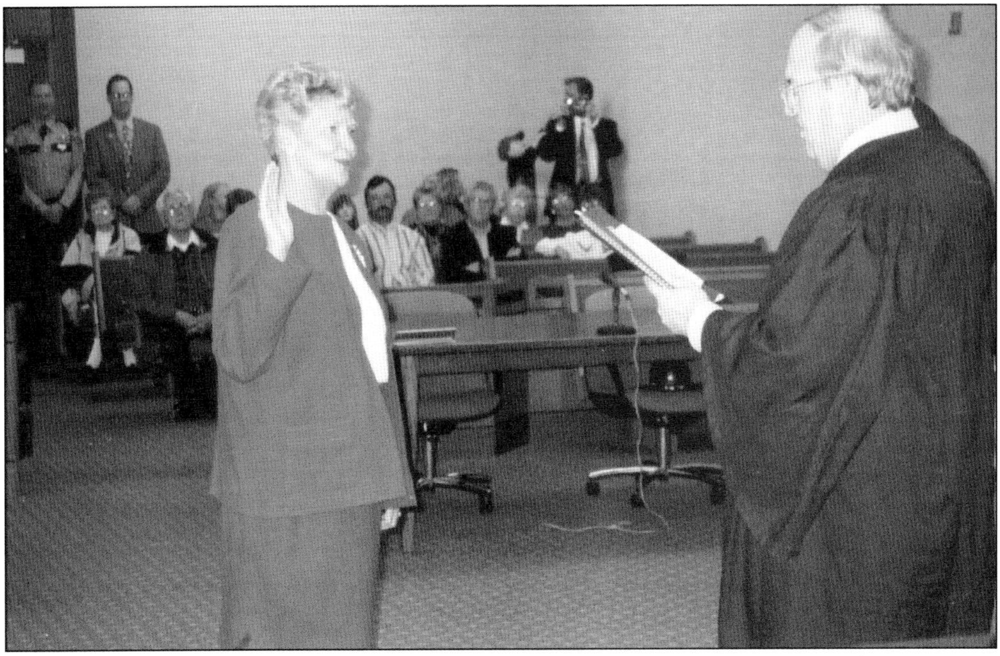

Ann Cline Deatherage takes the oath of office in 2002 as Carrollton's first female mayor. Her great-uncle Orville Monrow Wood, a Prestonville merchant, served as the city's very first mayor from 1894 until 1900, when the city government switched from a board of trustees to a city council. (Courtesy of Ann Deatherage.)

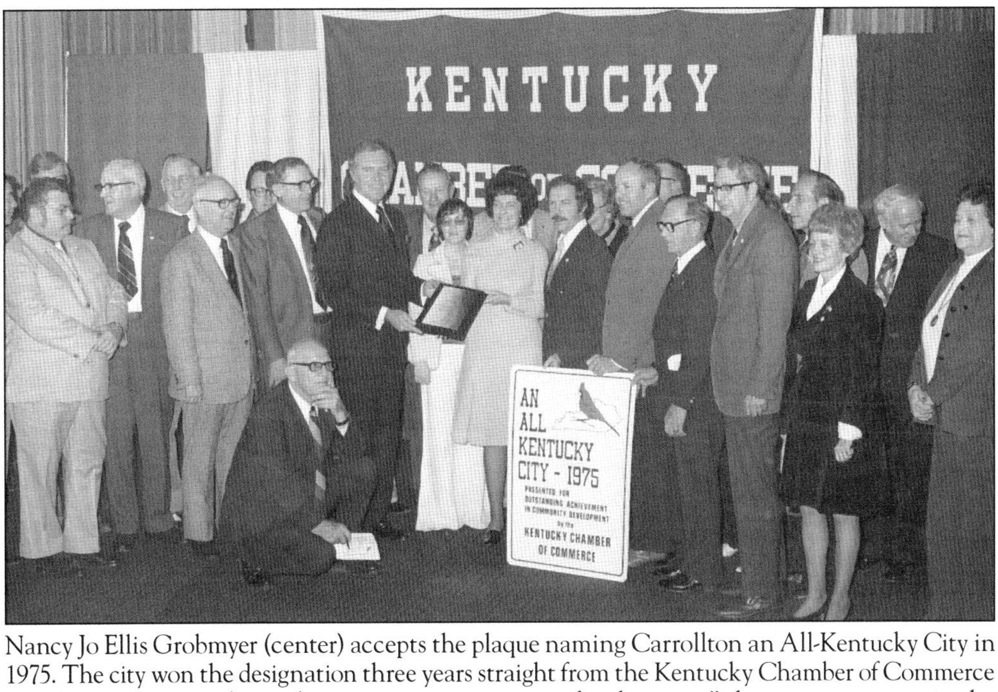

Nancy Jo Ellis Grobmyer (center) accepts the plaque naming Carrollton an All-Kentucky City in 1975. The city won the designation three years straight from the Kentucky Chamber of Commerce based on its "outstanding achievement in community development," thus earning a spot in the All-Kentucky City Hall of Fame. Other Carrollton residents attended, including Jim Fothergill, standing to Grobmyer's left. (Courtesy of Nancy Jo Grobmyer.)

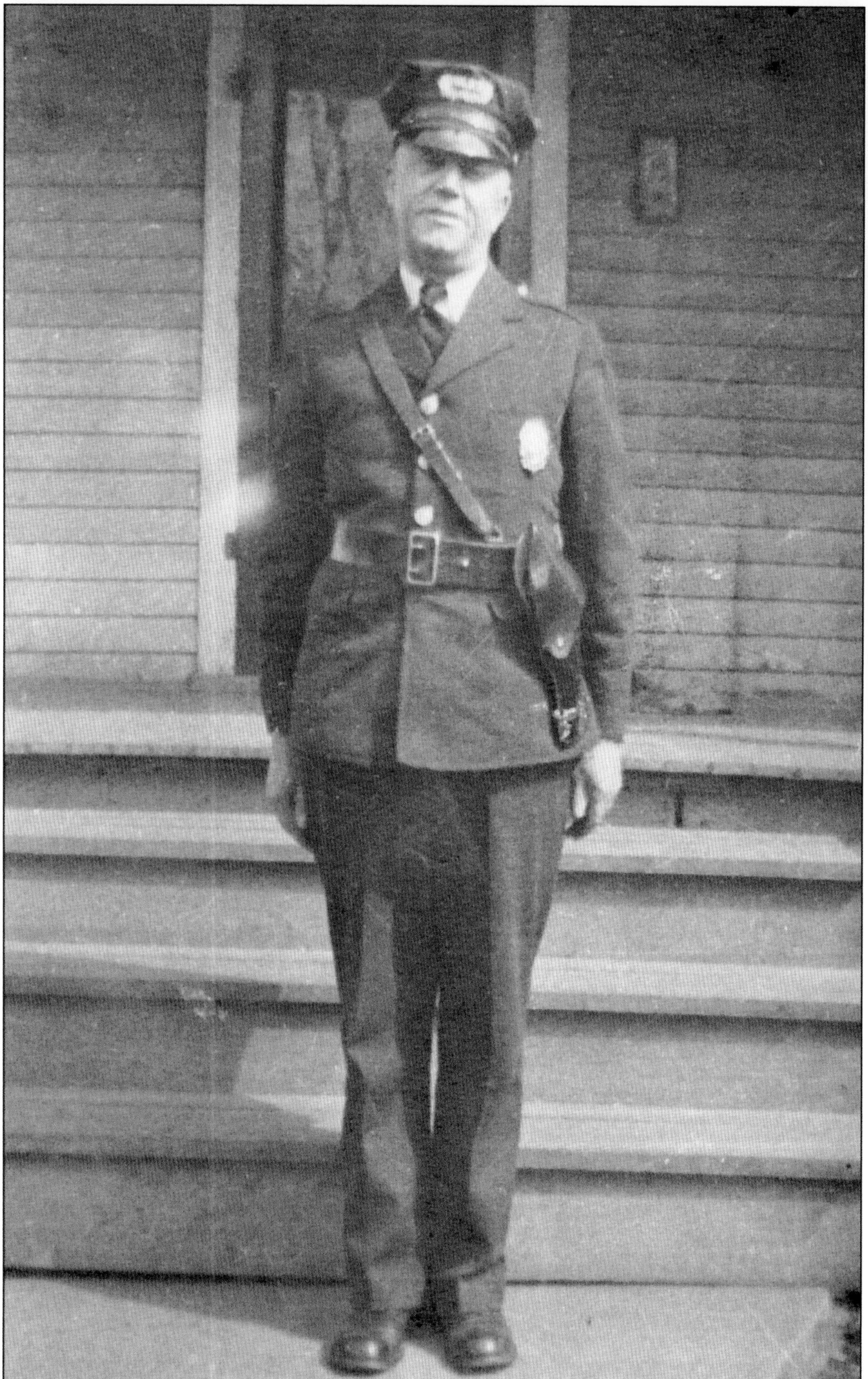

In 1929, Joseph Baker was Carrollton's only police officer. He is pictured here in front of his family's home on Fifth Street. Before entering law enforcement, Baker owned a general store in Worthville. (Courtesy of Carol Louden Shelton.)

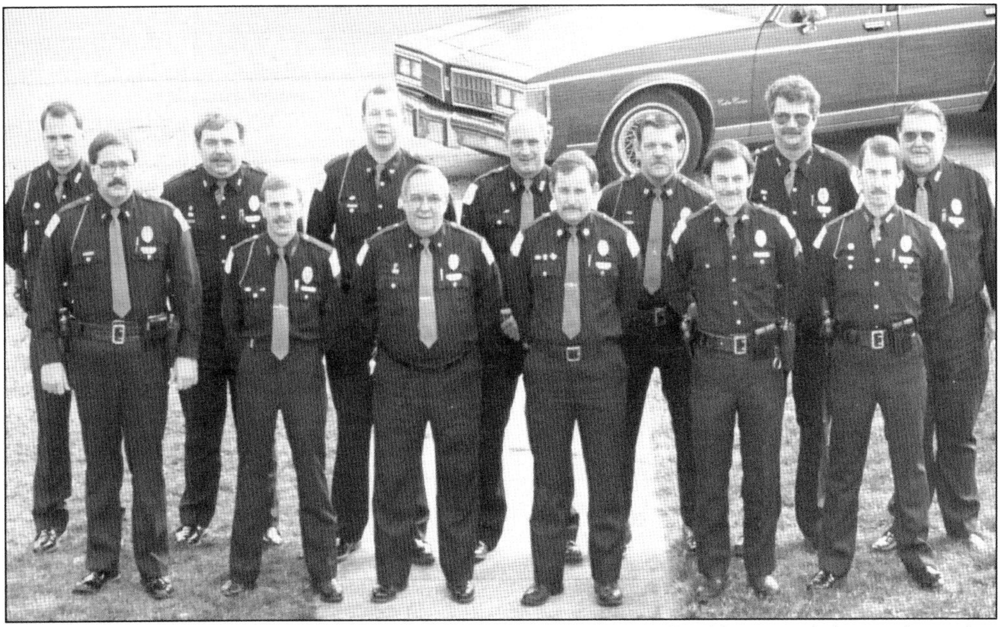

By 1990, the Carrollton Police Department had expanded considerably. From left to right in this photograph are (first row) officer John See, dispatcher Gary "Tick" Kindoll, dispatcher Jack Miles, dispatcher David Wilhoite, officer Rick Jackson, and officer Marty Souder; (second row) officer Greg Ford, officer Tim Ellis, Chief Laman Stark, officer Randy Culver, officer John "Tooter" Booth, and dispatcher Jess Maiden. (Courtesy of *News-Democrat*.)

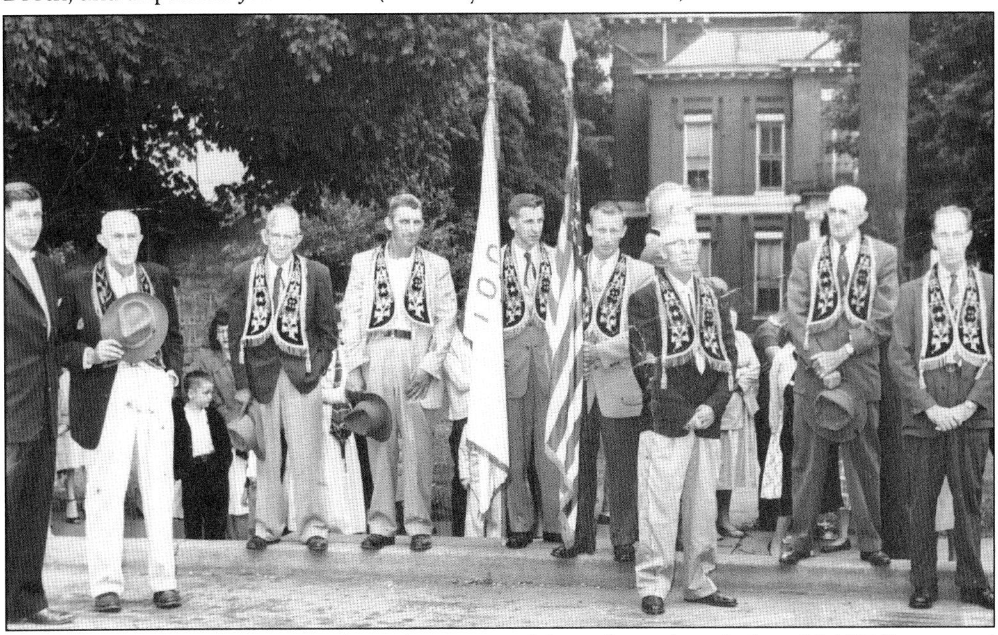

Members of Carrollton's Browinski Lodge No. 64 of the Independent Order of Odd Fellows stand on Highland Avenue in front of the courthouse during a parade in the 1940s. The lodge was founded in 1849 by Micholai W. Browinski, a native of Poland who moved his family to Carrollton. The lodge, at the corner of Seminary and Eleventh Streets, stands next to a cemetery, which the organization has operated since 1876. (Courtesy of Gary Ford.)

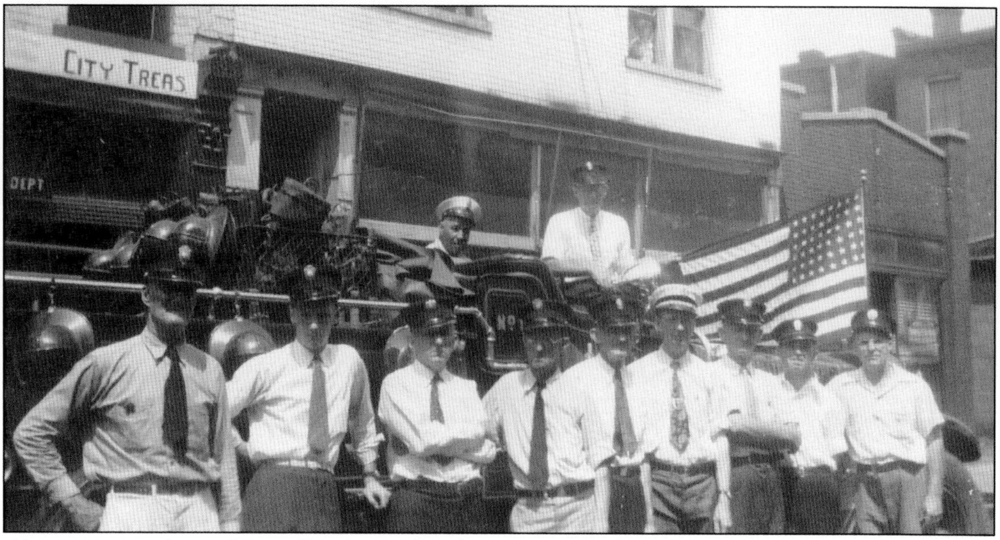

Above are members of Carrollton's city fire department in the 1930s in front of the old firehouse on Court Street. The building, which once housed all of the city's government offices, was abandoned and eventually torn down in 2008. Pictured below are members of the Carrollton Fire Department in 1951. From left to right are (first row) "Fats" Hamilton, Strother Stark, Orbie Calvert, and Eddie Marsh; (second row) Oscar Meadows, Andy Marsh, Foster Osbourne, Kirby House, and George Baker; (third row) Junior Courtney, Orville Hendricks, Adrian Danner, Tommy Ball, George Marsh, and Phillip Cayton. (Above, courtesy of Gary Ford; below, courtesy of Charles "Buck" Johnson.)

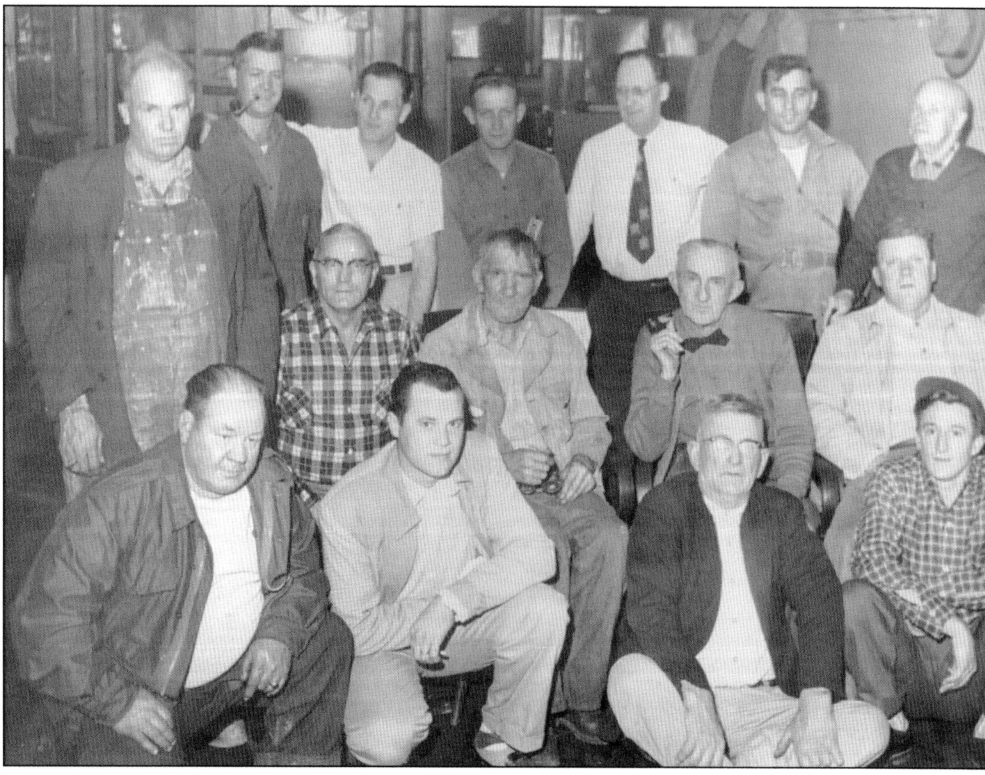

Five

The Rivers

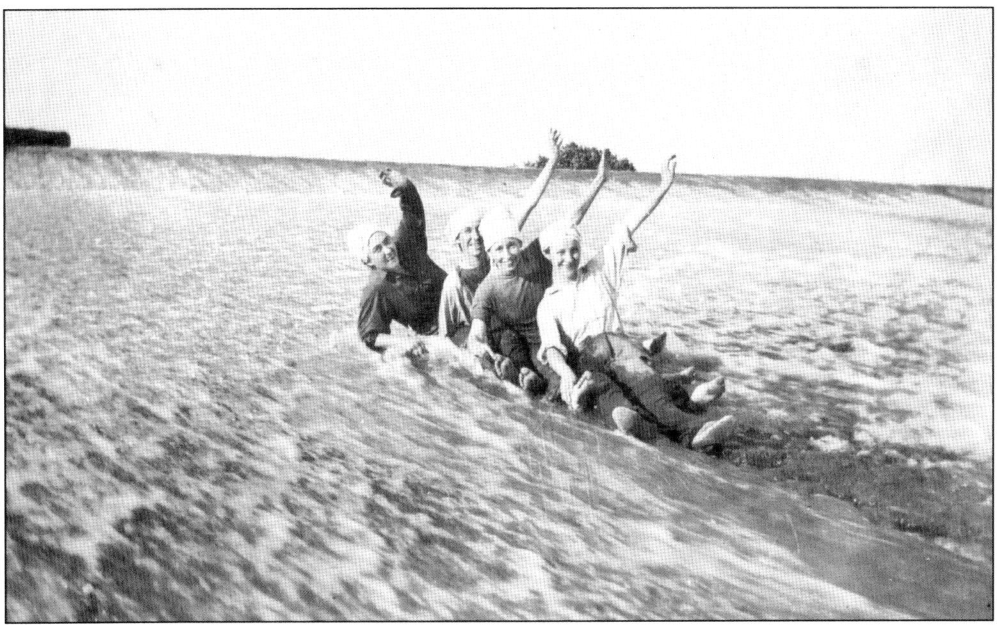

Four friends "slide the apron" in this photograph taken on the Kentucky River at Lock One about 1915. Leading the group is Florence Wood, who later would marry Herbert Morgan (see chapter four). The other girls are unidentified. (Courtesy of Rebecca Morgan Tull.)

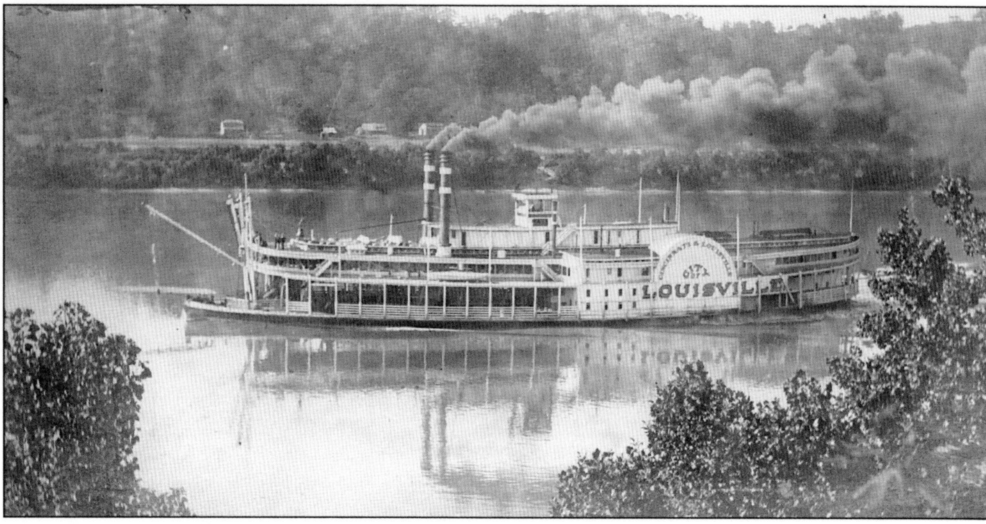

The *City of Louisville* steams past Pine View, a home on the Ohio River just east of town. Built by William and Adelaide "Ada" (sister of tobacco baron Ralph M. Barker) Fisher, Pine View was destroyed by fire. The Fishers began rebuilding, but Ada died before construction was finished. Barker completed the home, which he called Richlawn, and lived there until his death in 1952. (Courtesy of Don Mougey.)

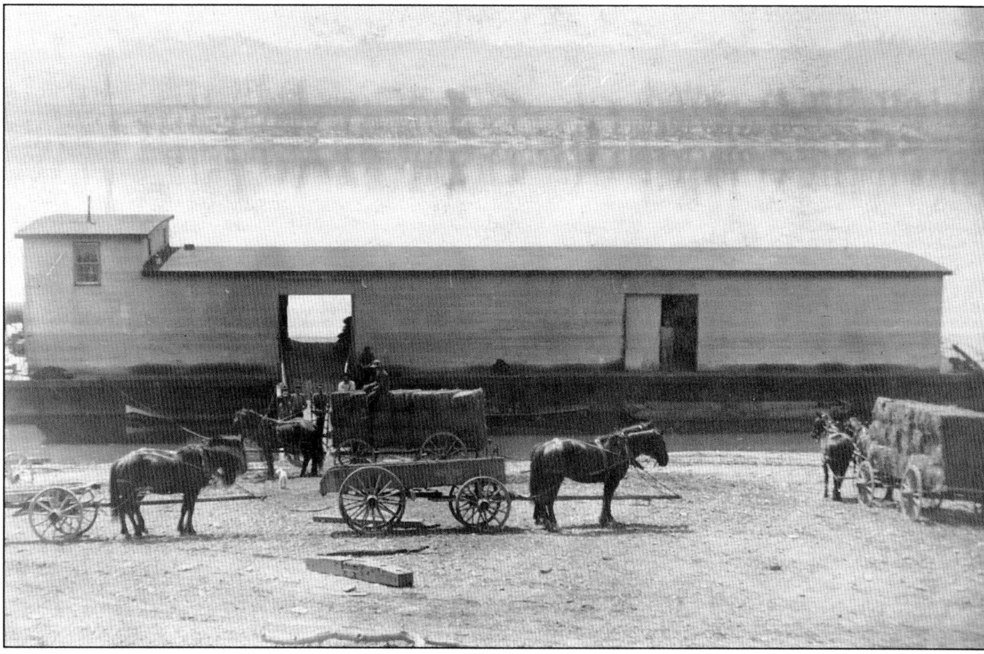

A barge stops on the Ohio River at Ghent for a load of hay. River transportation was the best way to move agricultural products and goods in the early days before the interstate highway system was built. (Courtesy of City of Ghent, James Bond Collection.)

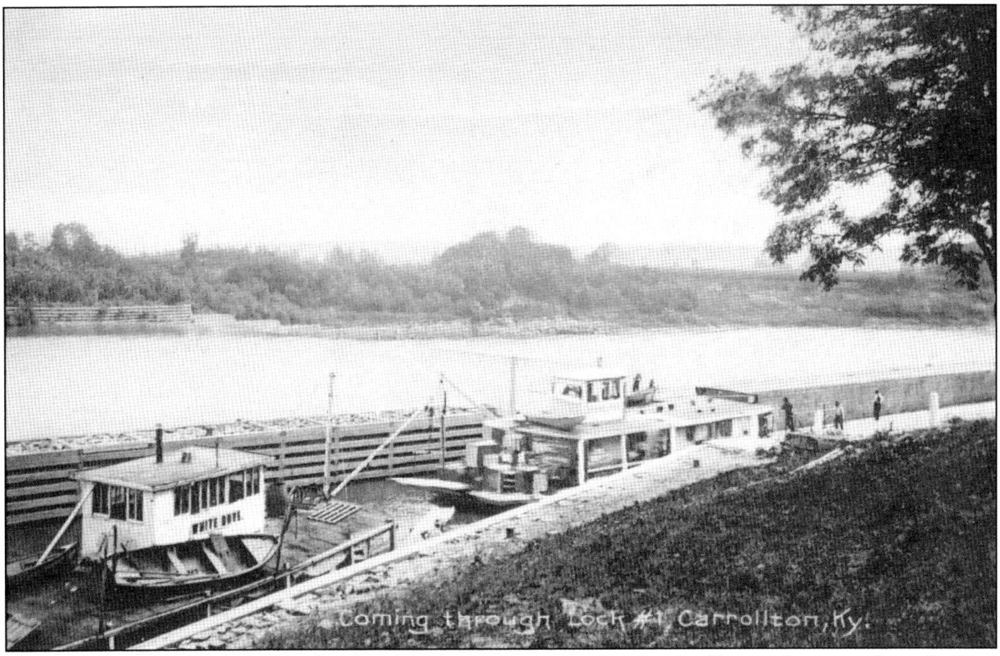

Locks helped river barges and other boats navigate the Kentucky River dams, and Lock One in Carrollton was built about 1836. In the early days of the county, the Kentucky River was as important a venue for shipping goods and resources as the Ohio River is today. (Courtesy of Jim Fothergill.)

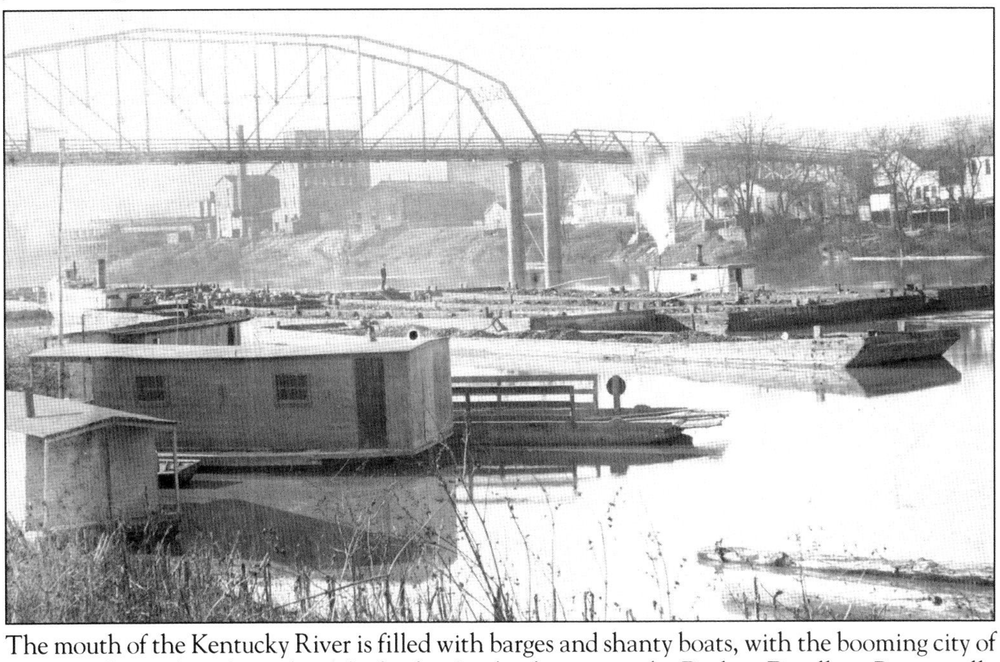

The mouth of the Kentucky River is filled with barges and shanty boats, with the booming city of Prestonville on the other side of the bridge. In the distance is the Darling Distillery. Prestonville actually was larger than Carrollton in the early days, but several major floods eroded its status and destroyed most of the buildings and businesses there. (Courtesy of General Butler State Resort Park.)

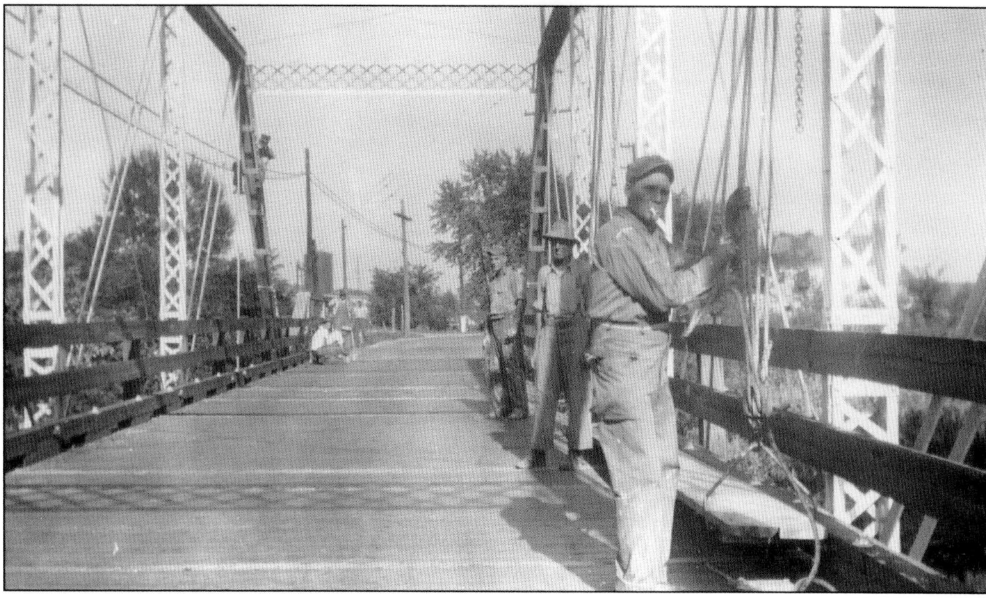

Above, a crew makes repairs and repaints the original Kentucky River bridge between Carrollton and Prestonville. Prestonville is in the background. Below, looking toward Carrollton, are the tollbooth and two tollbooth operators on the bridge. The toll eventually was eliminated. In the 1950s, the bridge was replaced by the one that exists today, which was better suited for the increasing motor vehicle traffic. (Above, courtesy of Gary Ford; below, courtesy of Carroll County Public Library.)

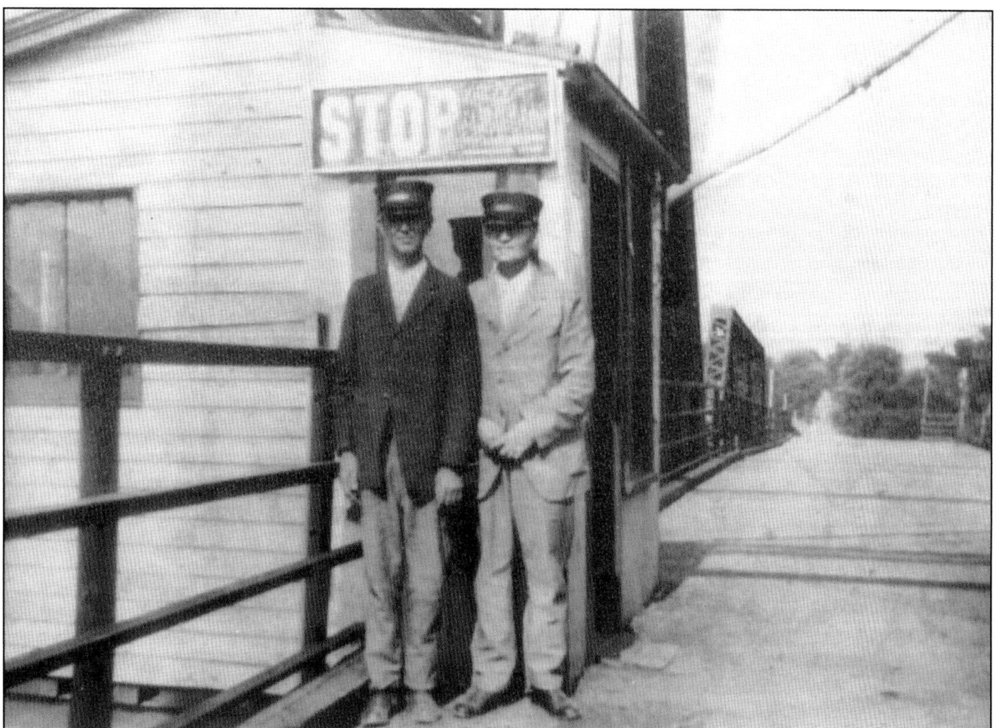

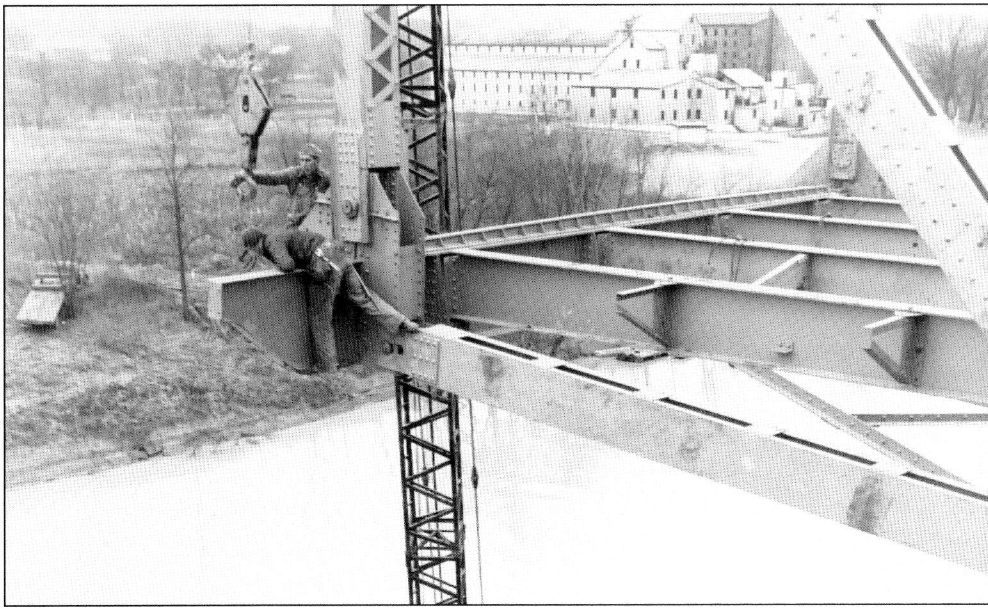

High above the Kentucky River, ironworkers build the new bridge between Carrollton and Prestonville. In the background is the Jett Distillery, which by this time was no longer owned by the Jett family. At right another view of the bridge, with Prestonville in the background, shows crews working to bring the two sides together. (Both, courtesy of Jimmy Supplee.)

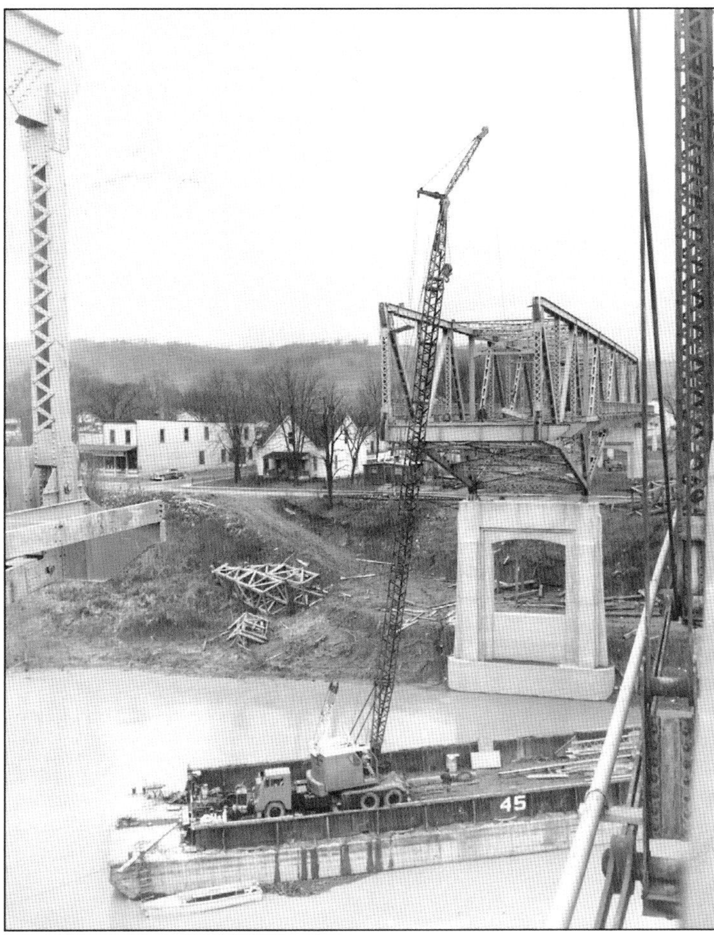

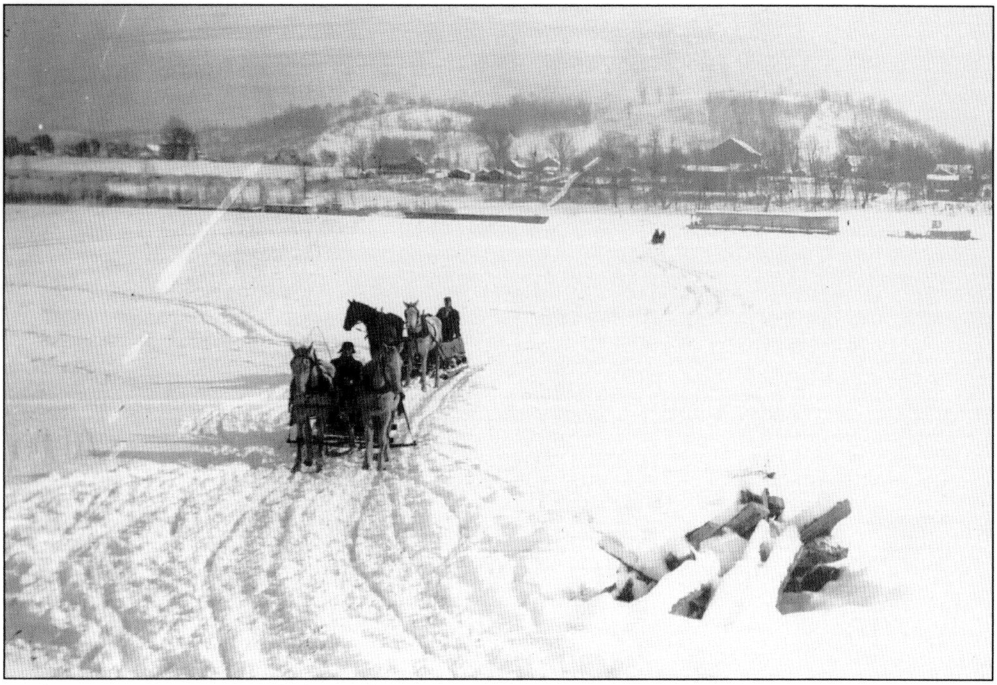

In the wintertime, particularly in the years before the Markland Locks and Dam were built in nearby Gallatin County in the 1950s, the Ohio River often froze over, eliminating the need for ferryboat transportation. People would walk across from Kentucky to Indiana, or, as in the photograph above, drive horse-drawn sleds across. (Courtesy of Darrell Maines.)

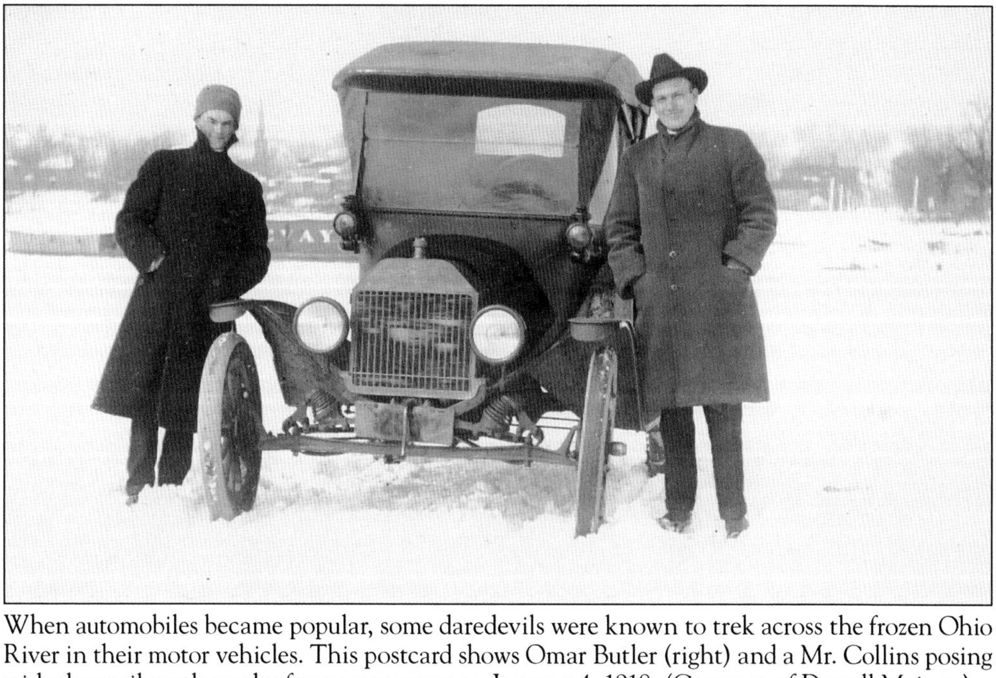

When automobiles became popular, some daredevils were known to trek across the frozen Ohio River in their motor vehicles. This postcard shows Omar Butler (right) and a Mr. Collins posing with the mail truck on the frozen waterway on January 4, 1918. (Courtesy of Darrell Maines.)

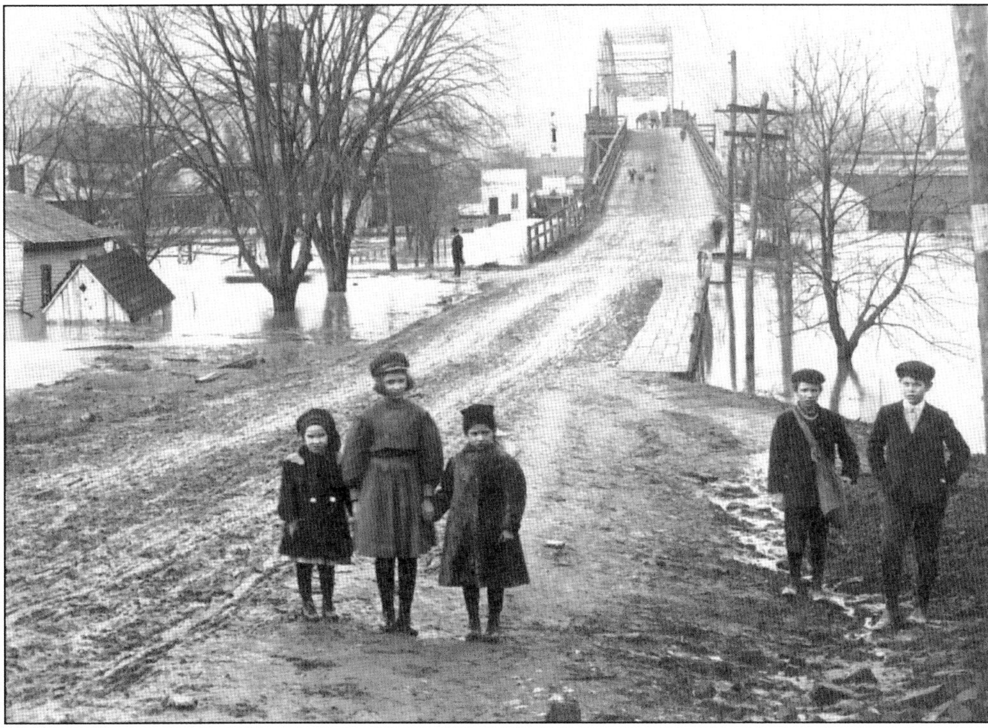

Beautiful rivers sometimes turn ugly, overflowing and causing destruction to the cities and towns along their banks. Above, children stand at the foot of the Kentucky River Bridge during the January 1907 flood. The city of Prestonville is visible on the other side of the toll bridge. Most of the buildings there were wiped away by subsequent floods in 1913 and 1937. Below, also pictured in 1907, onlookers stand at the edge of floodwaters that covered Main Street at the Second Street intersection to view Cincinnati's *Island Queen* steamer, seen in the background resting on its side near what is now Point Park. (Both, courtesy of Darrell Maines.)

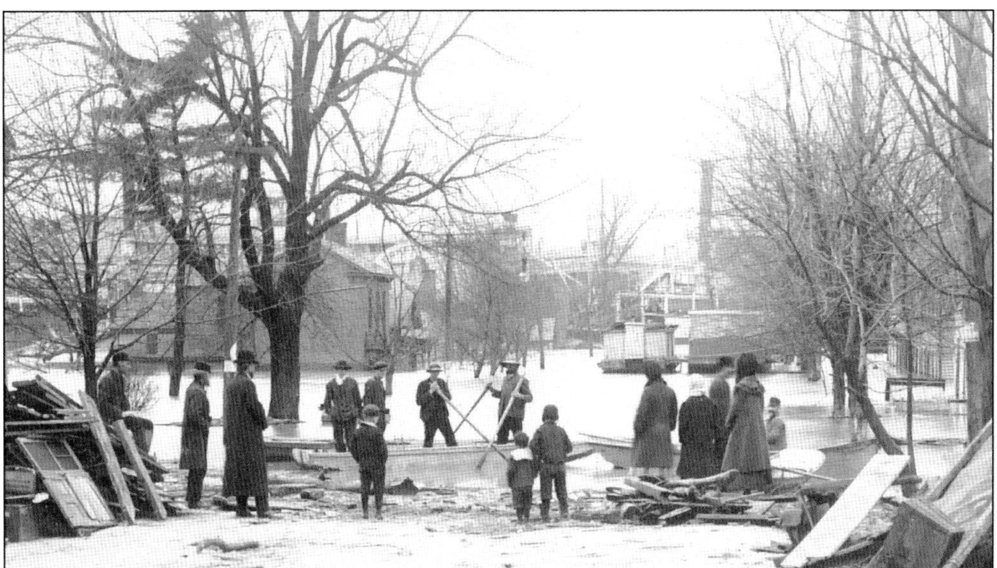

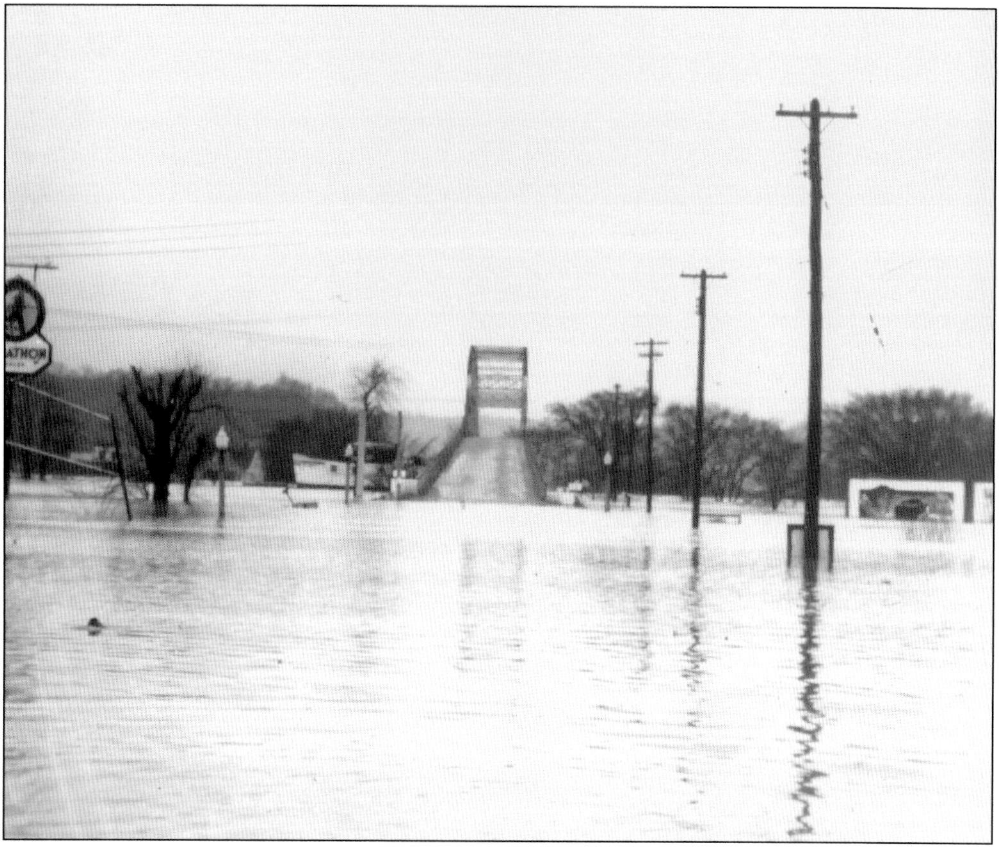

In 1937, the most devastating flood occurred since the city of Port William was founded in 1794. Floodwaters from the Ohio and Kentucky Rivers completely cut off the bridge between Carrollton and Prestonville, above. Below, downtown buildings along the north side of Main Street, between Court and Fifth Streets, are filled nearly to the second floor. (Both, courtesy of Gary Ford.)

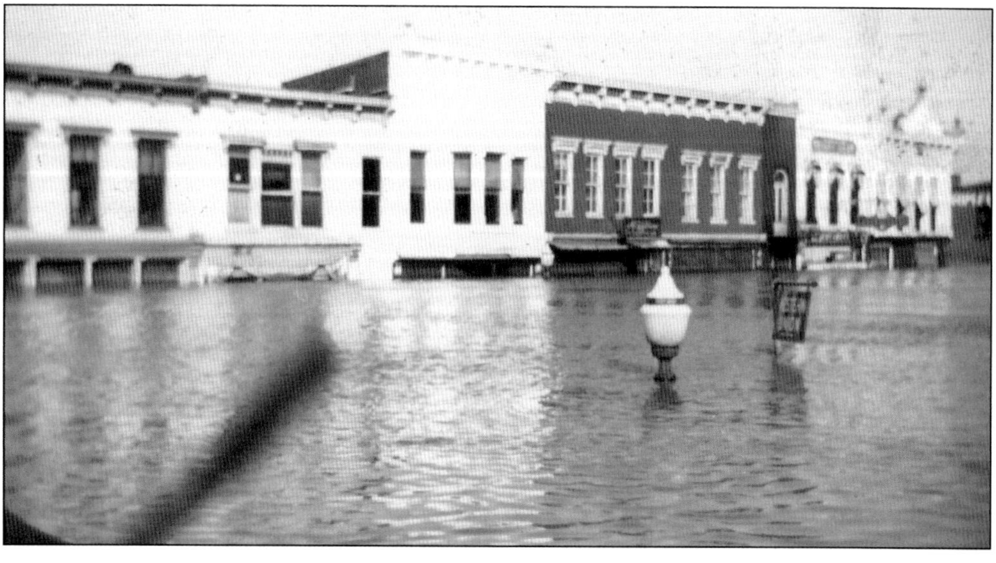

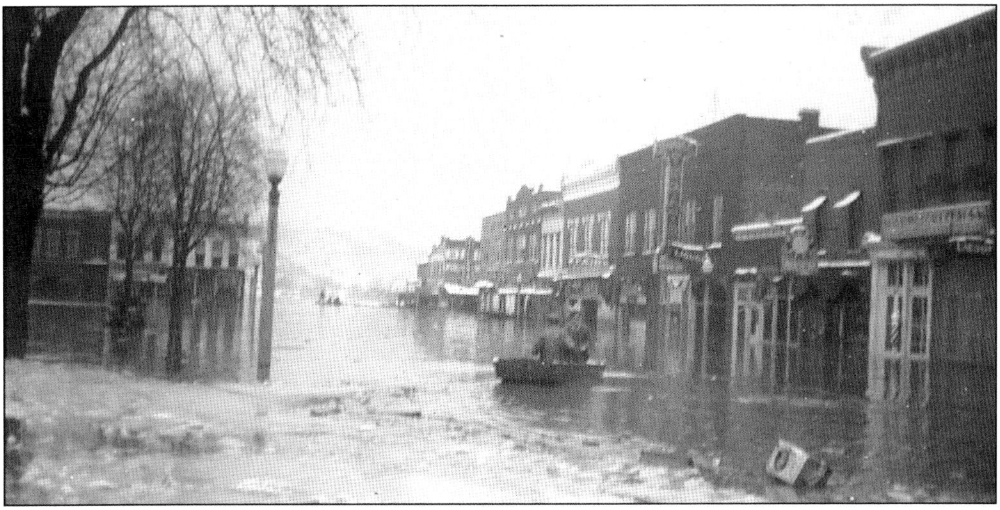

Above, rowboats were the only way for people to survey the damage during the 1937 flood. Two men are seen rowing down Fifth Street toward Main Street. This photograph and the one below were taken from a vantage point on Highland Avenue, where the floodwaters ended. Dr. ? Ryan, whose house was at the corner of Highland and Fifth Streets, is said to have rowed to his medical office on Main Street, entering through his second-floor office window. Below is the south side of the Carroll County Courthouse. Photographs published in the newspaper in 1937 show men rowing through the first floor of the courthouse. Today, a plaque in the courthouse shows the high-water mark. (Both, courtesy of Gary Ford.)

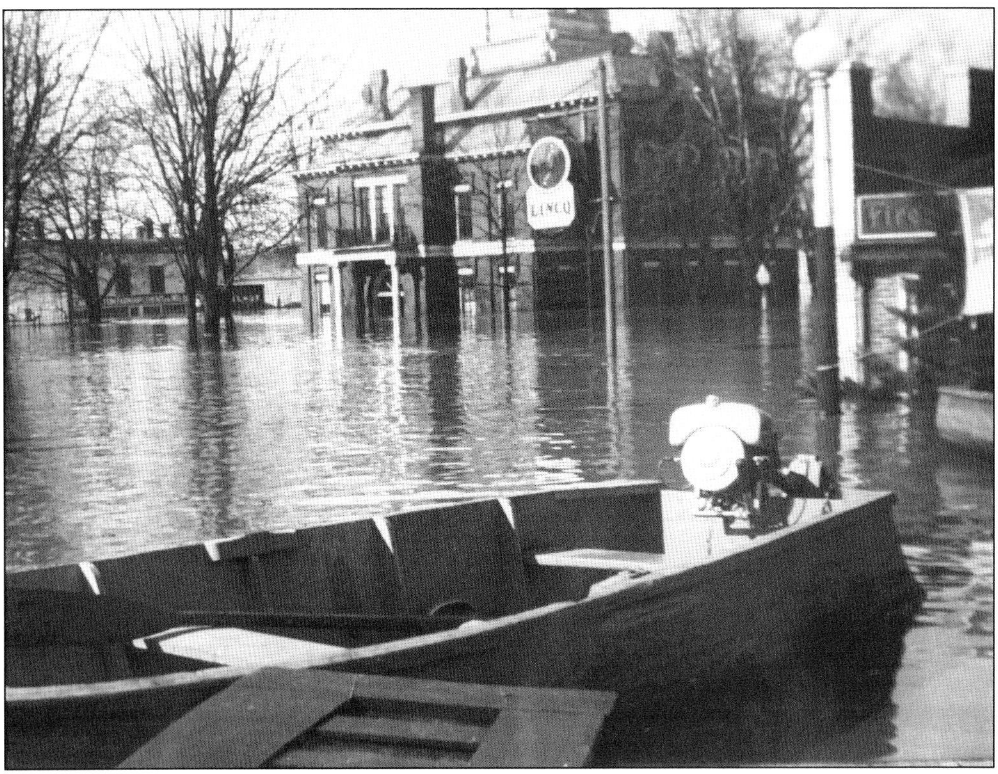

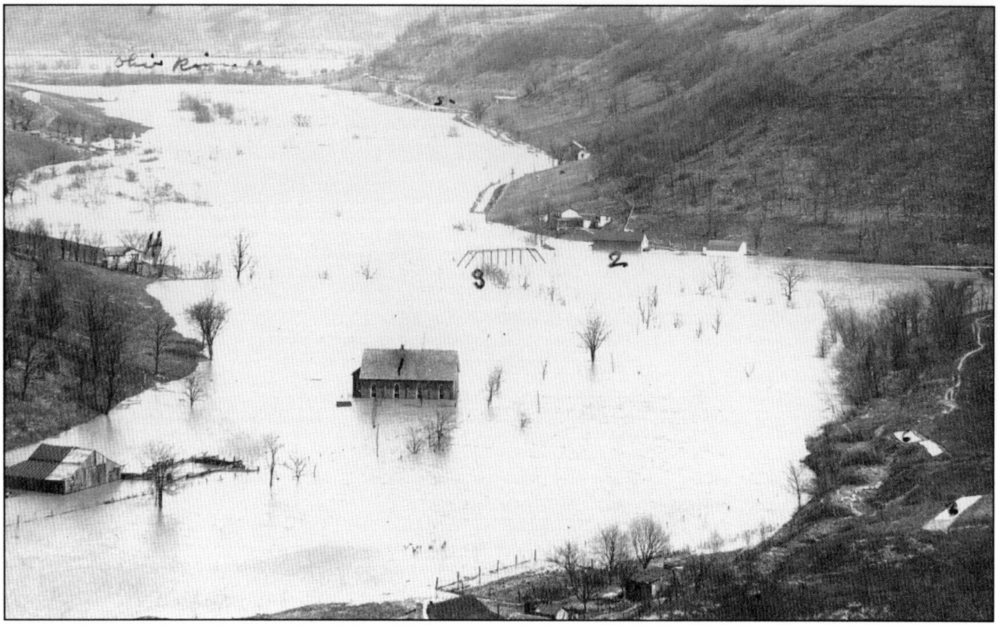

The 1937 flood also ravaged the small town of Locust, shown above, where Hopewell Methodist Church stands like an island in the midst of the devastation. Floodwaters backed up from the Ohio River into the valley and into both the east and west prongs of Locust Creek. Below, the Ohio River overtakes the flour mill, which was located at the bottom of Fishing Street in Ghent. (Above, courtesy of Darrell Maines; below, courtesy of City of Ghent, James Bond Collection.)

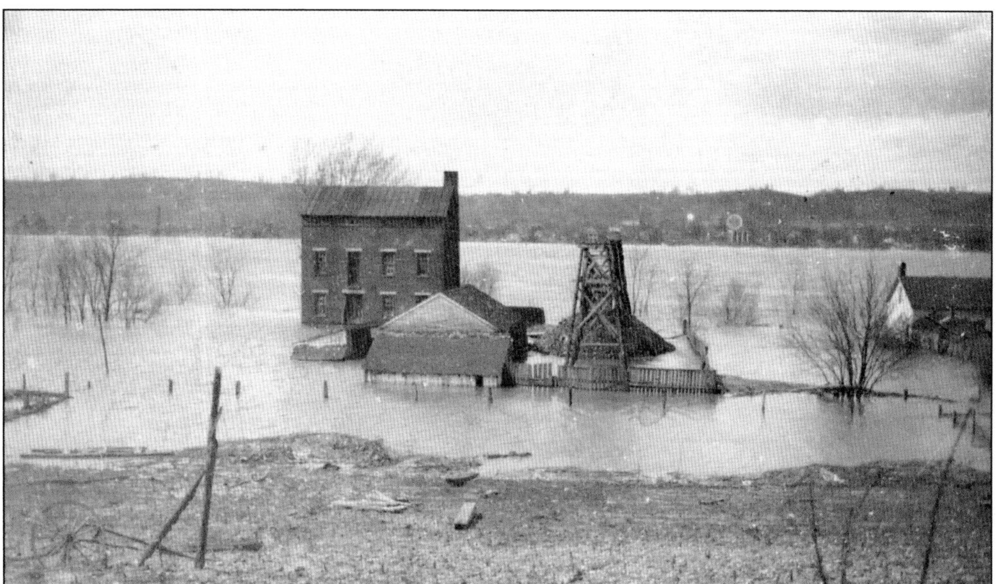

Six

A CALL TO WORSHIP

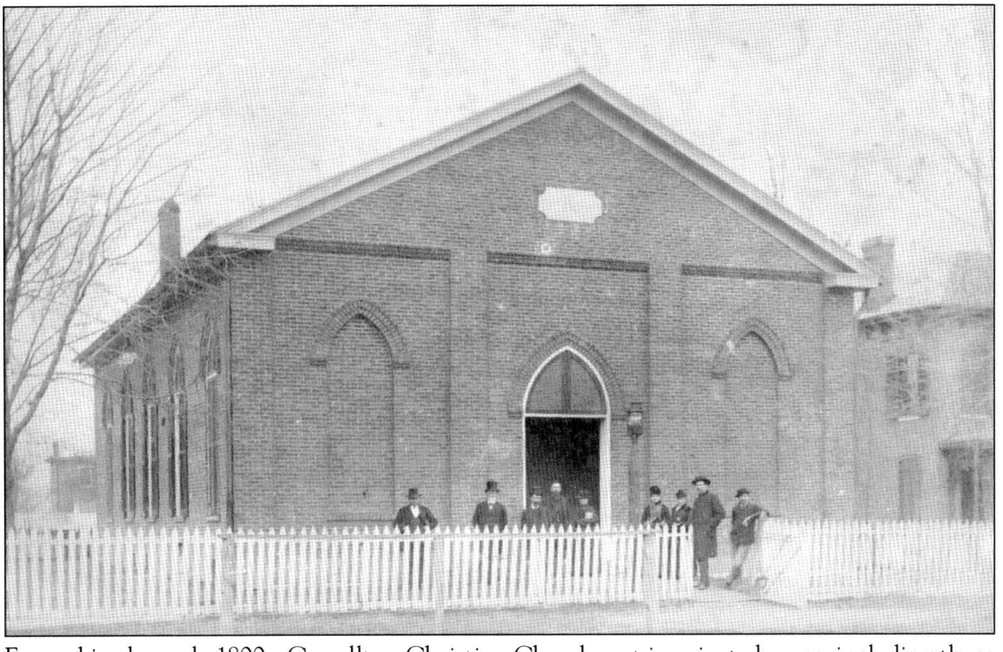

Formed in the early 1800s, Carrollton Christian Church met in private homes, including those of Robert Darling and Amelia Salyers, and later at the Carroll County Courthouse until 1870, when it built a church on Fifth Street. In 1889, some members pose in front of the structure, which originally did not have a steeple. They are, from left to right, Frank Morrow, F.H. Gaines, Will Salyers, Cyrus Hanks, Mittie Hanks, Mrs. Perry Corn, Atha Hanks Gullion, Brother Pinkerton, and John Corn. (Courtesy of Carrollton Christian Church.)

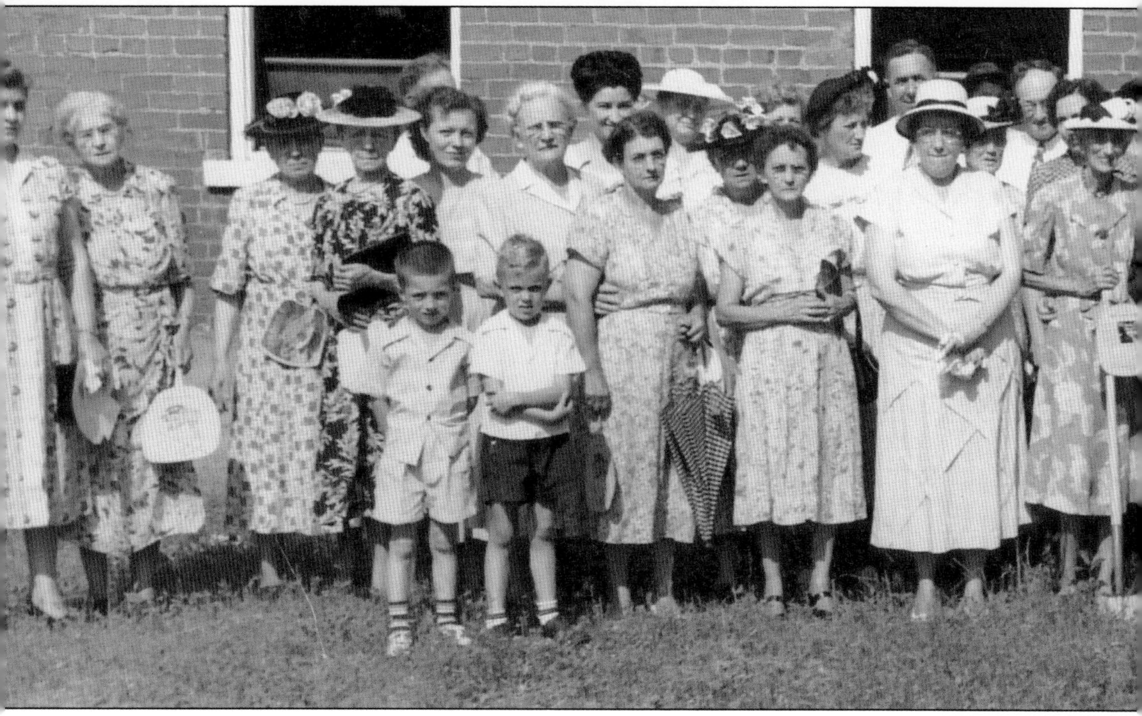

Membership homecoming is an annual tradition at Carrollton Christian Church on Fifth Street.

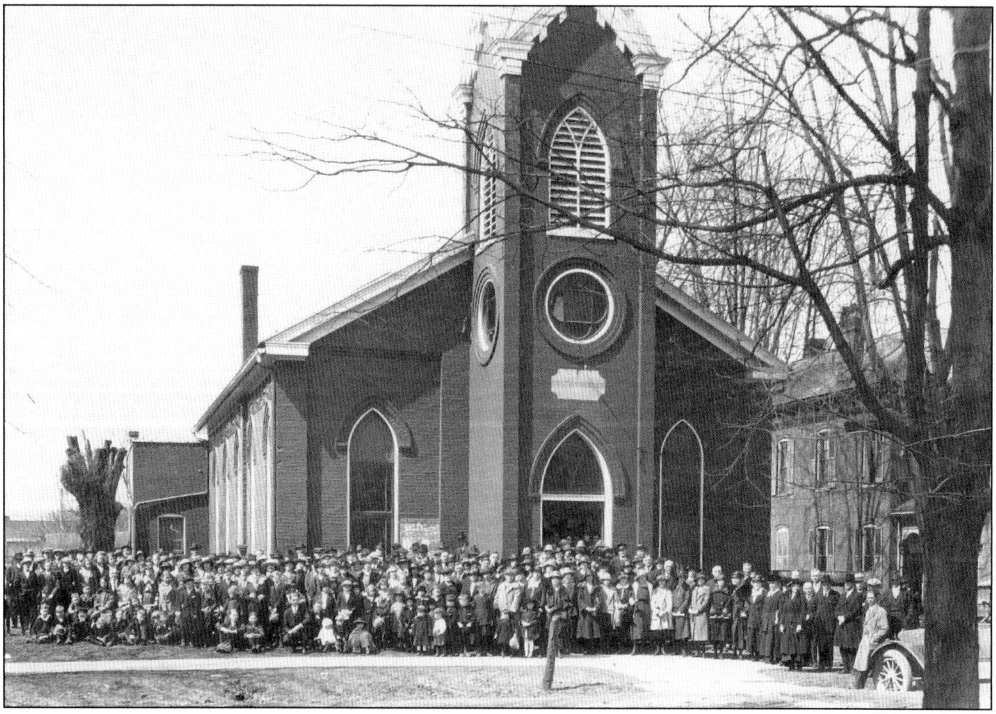

This 1916 photograph of the annual Carrollton Christian Church homecoming shows the church with its recently added bell tower. The home to the right was torn down for the addition of classrooms and office space in the 1960s. (Courtesy of Carrollton Christian Church.)

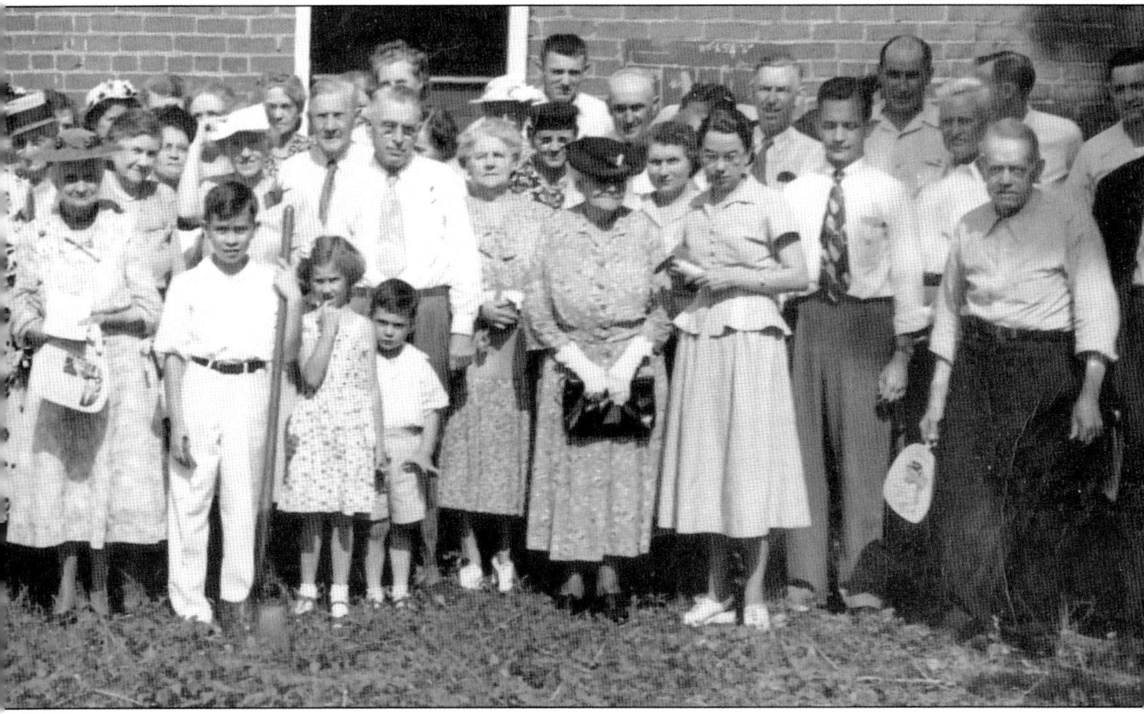

This group photograph is from the 1950s. (Courtesy of Carrollton Christian Church.)

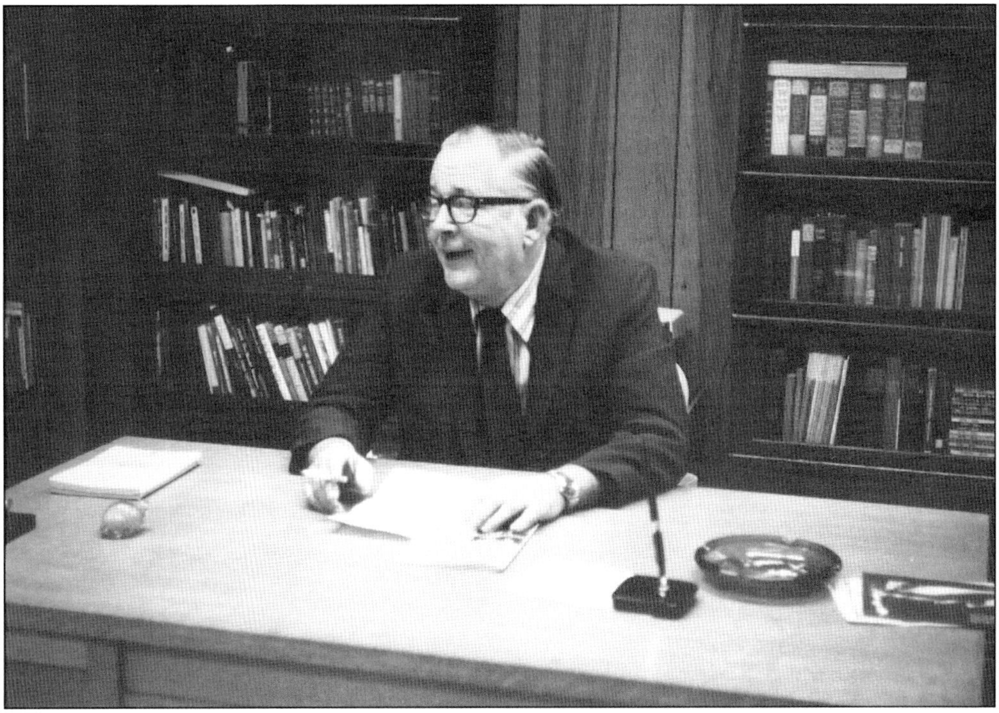

The Reverend Paul Livesay, a World War II US Army veteran of the 41st Division, became pastor of the Carrollton Christian Church in 1962 and served the congregation until his retirement in 1982. (Courtesy of Carrollton Christian Church.)

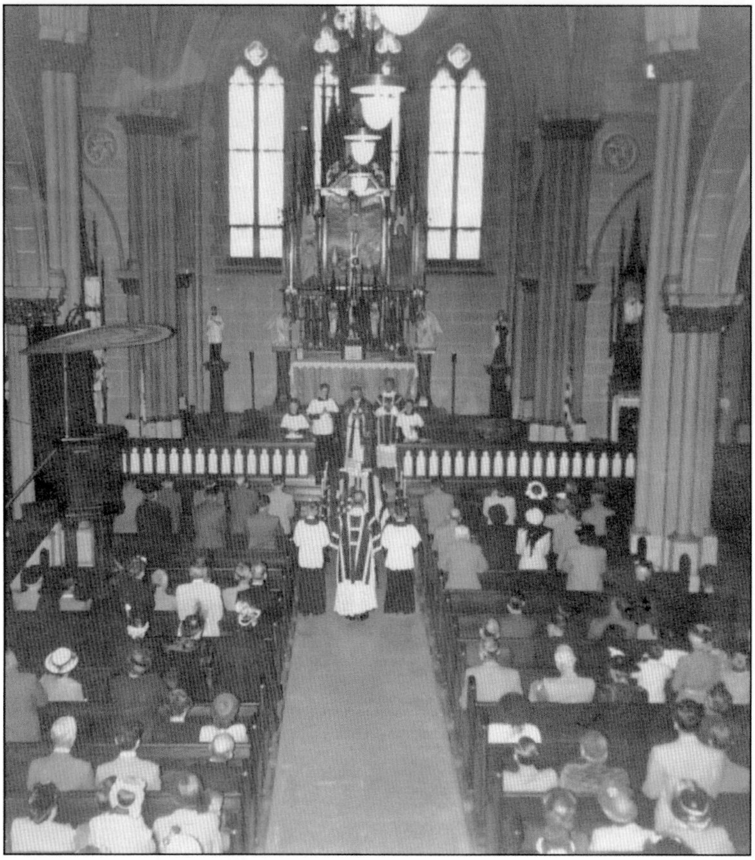

This 1940s photograph of a funeral service shows the interior of St. John the Evangelist Catholic Church on Fifth Street in Carrollton. Built in 1900, the church underwent a major renovation in the 1970s. Pictured below is St. John Catholic School, located next to the church, at the corner of Fifth and Clay Streets. The original school building was razed in the 1950s and replaced with a modern brick structure. (Left, courtesy of Nancy Jo Grobmyer; below, courtesy of Amy Baglan.)

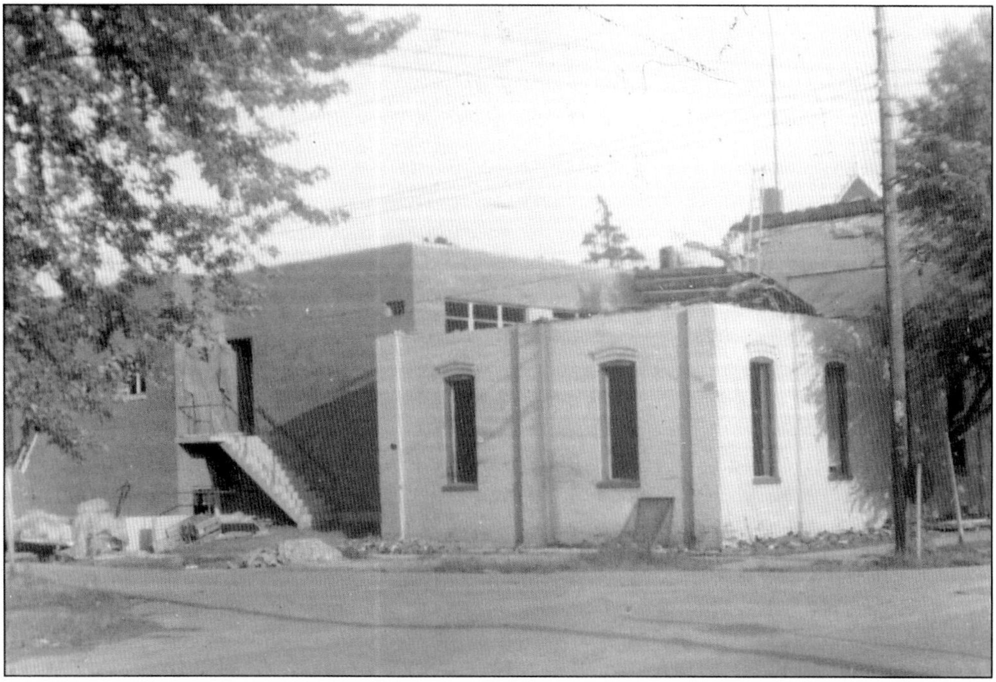

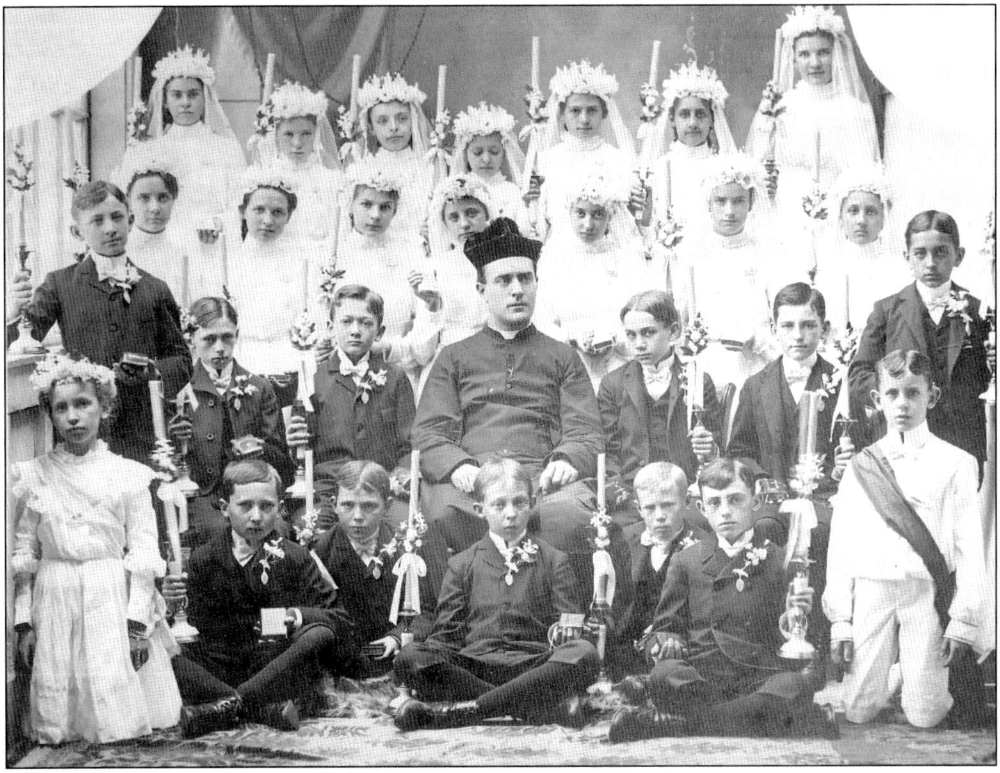

At one point, there were as many as 1,500 Catholics living in Carroll County. Above, Fr. Ignatius Mary Ahmann, who served from 1894 to about 1907, sits with one of his first communion classes for a photograph likely taken before the turn of the century. Father Ahmann is responsible for construction of the existing church. At right is Marianna Emma Glauber, a daughter of shoe store founder John Glauber. Born in 1876, Emma entered the convent in Newport, Kentucky, March 25, 1897 and took her vows as Sr. Mary Pascal on March 13, 1898. She is buried in St. Anne Convent Cemetery in Campbell County, Kentucky, where she died in 1942. (Both, courtesy of John and Carolyn Glauber.)

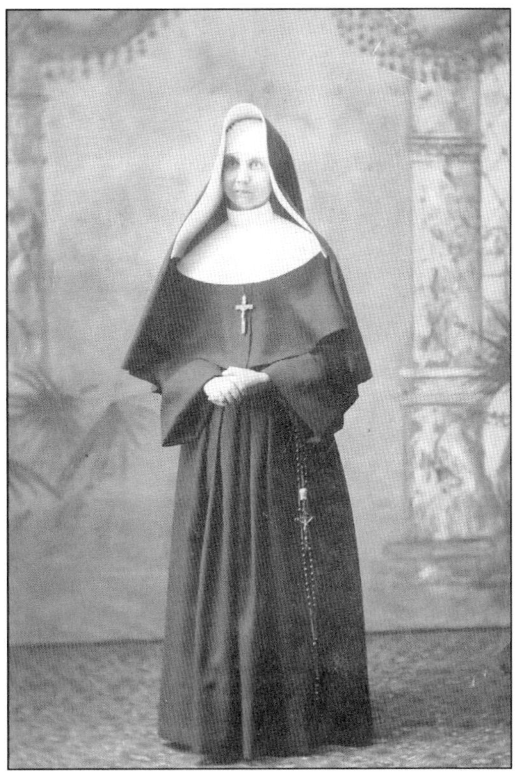

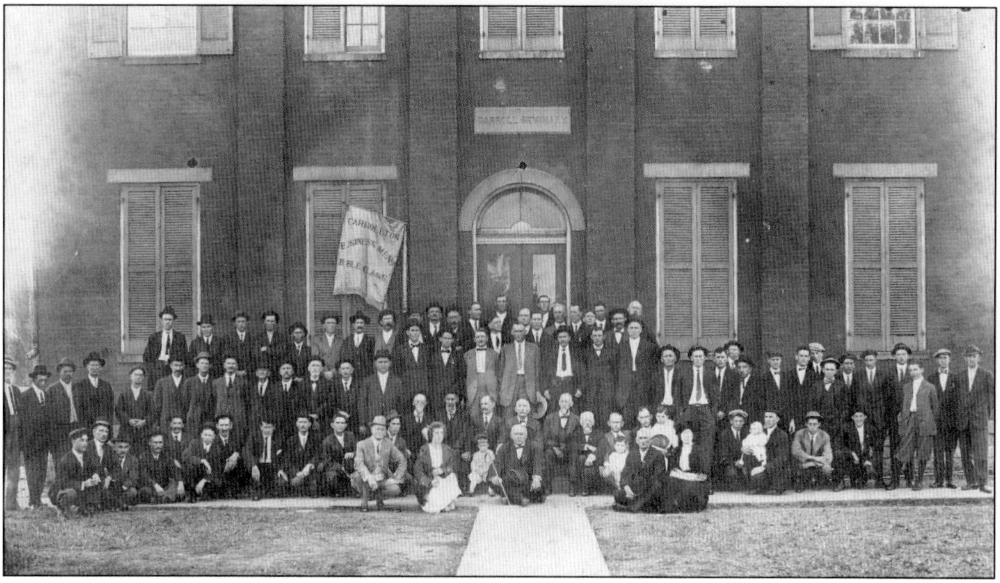

The Carrollton Businessmen's Bible Class poses for a group portrait in 1916 in front of the Carroll Seminary on Seminary Street, between Fourth and Fifth Streets. The location previously was the site of Gallatin Academy and later was the site of Carrollton High School. It is now the location of Carroll County Middle School. In front are, from left to right, unidentified, Katie Jett (organist), Ernest C. Smith (teacher), Albert N. Jett (class president), and Daisy Jett (vocalist). (Courtesy of Jim Fothergill.)

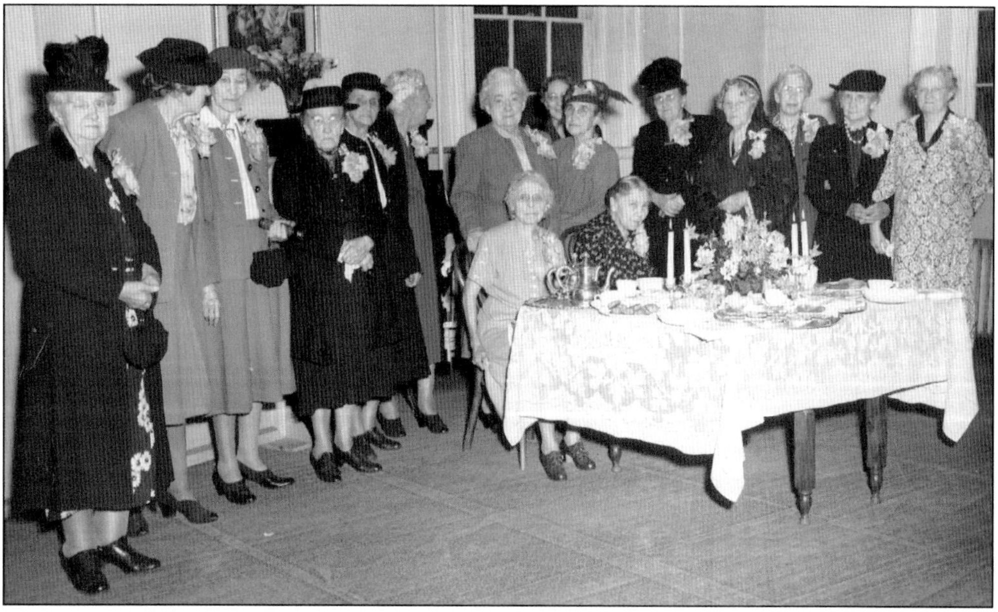

The women of the Carrollton Methodist Church gather for a missionary meeting at the church in October 1949. They are, from left to right, (standing) Laura Powers, Mary Masterson, Margaret Masterson, Cora Neblett, Alice Hanlon, Mrs. Henry Phillips, Mrs. O.W. Smith, Mary Lacy, Mrs. Robert Kendall, Mrs. C.M. Dean, Mrs. R.T. Stafford, Mrs. T.E. Mathews, Lenora Kipping, and Ora Chatham; (seated) Lydia Shaw and Hallie Masterson. (Courtesy of Carrollton Methodist Church.)

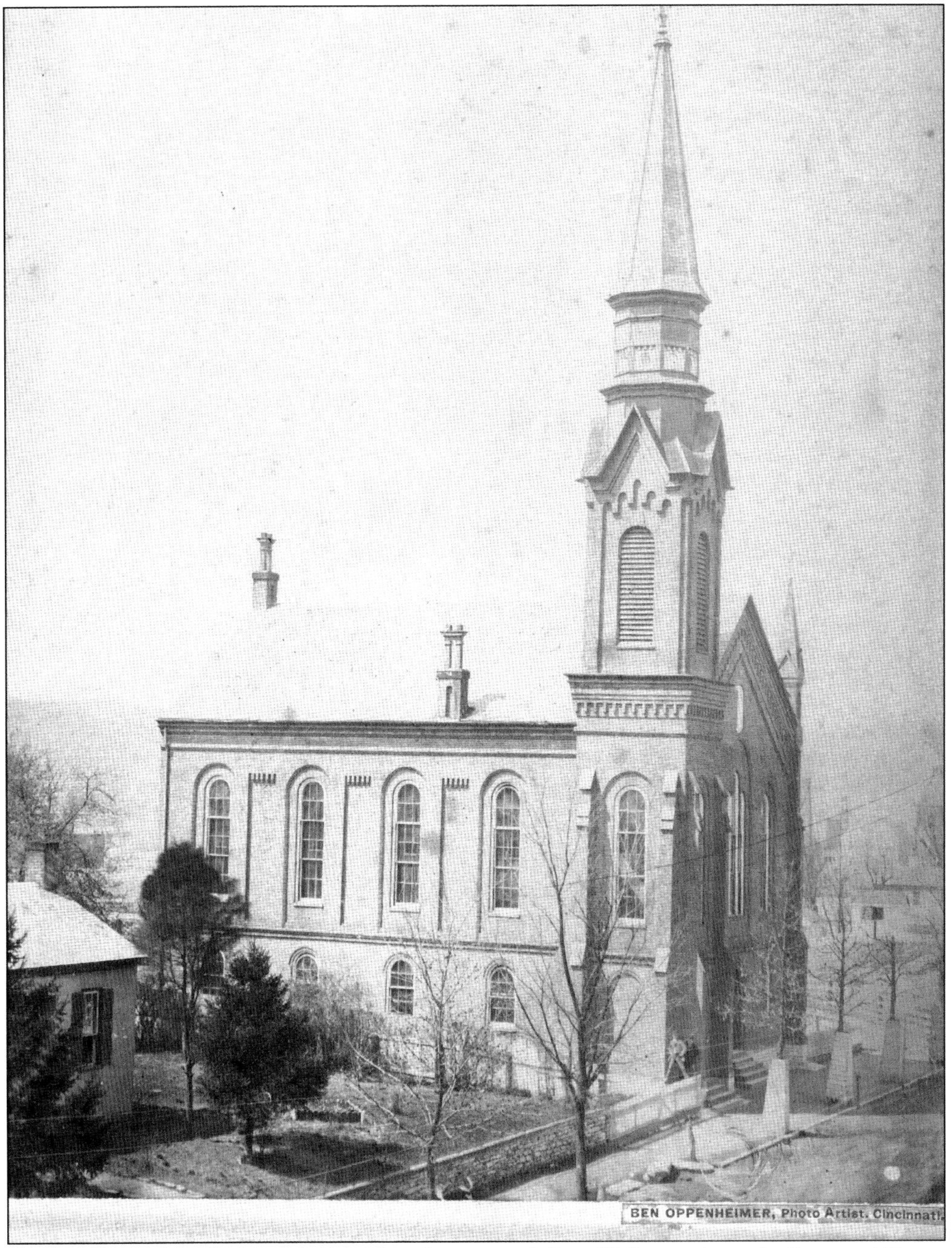

The history of Carrollton Methodist Church starts with Port William, where the Reverend Henry Ogburn held services in the home of Richard and Sarah Masterson in the 1790s. A log church building was constructed in 1810 on Ogburn's farm. The congregation later moved to 405 Sixth Street in 1818 and then to its present location at 320 Highland Avenue in 1830. The original church at this site was replaced with this one in 1870. Stained-glass windows were added in 1892. A fellowship hall was added in 1957, and a parsonage was built at the corner of Fourth and Highland Streets in 1961. Storms have wreaked havoc on the church steeple, which was toppled and replaced in 1943 and again in 2003. (Courtesy of Carrollton Methodist Church.)

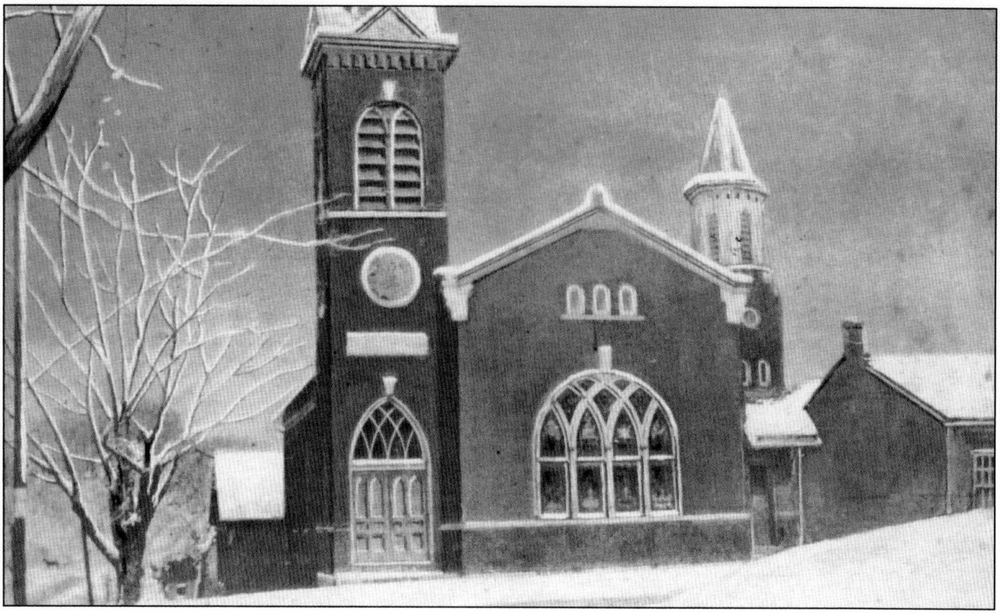

First Baptist Church of Carrollton was formed June 30, 1849, and its first meetings were held in the Carroll County Courthouse. The Reverend L.D. Alexander was named the first pastor. In January 1850, the church committee bought a lot at the corner of Fourth and High Streets (Highland Avenue), and the existing church was built in 1852. The annex was added in 1932. (Courtesy of Darrell Maines.)

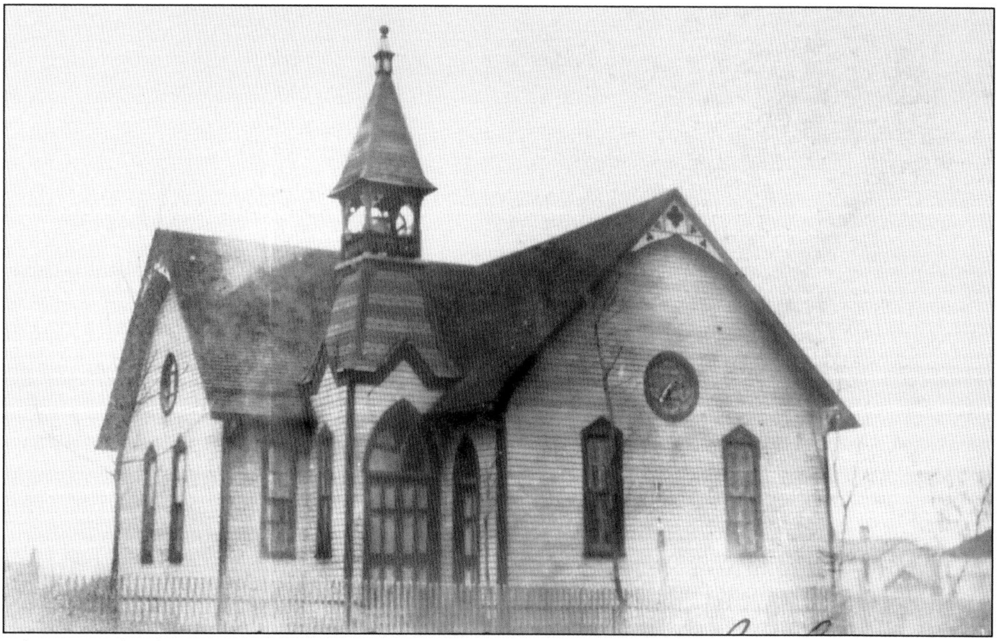

Ghent Methodist Church was founded in 1833, with the congregation meeting in a log house. Members later moved to a brick school building, built in 1859, which subsequently became Ghent Deposit Bank and is now the post office. This building was constructed in 1889. The congregation disbanded in the 1960s, and the building was left to ruin. Recently, it was purchased by David Hendren and is now the Gen. J.T. Ellis Banquet Hall. (Courtesy of Darrell Maines.)

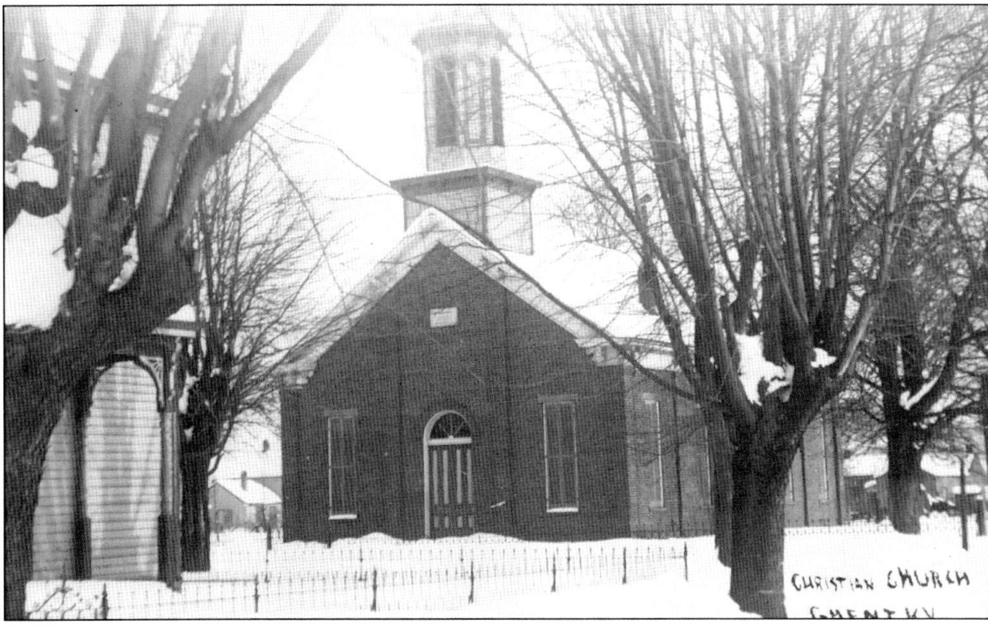

The Ghent Christian Church, formed in 1836, was built on Union Street after the congregation grew too large for the first church building, which stood on Main Street (now US 42). Constructed in 1872, the church building had a steeple and an iron fence, both of which were removed when the structure was owned by an Amish congregation in the 1980s. The building is now owned by the City of Ghent and houses city offices in an addition at the back. City leaders plan to renovate the sanctuary for a community center. (Courtesy of City of Ghent, James Bond Collection.)

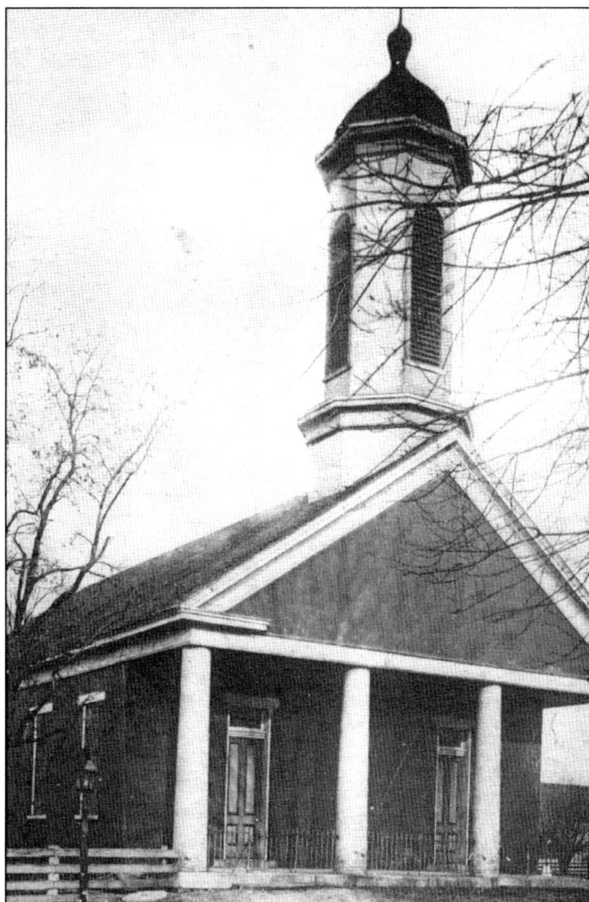

The Ghent First Baptist Church was founded in 1800, and the congregation built the existing church in 1843. Records from 1845 show a membership of 200, of whom 50 were African Americans. That group later began its own church, the Ghent Second Baptist Church, which still serves its congregation today on Liberty Street. (Courtesy of Ben Collett.)

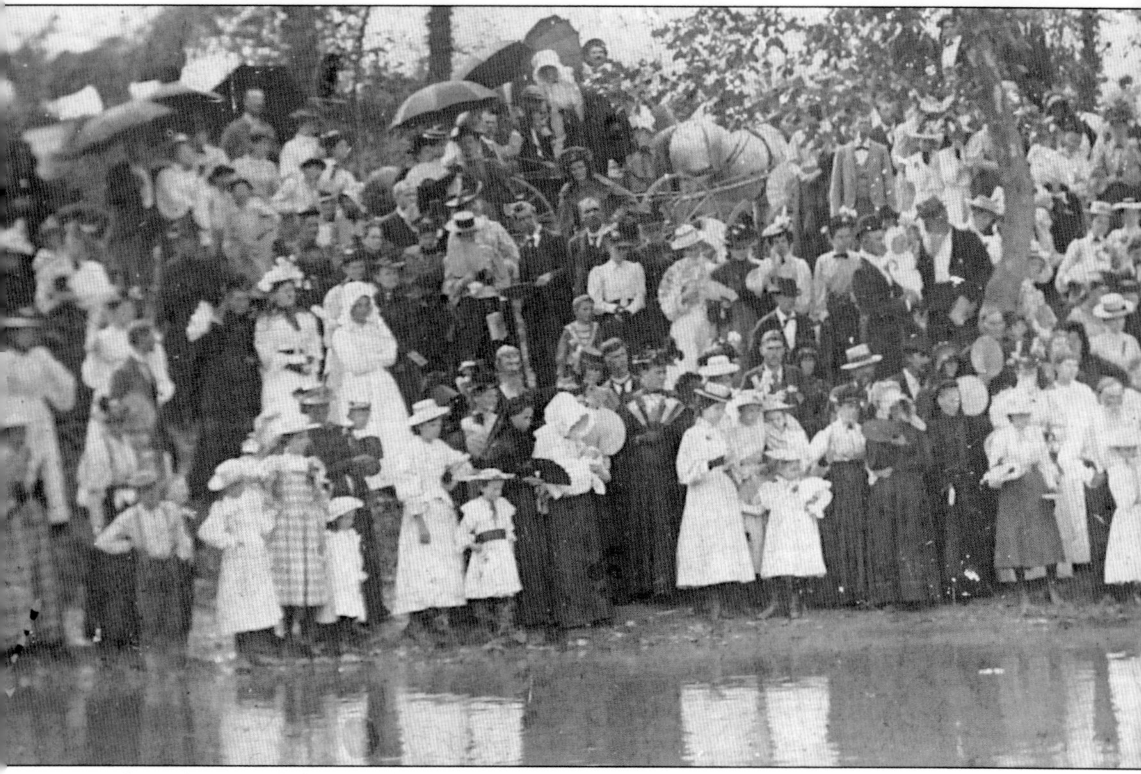

In this cabinet card photograph taken by a Sanders photographer, a large congregation gathers by the river—or, most likely, Eagle Creek—for a baptism. The church affiliated with the ceremony

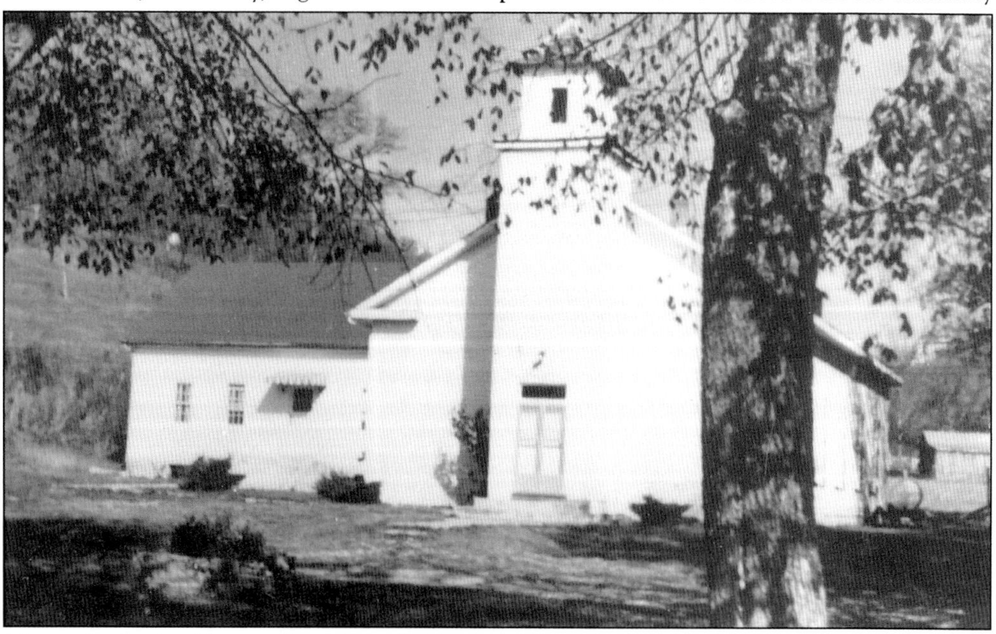

This is the Jordan Baptist Church in Sanders in the 1960s. According to an 1884 county atlas, Jordan was one of eight precincts, along with Ghent, Carrollton, Worthville, Liberty Station (now Sanders), Prestonville, Mill Creek and Locust. (Courtesy of Ida Lewis.)

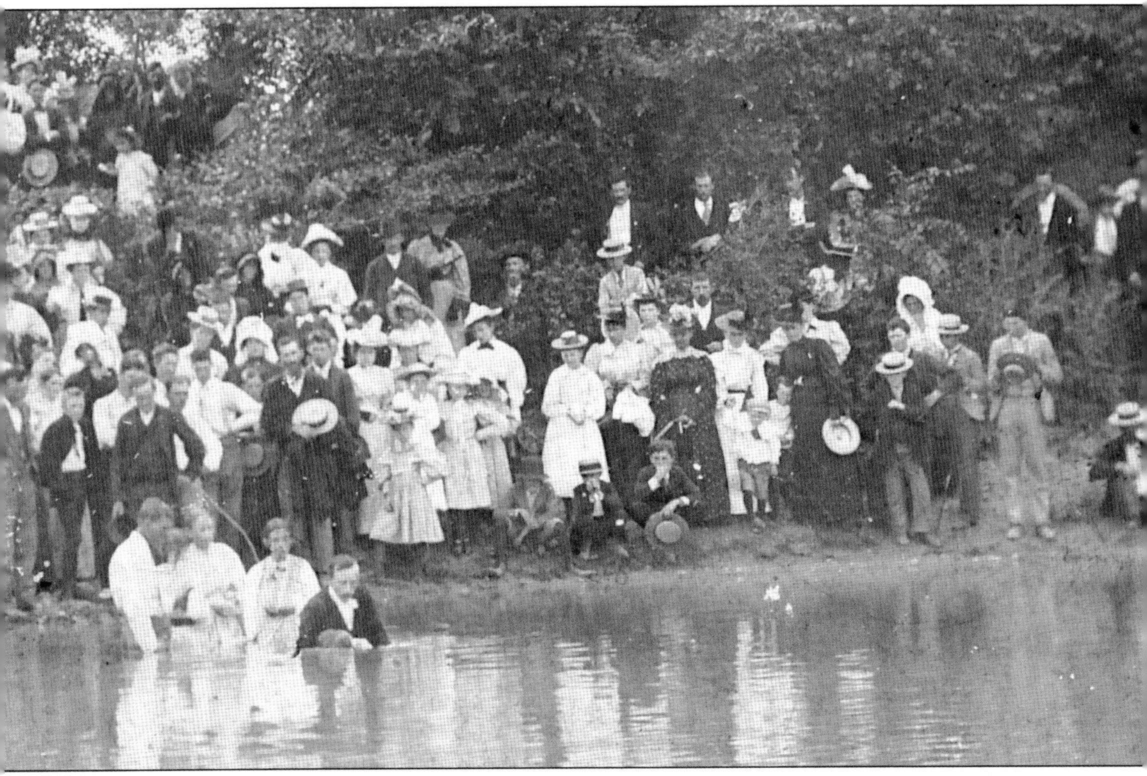

in this image is not identified. Clothing styles suggest the photograph was taken near the turn of the 20th century. (Courtesy of Darrell Maines.)

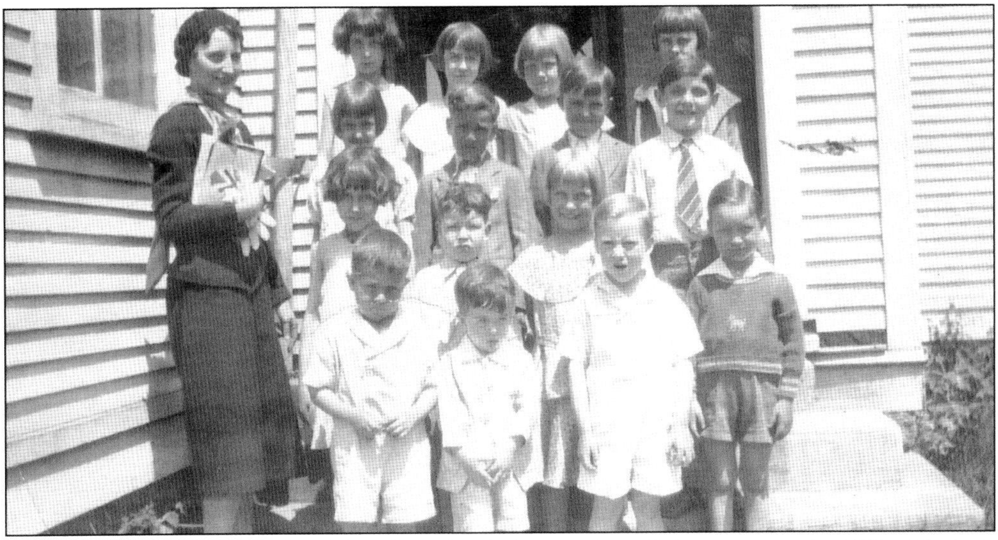

Well-dressed children in a local Sunday school class in Carroll County pose in 1931 with their teacher outside their church. (Courtesy of *News-Democrat*.)

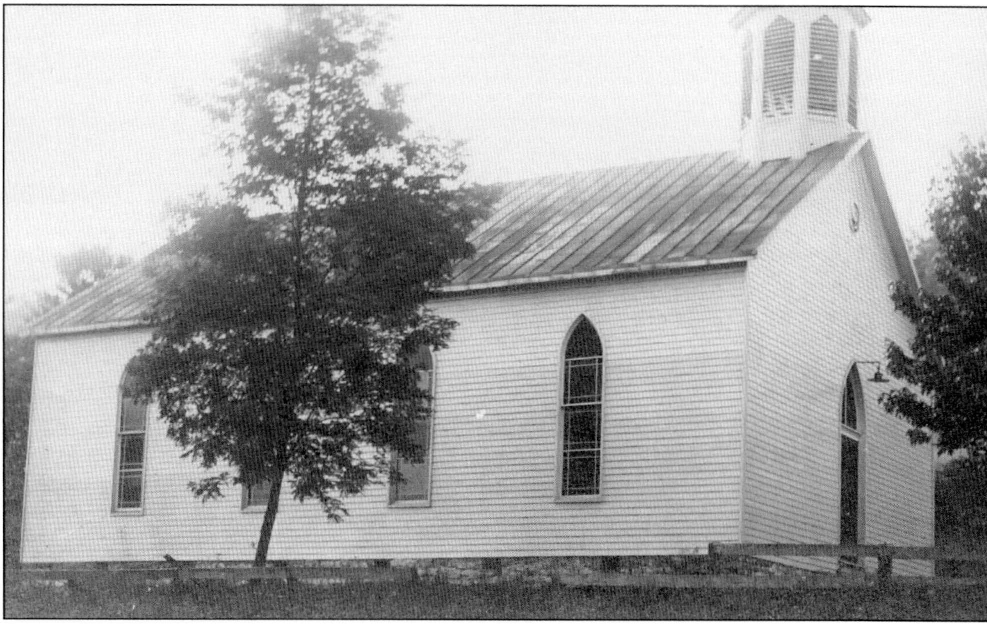

In 1935, Cora Gentry Smith wrote a history of the Worthville Baptist Church, which was formed in July 1883 following an 1882 revival promoted by Baptists from Owen, Henry, and Carroll Counties. The first pastor was the Reverend Thomas A Spicer, and this church was completed in June 1885. The dedication ceremony was led by the Reverend T.T. Eaton, pastor of the Walnut Street Baptist Church in Louisville. (Courtesy of Darrell Maines.)

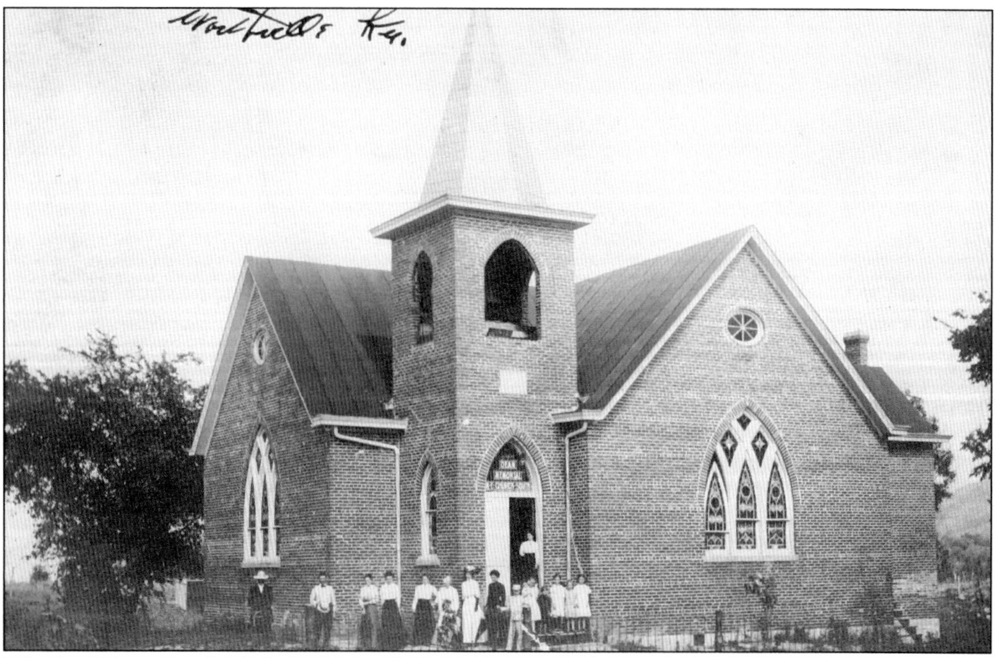

Worthville's original Methodist church, known as Dean Chapel, was built by Chatz T. Dean, a well-to-do landowner devoted to the Methodist Episcopal denomination. The chapel, built near his homestead, was replaced about 1910 by the present brick building, called Dean Memorial Methodist Church, South. (Courtesy of Darrell Maines.)

Seven

Schools

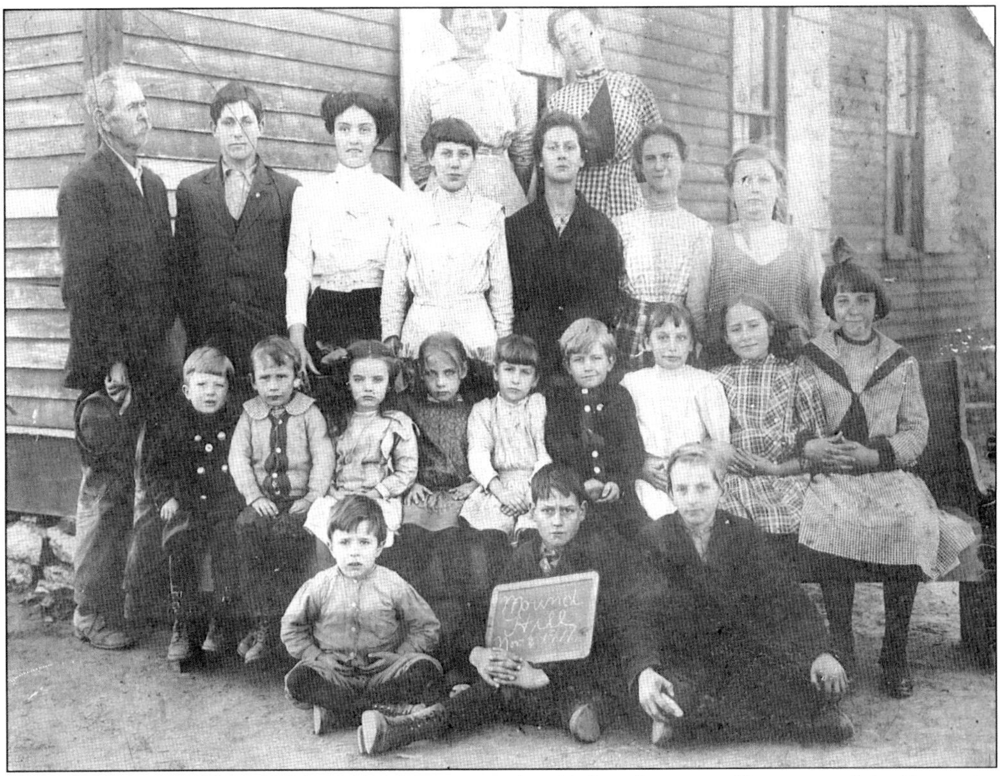

Carroll County's public school system was organized in 1867 and approved by an act of the Kentucky Legislature. Each district in the county had its own trustee, who was in charge of maintaining the school buildings, providing footbridges across creeks, and recommending teachers. By 1895, there were 32 elementary schools scattered throughout the county for whites and five schools for African Americans, educating a total of 3,002 children. This image includes the students of Mound Hill School in 1911. Consolidation began in the early 1900s. The board of education mandated that schools attended by fewer than 25 children be closed. In accordance with this, Mound Hill, Buffalo, South Fork, and Bersot schools were closed in 1927. (Courtesy of Gary Ford.)

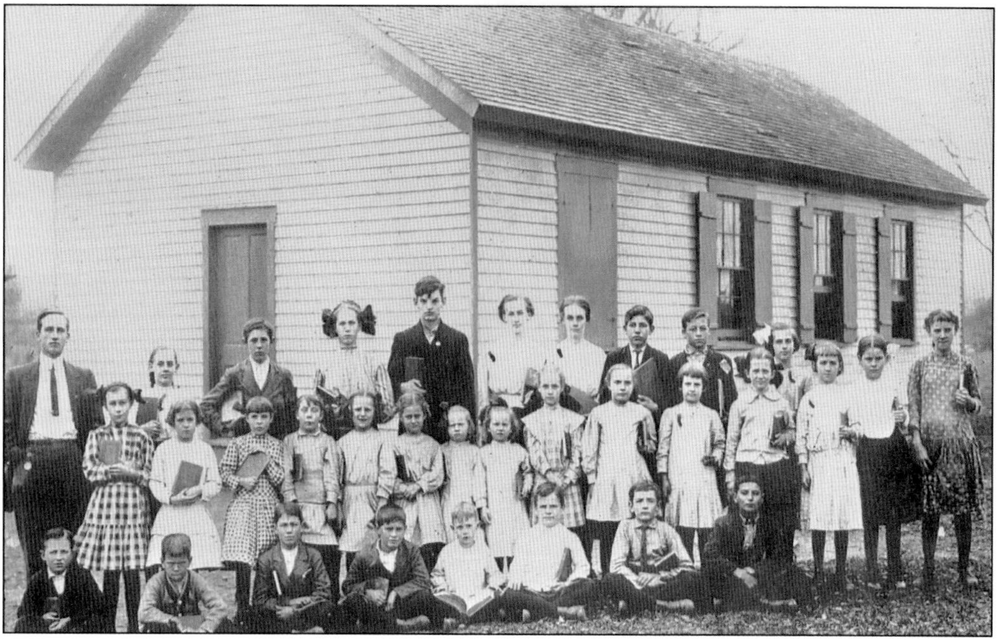

The Tandy School, above, was located on Ghent-Eagle Station Road. Below, unidentified classmates from the sixth, seventh, and eighth grades pose on the steps of the Ghent Independent School, formerly Ghent College. After 1890, the three-story Ghent school building housed primary grades through high school. The Ghent schools eventually were consolidated into Carroll County Schools, and students were bused to new elementary, middle, and high school buildings in Carrollton. (Above, courtesy of Gary Ford; below, courtesy of Charles "Buck" Johnson.)

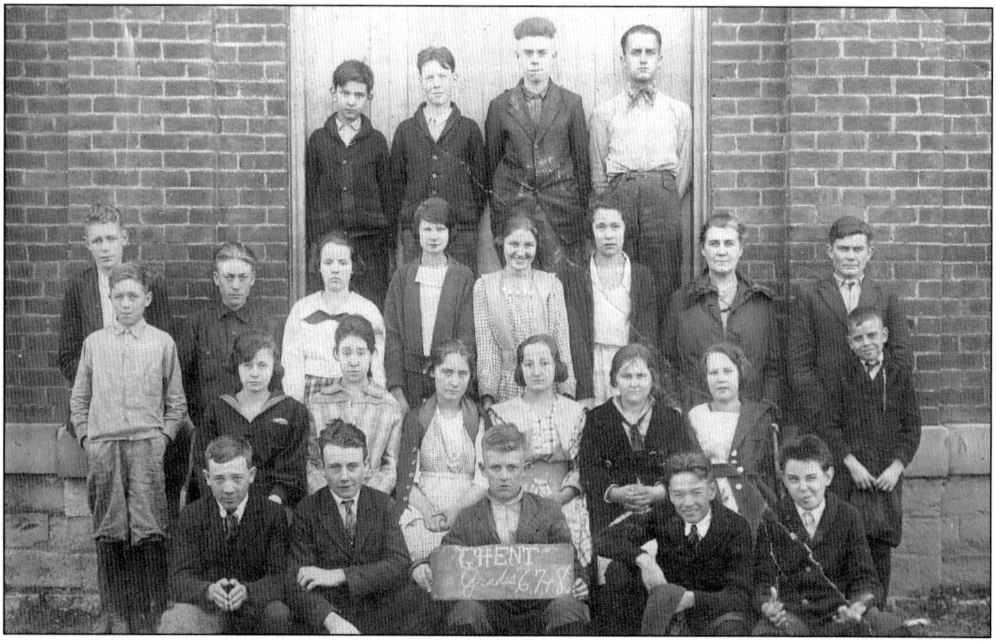

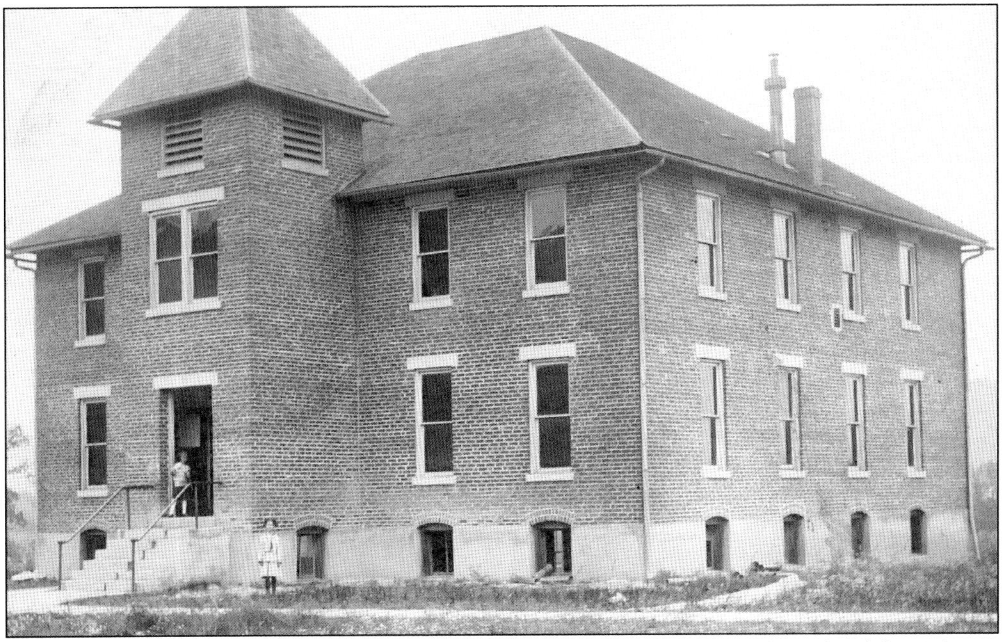

Worthville High School, above, was built in 1911. Worthville also had a school for African American children; however, in 1921, that school was closed and the children from Worthville were transported by the C&W Railway to the Dunbar School in Carrollton. In 1949, a new elementary school for African American children was dedicated in Ghent and named for superintendent Richard E. Cartmell. High school–age blacks were sent to the Lincoln Institute, a boarding school near Shelbyville, Kentucky. That school was discontinued after integration was mandated in the 1950s. Below, students at the Worthville School include members of the Mefford, Gullion, and Brock families. (Above, courtesy of Darrell Maines; below, courtesy of Reba Brock.)

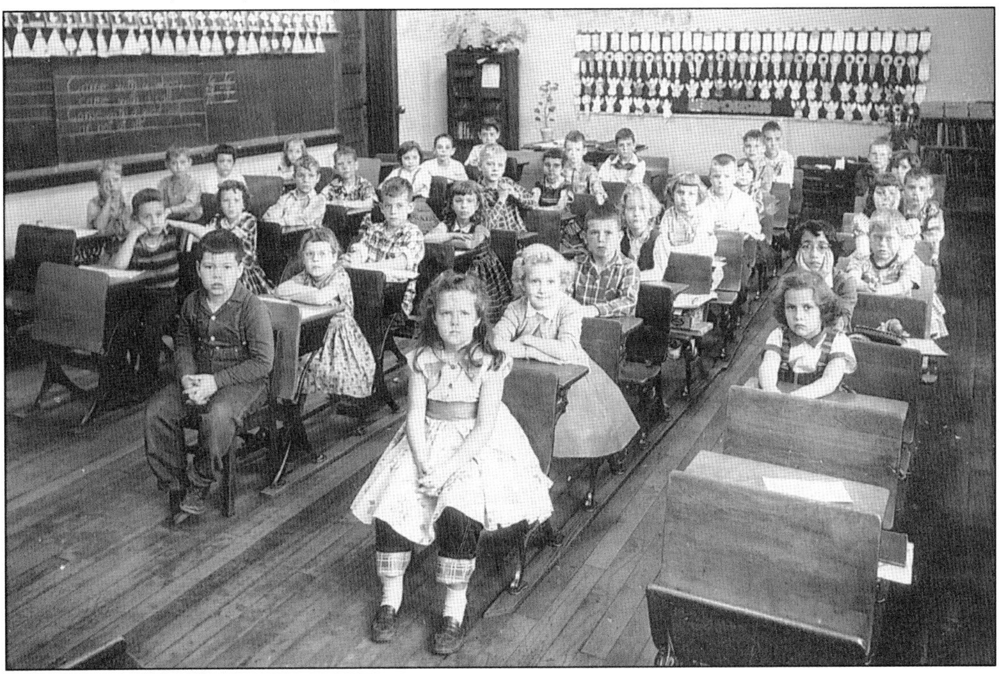

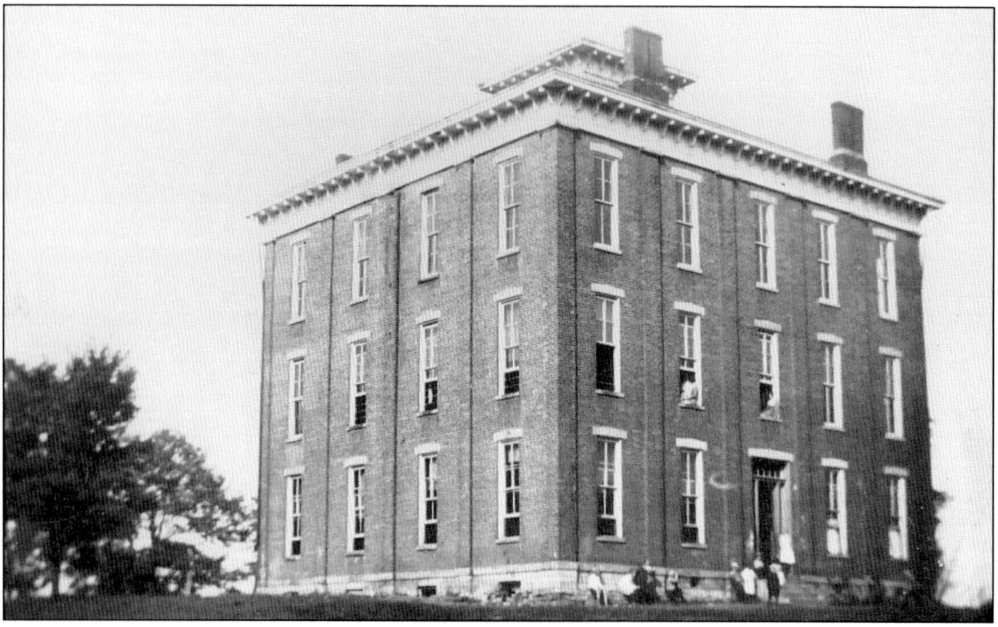

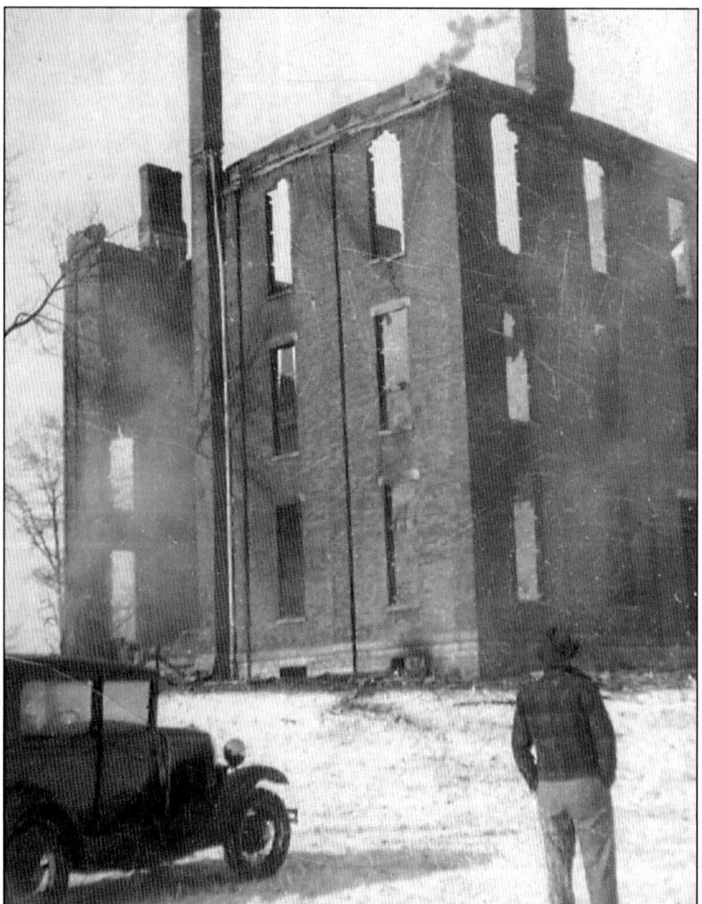

Ghent College, above, was built in 1868 after $31,700 was raised through the sale of local subscriptions of stock at $100 each. For 22 years, it enjoyed a reputation as a top college, offering one of the best music departments and "high standards of leadership," according to one local history. After the college closed, the structure housed the Ghent Independent graded and high schools until it was destroyed by fire on New Year's Day, 1940. Ray Taylor observes the ruins in the photograph at left. In 1940, with a $12,000 bond, the federal Work Projects Administration set to work building a new school near the site of the old college. That building was used until 1972. (Both, courtesy of City of Ghent, James Bond Collection.)

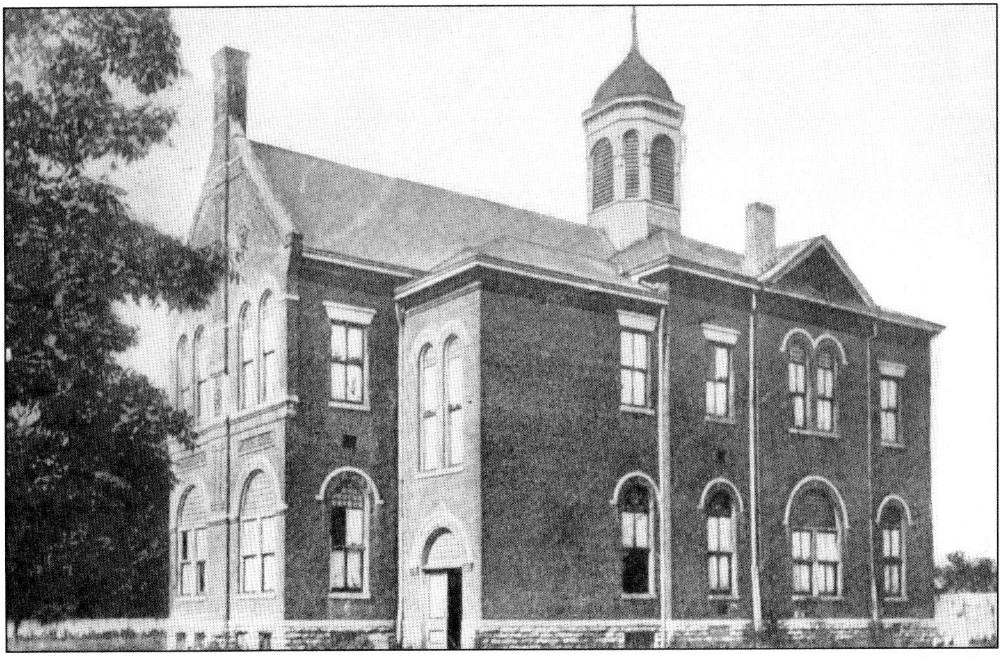

The first Carrollton High School was a two-story Victorian built in 1887 at Sixth and Taylor Streets. In 1912, it was one of four 4-year high schools in the county; the others were in Sanders, Worthville, and Ghent. Two 2-year high schools were located in English and Locust. Until after the turn of the century, the building also housed upper elementary grades. (Courtesy of Jim Fothergill.)

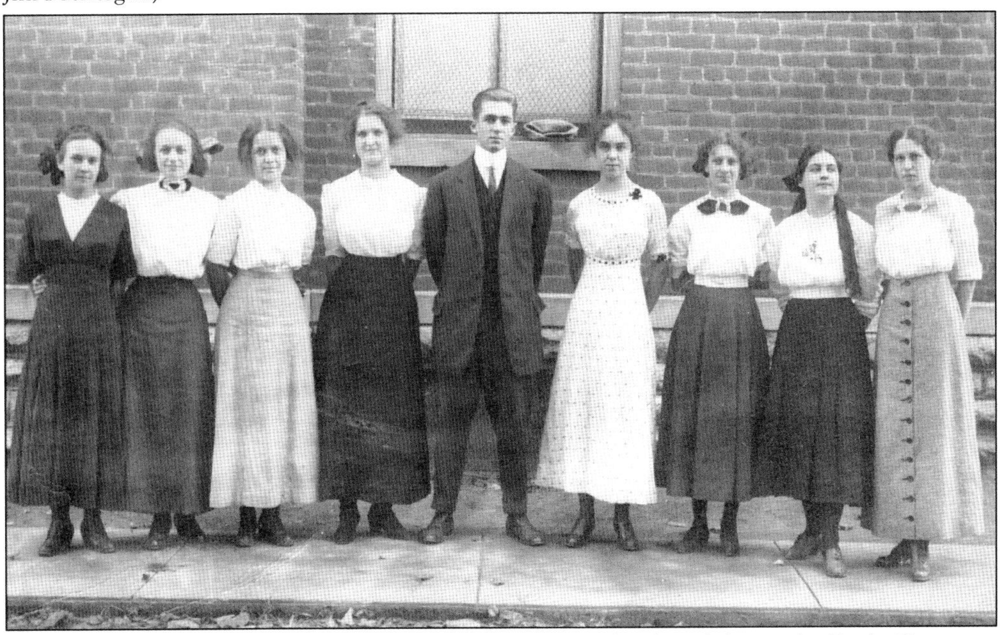

The Carrollton High School graduating class of 1914 includes, from left to right, Ruth Chapman; unidentified; Maude Johnson; Lillie Mae Powers; Robert L. Gaines, son of Kentucky senator Perry B. Gaines; Hester Bruce; Hallie Bishop; Vivian Delane; and Dorothy Adkinson. In 1950, Gaines built the Riverview Drive-In Theater. (Courtesy of Amy Baglan.)

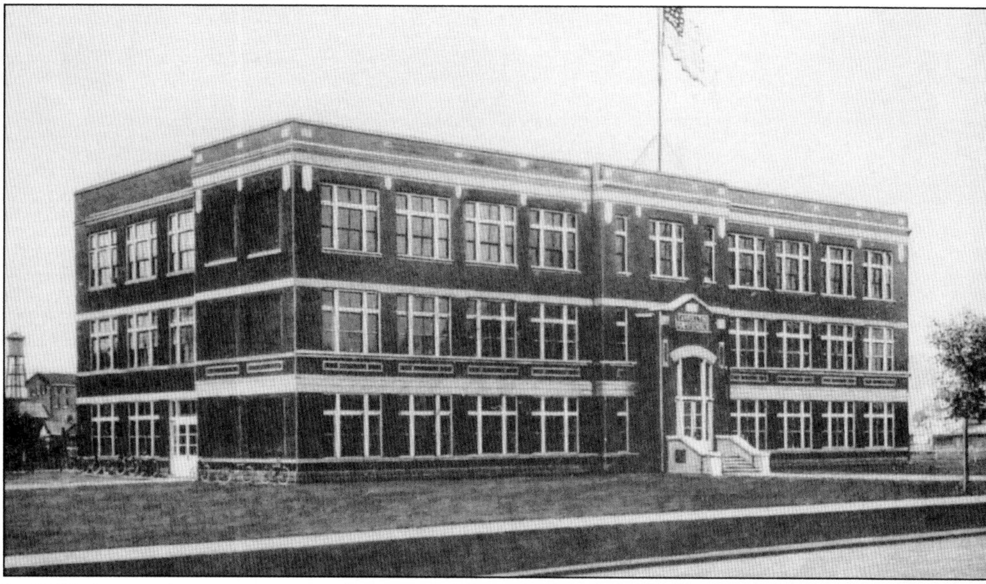

In 1917, this modern structure on Seminary Street replaced the first Carrollton High School. Built for $25,000, it first held all grades of Carrollton students in 16 classrooms. In 1935, the Works Progress Administration built an addition of 12 classrooms, a laboratory, a gymnasium, and a library; by 1939, the county's high schools were consolidated and students were transported to the Carrollton school. (Courtesy of Darrell Maines.)

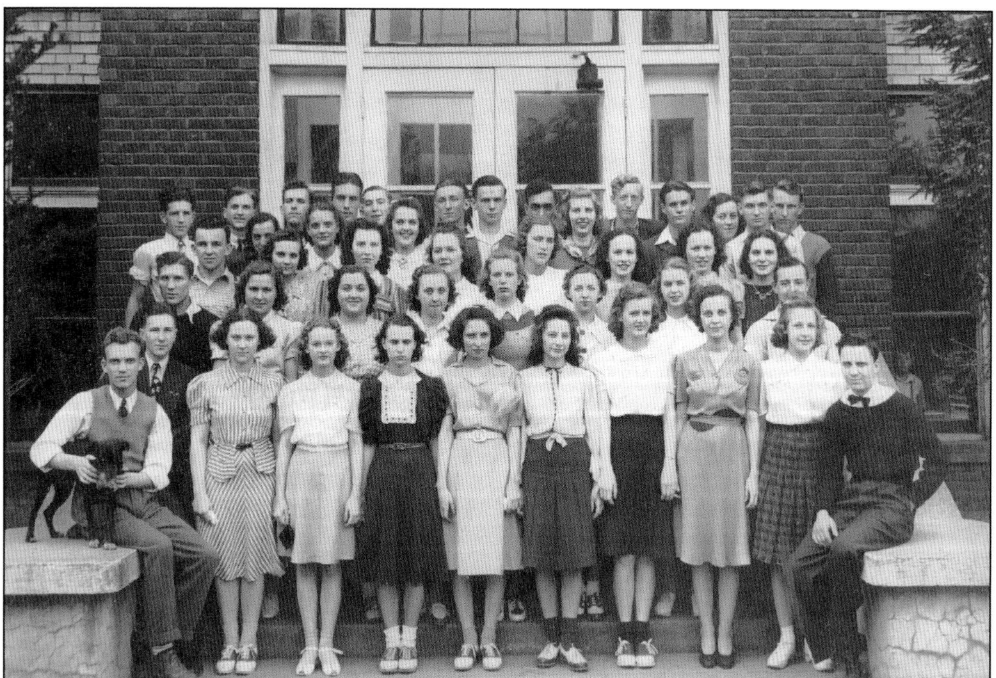

The class of 1940 stands in front of Carrollton High School. It was customary for seniors to have a class photograph taken, which was then published each year in the *News-Democrat*. (Courtesy of Gary Ford.)

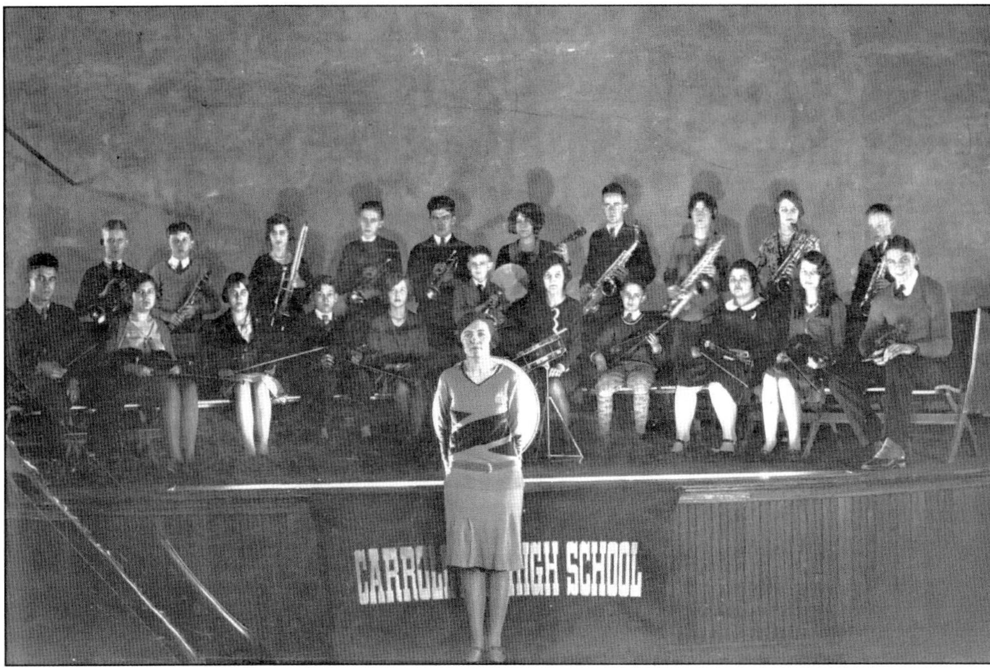

Above, the Carrollton High School concert band poses for this impressive 1931 photograph taken on the stage at the school on Seminary Street. Below, the CHS marching band in 1939 includes many of the students from the graduation class photograph on the previous page. (Both, courtesy of Amy Baglan.)

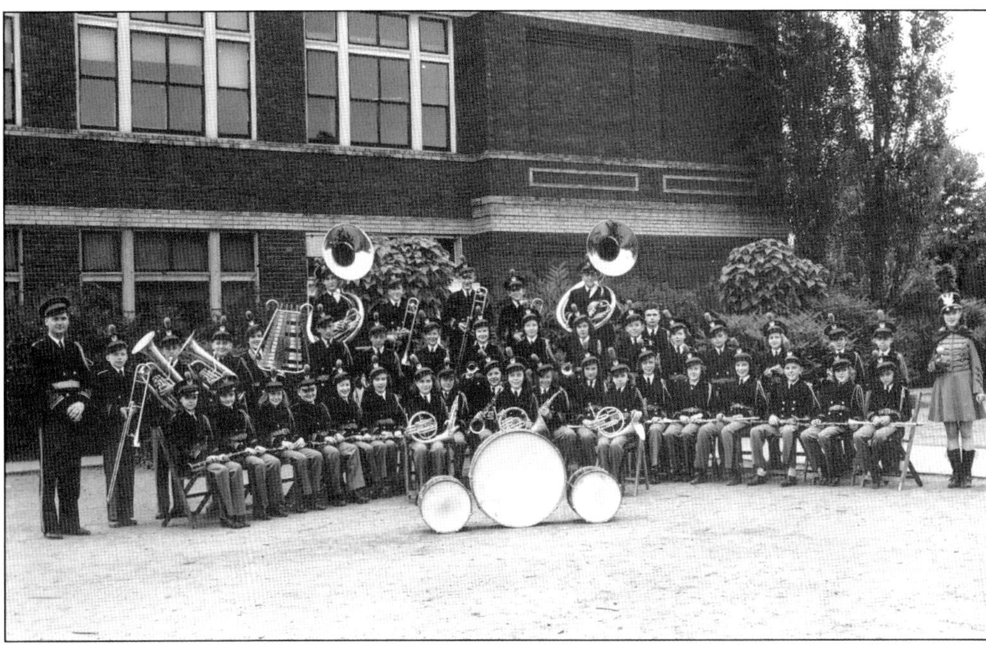

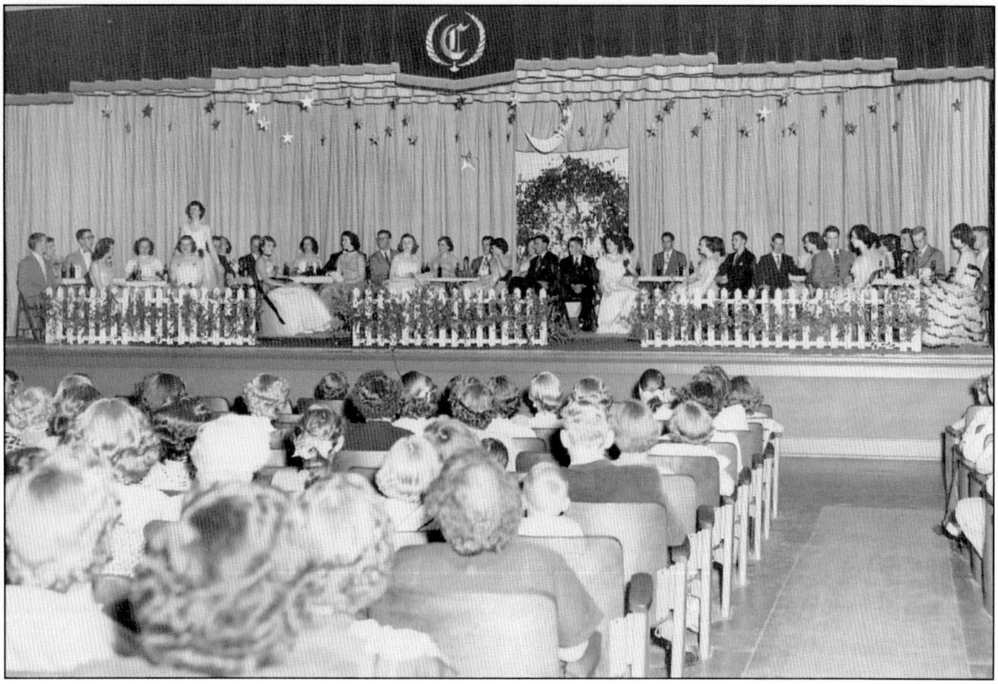

Senior Class Night was a tradition in the 1940s and 1950s. Above, the class of 1952 participates in the event, with friends and family members seated in the auditorium of Carrollton High School. Another tradition was the senior play, with members of the cast appearing in the 1952 production posing below. (Both, courtesy of Charles "Buck" Johnson.)

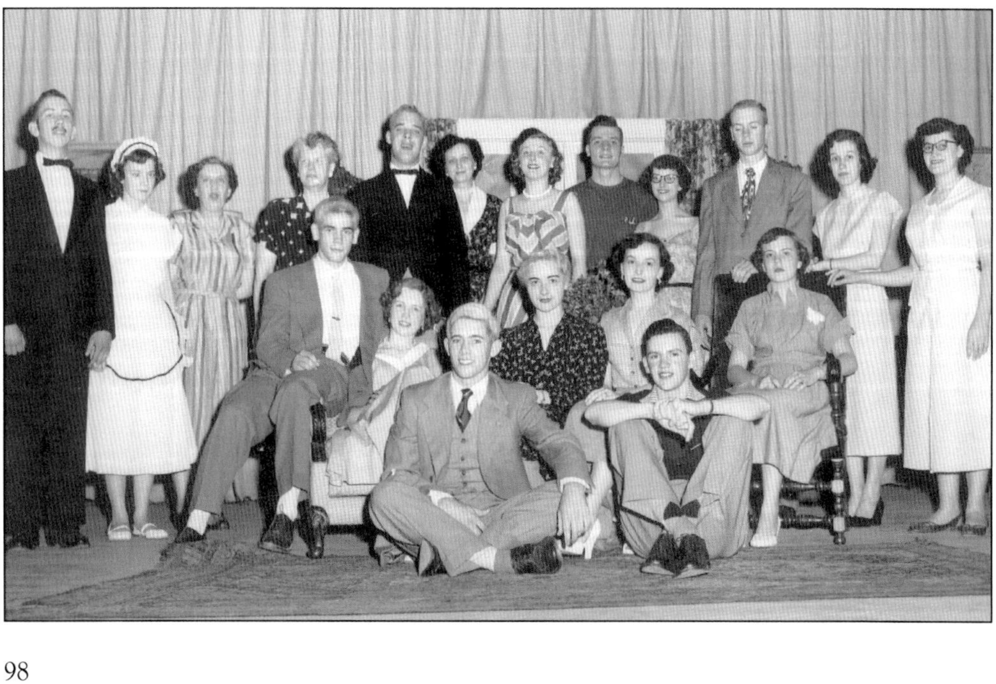

Eight

From Tobacco to Stainless Steel

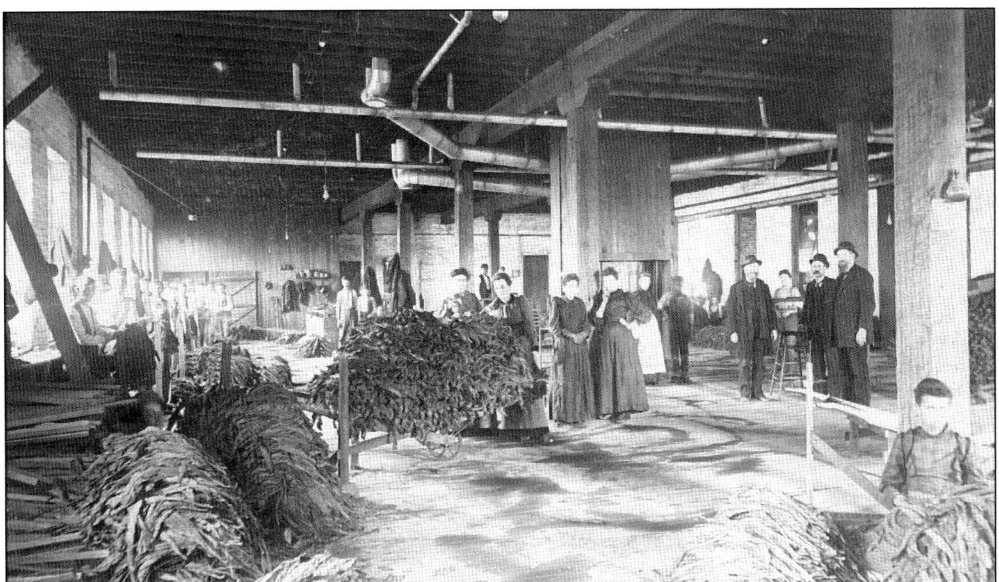

This photograph was taken inside the Carrollton Redryer facility in the early 1900s. Tobacco has been a traditional crop in Carroll County, and became even more important as an agricultural product during Prohibition, which shut down the local distilleries and reduced the need for corn, rye, and other grains used to make whiskey. By the 1970s, Carrollton was the second-largest burley tobacco market in the world. (Courtesy of Jean Yager and Junior Welch.)

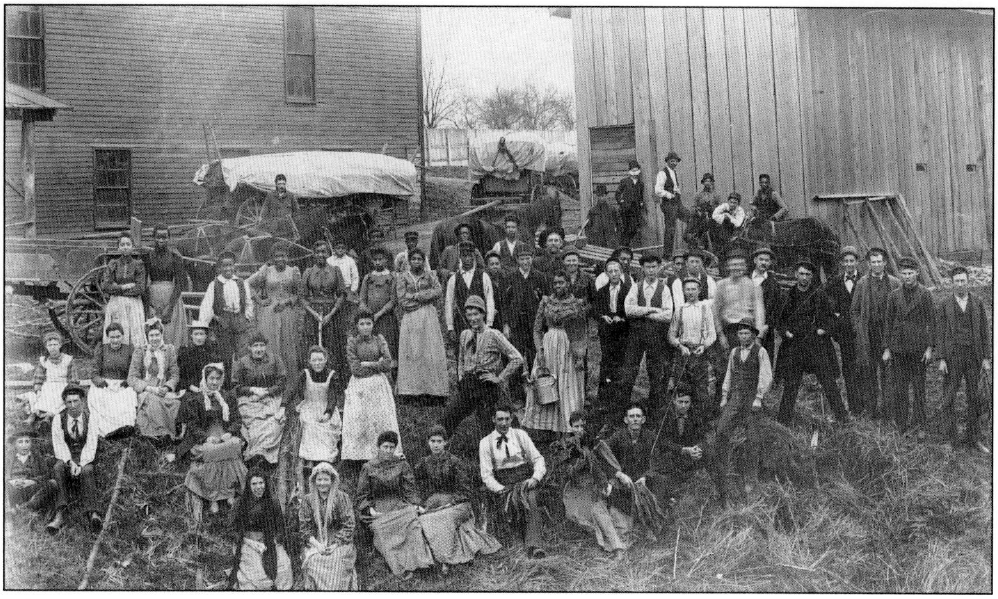

All the employees pose outside the Carrollton Redryer. Because of requirements for growing, cutting, stripping, and drying tobacco, the industry was probably the biggest employer in Carroll County for most of the 20th century. (Courtesy of Jean Yager and Junior Welch.)

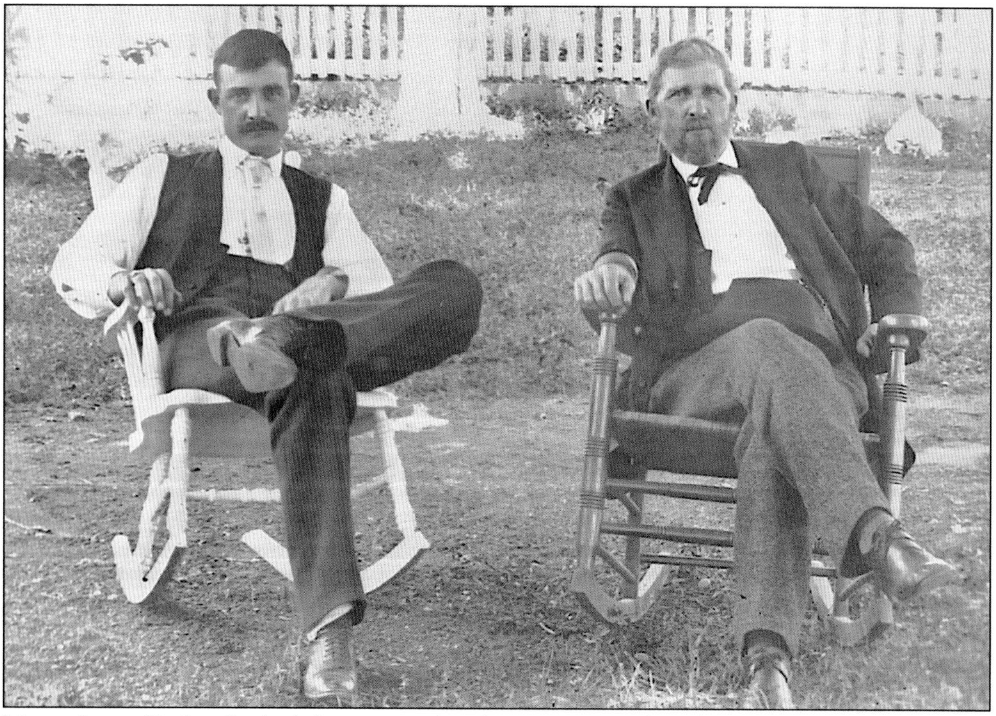

Myron Irving Barker Sr. (right) was considered an expert on the tobacco industry, learning the business from the ground up in the mid-1800s. In 1878, he began his own production and warehouse business, which he passed on to his son Ralph Malcolm Barker (left). A 1917 biography states that M.I. Barker "expended about $125,000 in buildings alone, and gave employment to two hundred hands." (Courtesy of Don Mougey.)

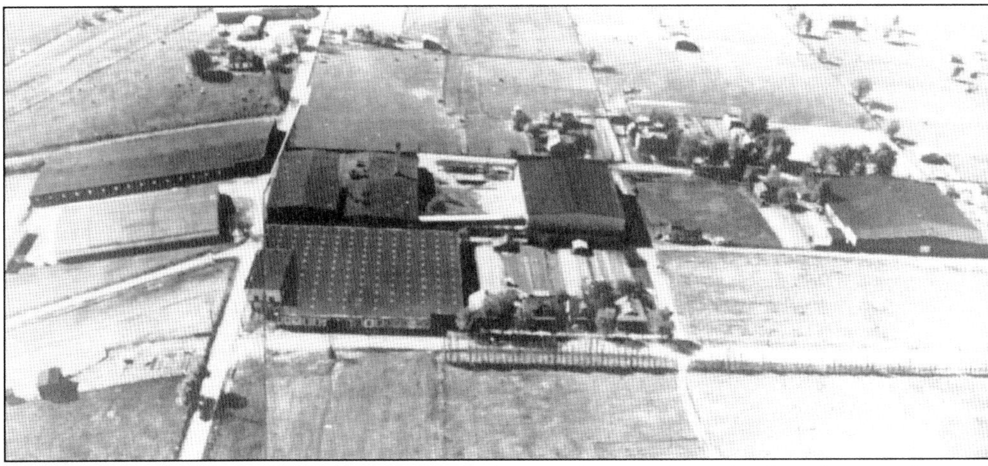

An aerial view shows the Barkers' tobacco warehouses that stood on what later became Eleventh Street (the vertical thoroughfare on the left) and Clay and Polk Streets (the two horizontal roads in the center of the photograph). The surrounding fields are now residential streets in Carrollton; the lots in the bottom right of the photograph are where the Carrollton Independent Order of Odd Fellows Cemetery is located. (Courtesy of Don Mougey.)

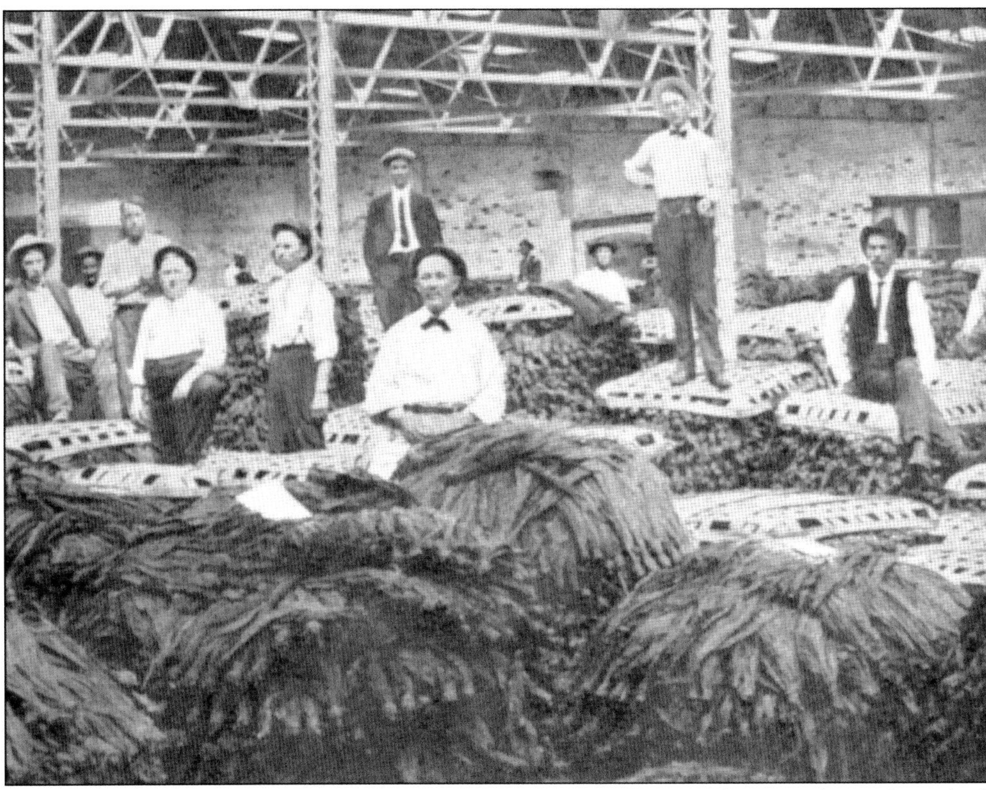

Inside one of the warehouses, men pose with large bales of tobacco as they wait for market, which opened annually around Thanksgiving and drew buyers from all over the country. While Carroll County has never been a top producer of tobacco, Carrollton warehouses at one time handled 15 million pounds of tobacco annually. In the 1970s, it became the second-largest burley tobacco market in the world. (Courtesy of Jim Fothergill.)

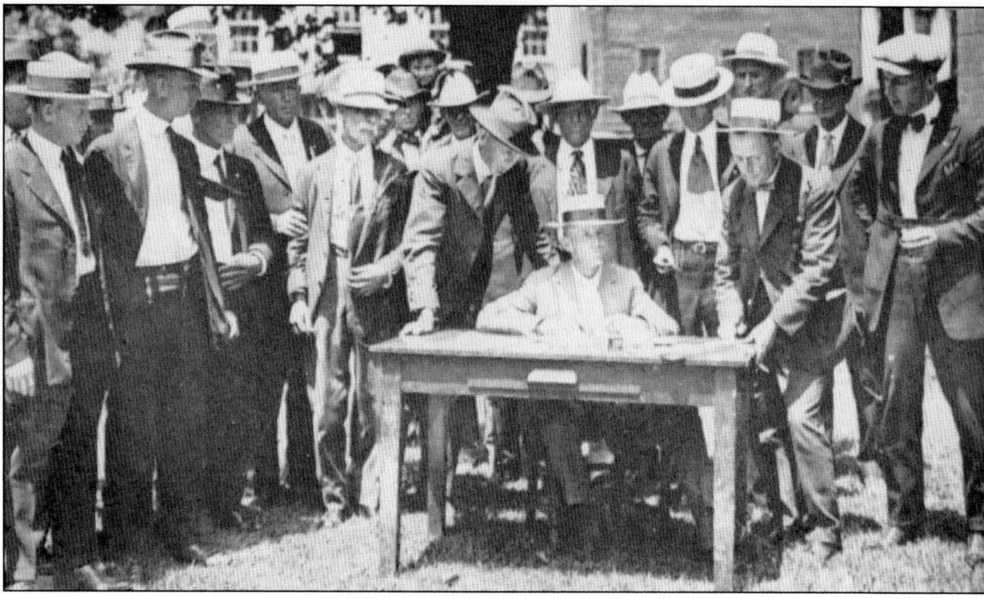

Formed in 1921, the Burley Tobacco Growers Cooperative signed a five-year contract with more than 75 percent of the growers in five states—Kentucky, Indiana, Ohio, West Virginia, and Missouri—in an attempt to stabilize the market, which had seen prices drop as low as 3¢ per pound in 1904. Above, farmers gather in Carrollton to sign a burley marketing contract on Rally Day, June 4, 1921, at Carroll County Courthouse. Business continued to boom among the warehouses built throughout Carrollton, including those shown below. Big Burley 2 still stands at Seventh and Railroad Streets, but its sibling Big Burley (below) is one of many that have been razed, along with the brick warehouse building behind it, where Billy Sunday once preached in the 1920s. (Above, courtesy of Darrell Maines; below, courtesy of General Butler State Resort Park.)

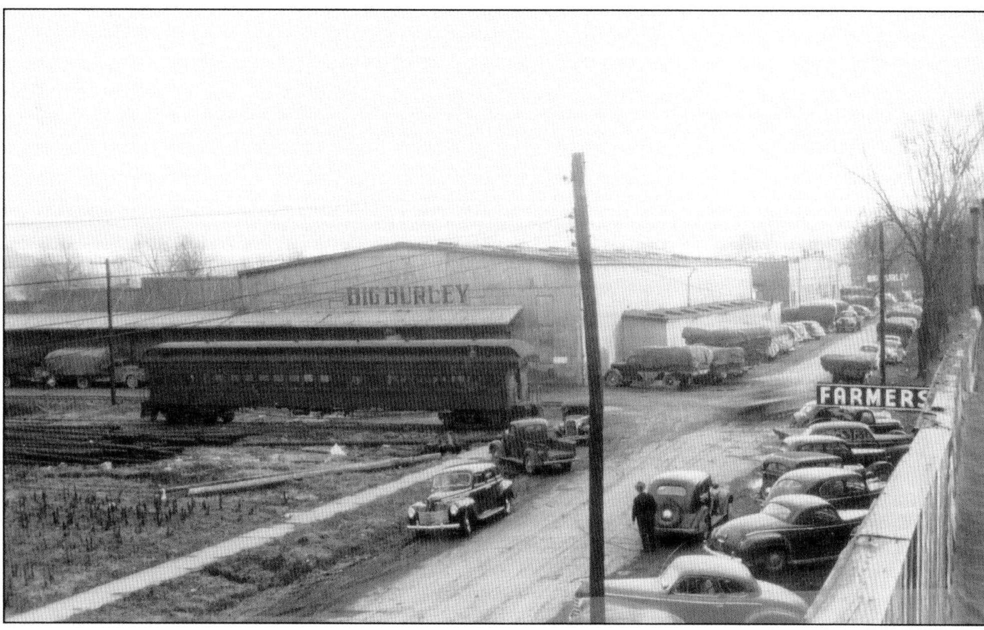

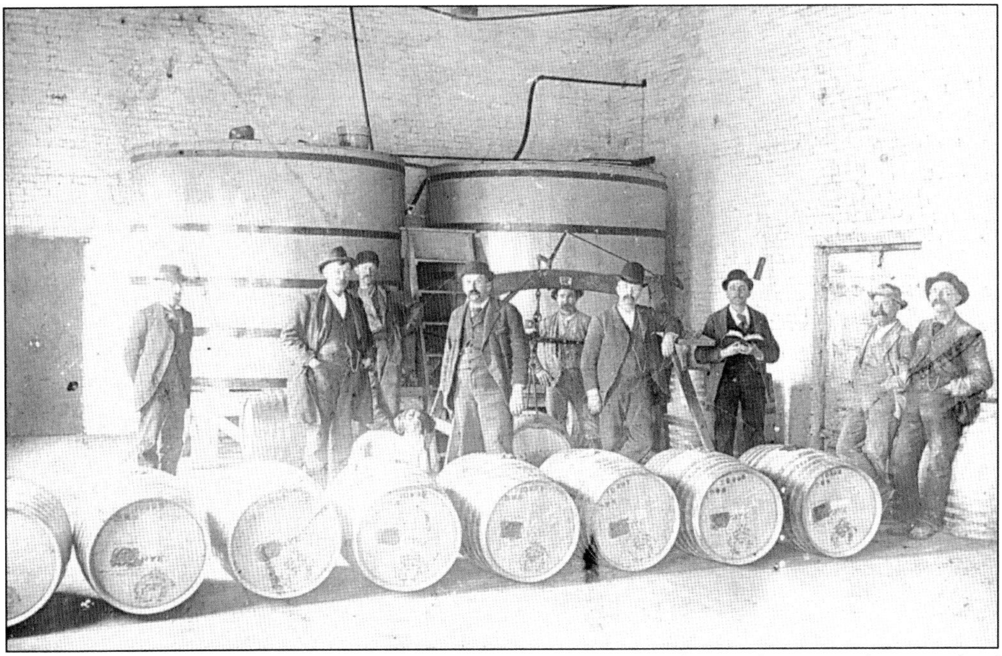

Bourbon whiskey was not the only spirit distilled by the Jett Brothers. Above is a photograph of company employees and a dog, standing with barrels labeled "rye" in one of the distilling rooms. In 1898, the brothers built an electric plant to power streetlights for Carrollton. (Courtesy of Jim Fothergill.)

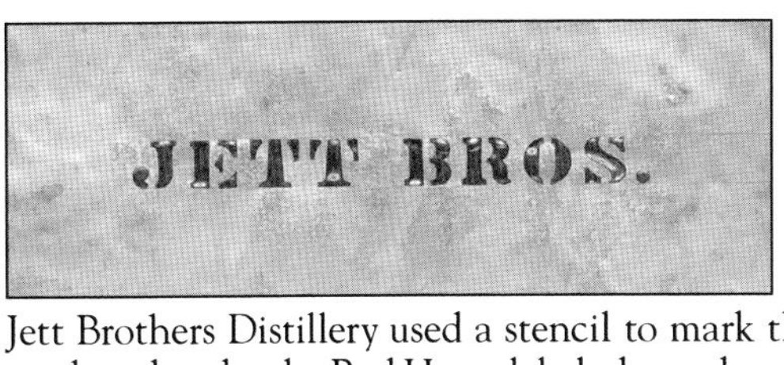

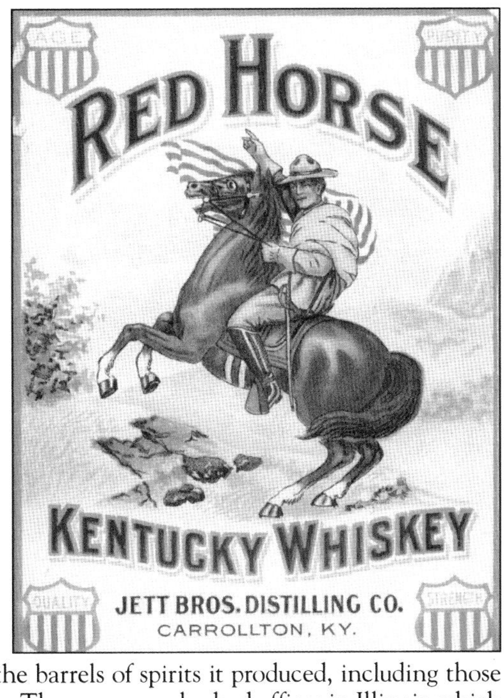

Jett Brothers Distillery used a stencil to mark the barrels of spirits it produced, including those marketed under the Red Horse label, shown here. The company also had offices in Illinois, which helped distribute the products throughout the country. A 1908 Carroll County yearbook states that Jett Brothers products also were well known in Europe. (Both, courtesy of Jim Fothergill.)

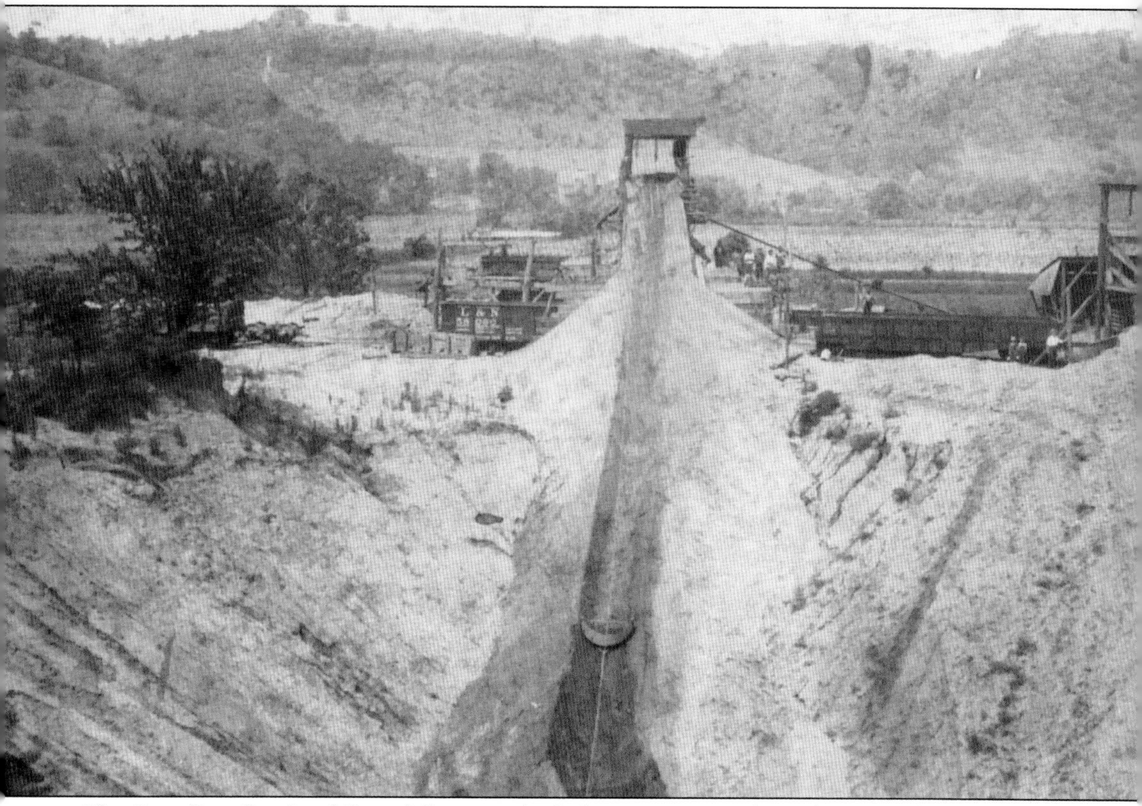

The Carrollton Sand and Gravel Company had a huge operation along the Kentucky River, across from where General Butler State Resort Park is located. Long since gone from this location, the industry remains on State Highway 36 in the Hunters Bottom area of Carroll County, where

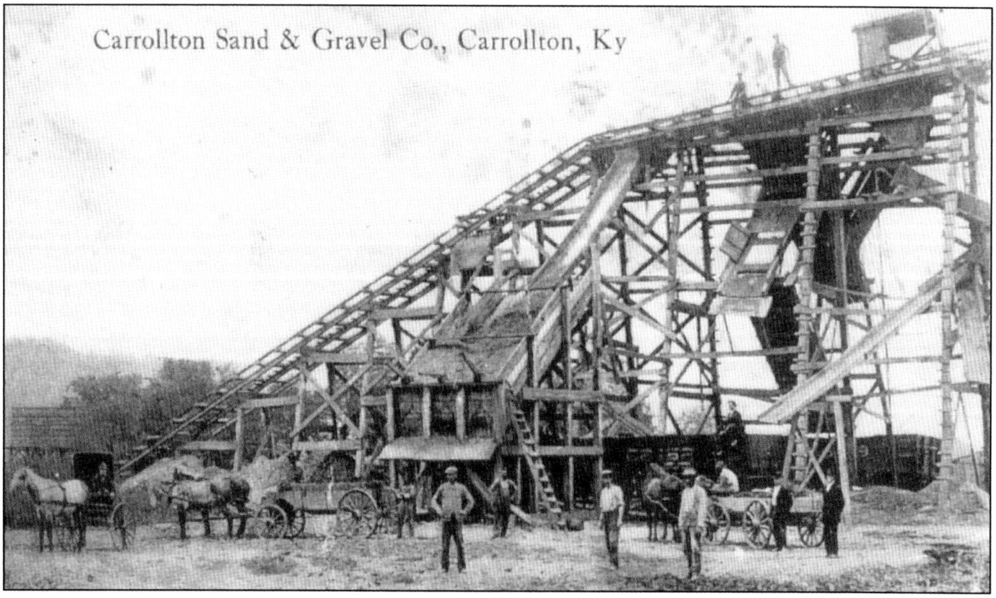

Workers at Carrollton Sand and Gravel Company take a break to pose next to the mine. (Courtesy of Gary Ford.)

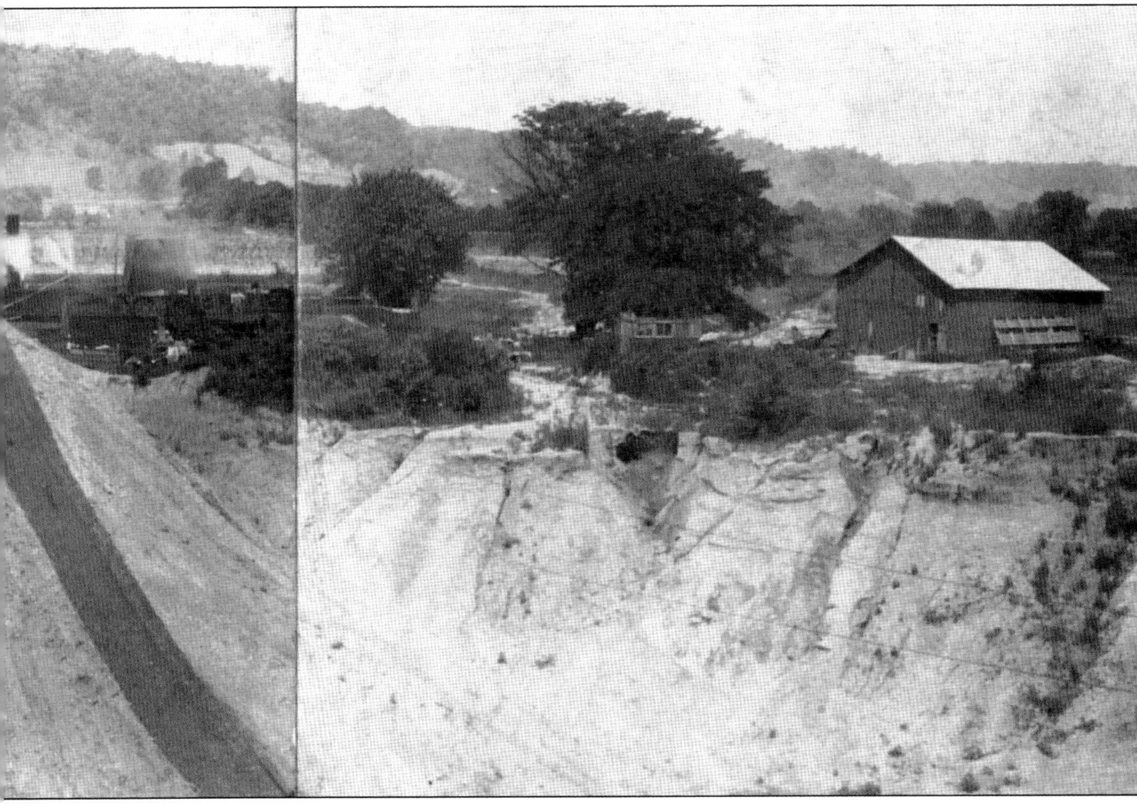

Louisville-based Nugent Sand Company operates a facility that takes up hundreds of acres of land in western Carroll County and ships products by barge from its dock on the Ohio River. (Courtesy of Gary Ford.)

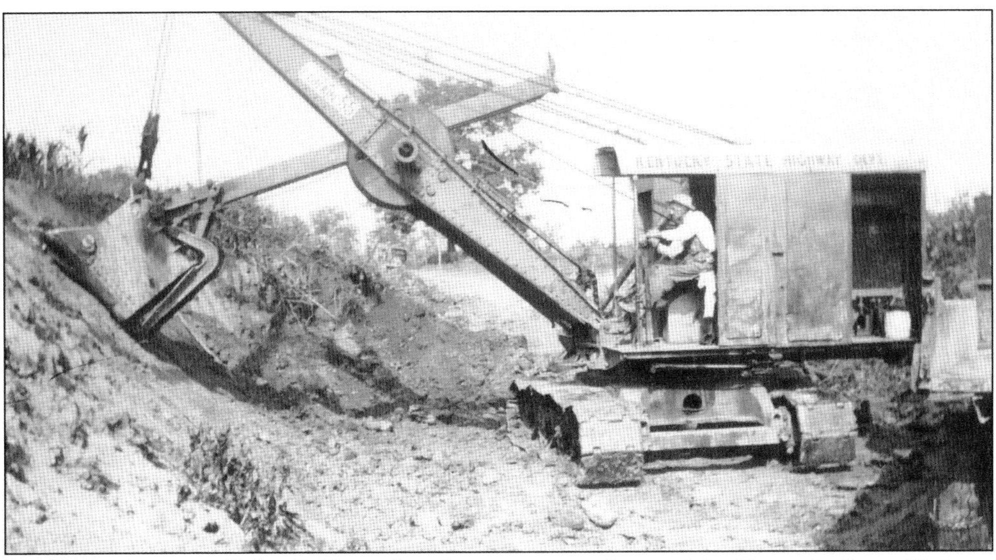

World War I veteran Kirbie F. House later became an employee of the Kentucky State Highway Department. Here, he uses a steam shovel on a road project out in the county. (Courtesy of Gary Ford.)

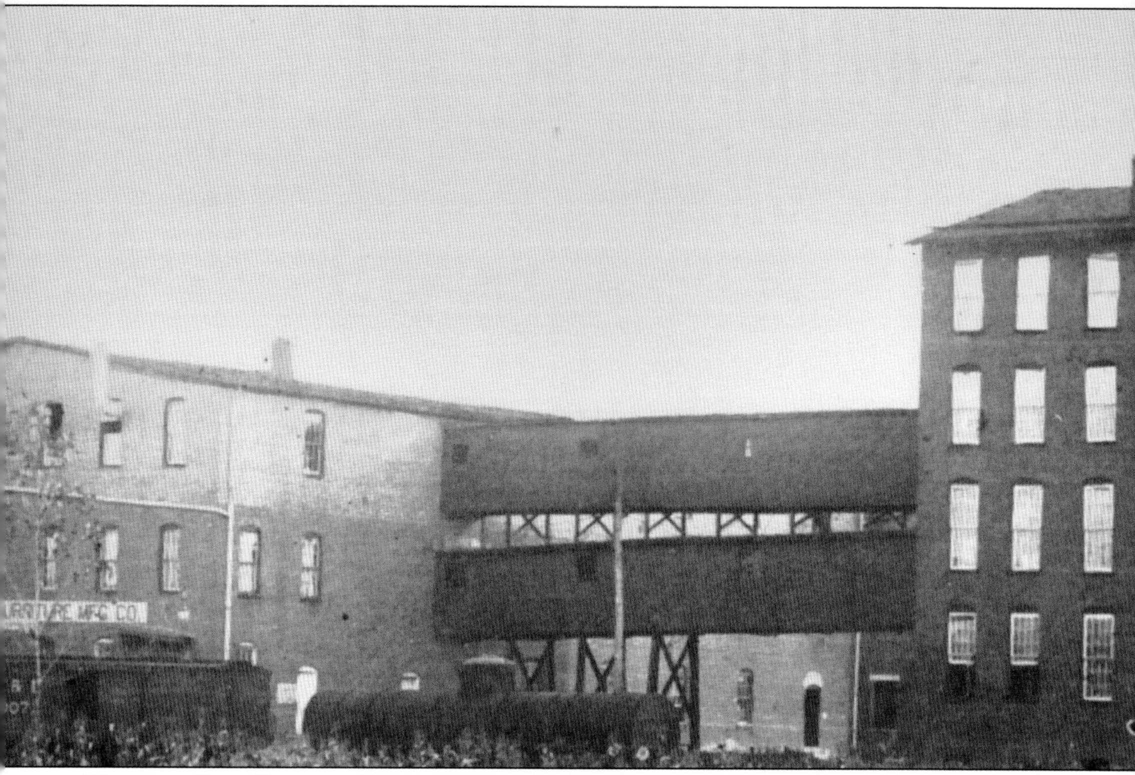

The Carrollton Furniture Factory was established by a committee of prominent businessmen who raised $20,000 from the sale of stock in 1883 to begin building the facility on four acres along Fourth Street, south of Clay Street. Operated by superintendent Henry Schuerman, the factory employed top craftsmen who built Louis XV– and Louis XVI–style bedroom suites

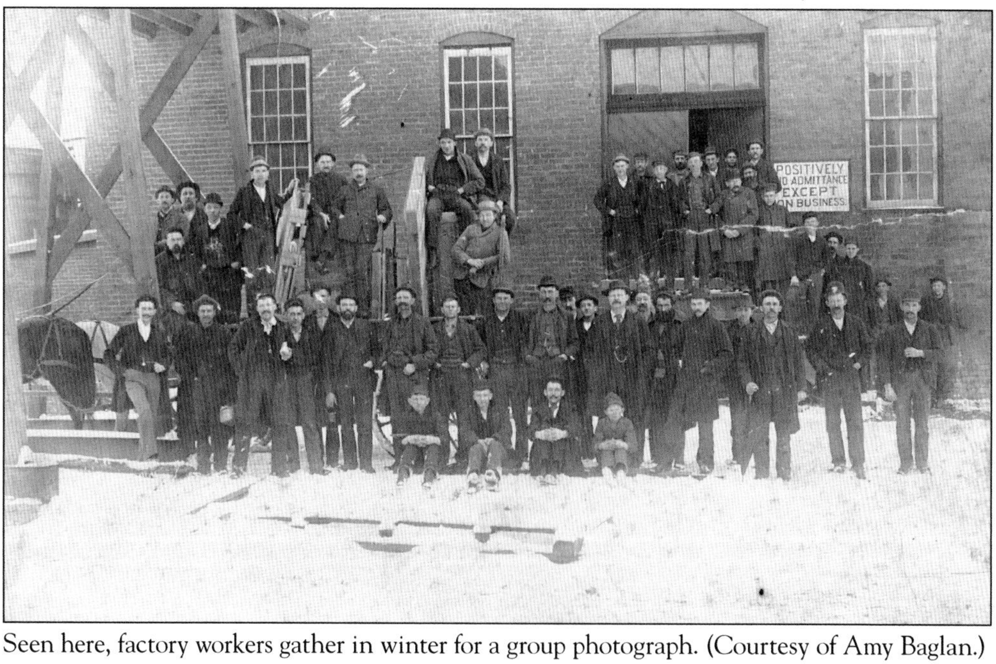

Seen here, factory workers gather in winter for a group photograph. (Courtesy of Amy Baglan.)

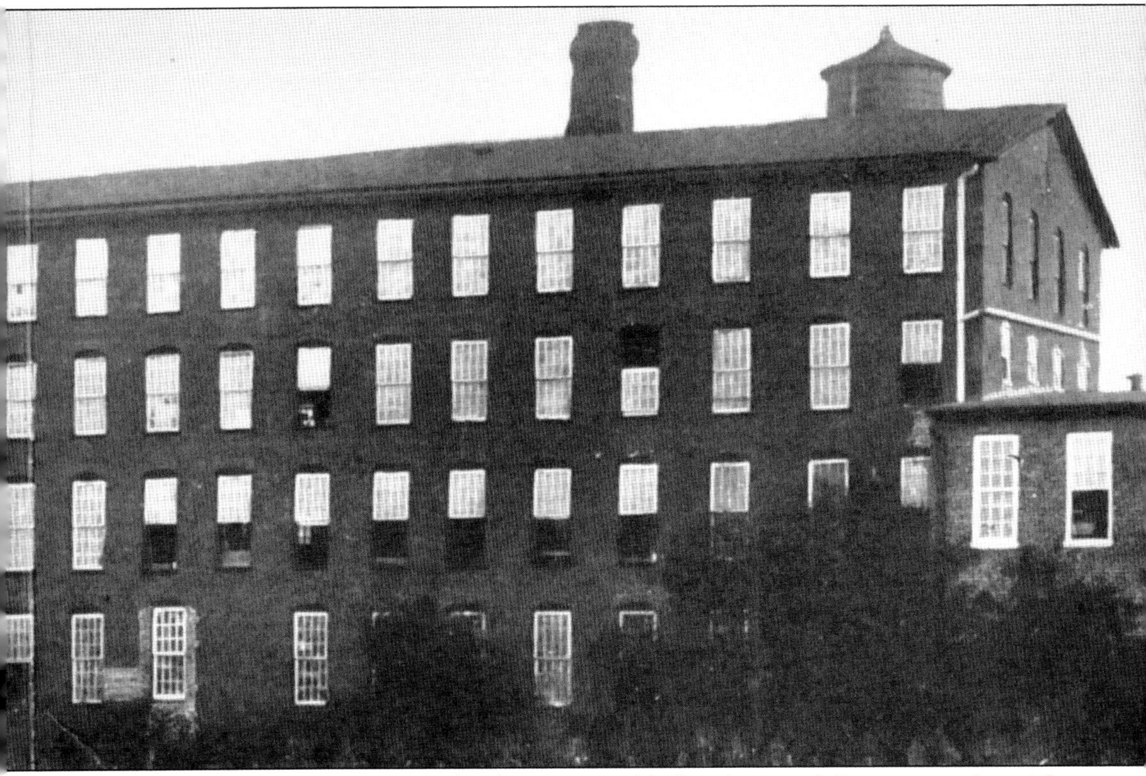

from mahogany, bird's-eye maple, birch, American black walnut, and Circassian walnut. These products were shipped to markets in New Orleans and Grand Rapids, Michigan. (Courtesy of Robin Caldwell Welch.)

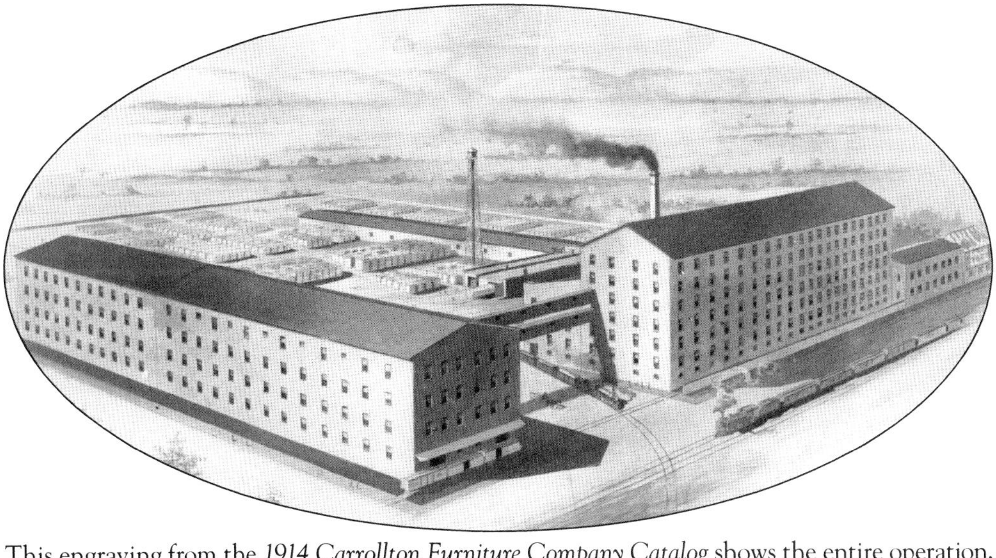

This engraving from the *1914 Carrollton Furniture Company Catalog* shows the entire operation, which stood on Fourth Street in the south section of Carrollton next to the Kentucky River. The company took a blue ribbon for its products at an industrial exposition in New Orleans in the mid-1880s. One bedroom in Grover Cleveland's White House was furnished with furniture from the Carrollton factory. (Courtesy of Courtesy of Robin Caldwell Welch.)

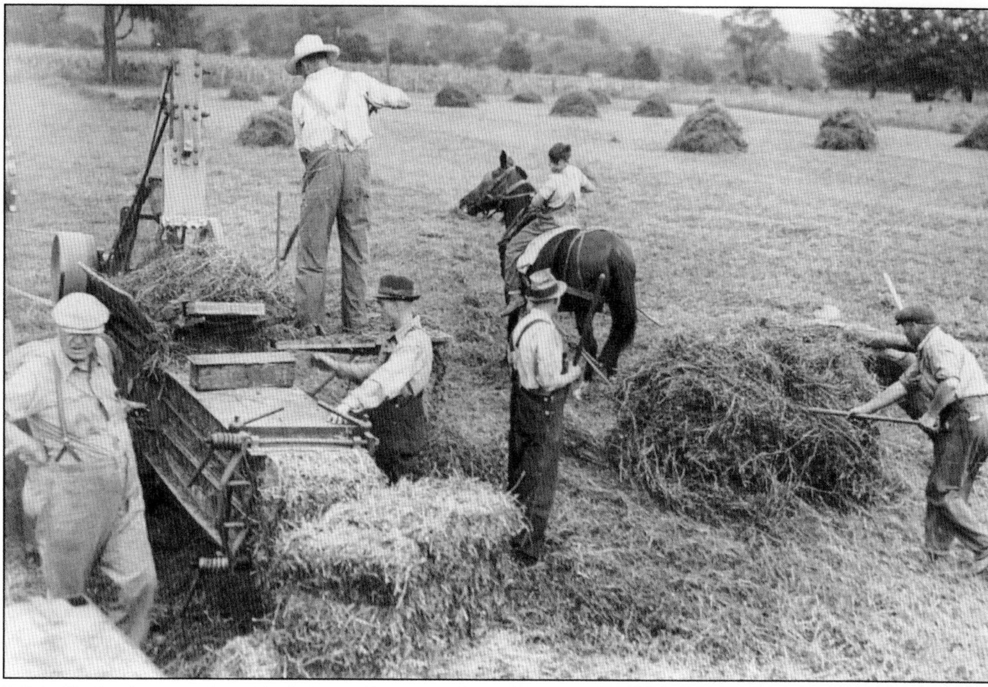

R.M. Barker's sprawling Richlawn farm produced hay to feed Barker's prizewinning horses and livestock. Here, workers man a baling machine. From left to right are Barker, Hubert Hackett, Woodrow Harmon, a Mr. Tingle, Everett Bright, Jim Adams, and Elois "Carroll" Hackett on horseback. Barker donated a large portion of the farm for use as the Carroll County Fairgrounds, now the location of the Carroll County High School campus. (Courtesy of Don Mougey.)

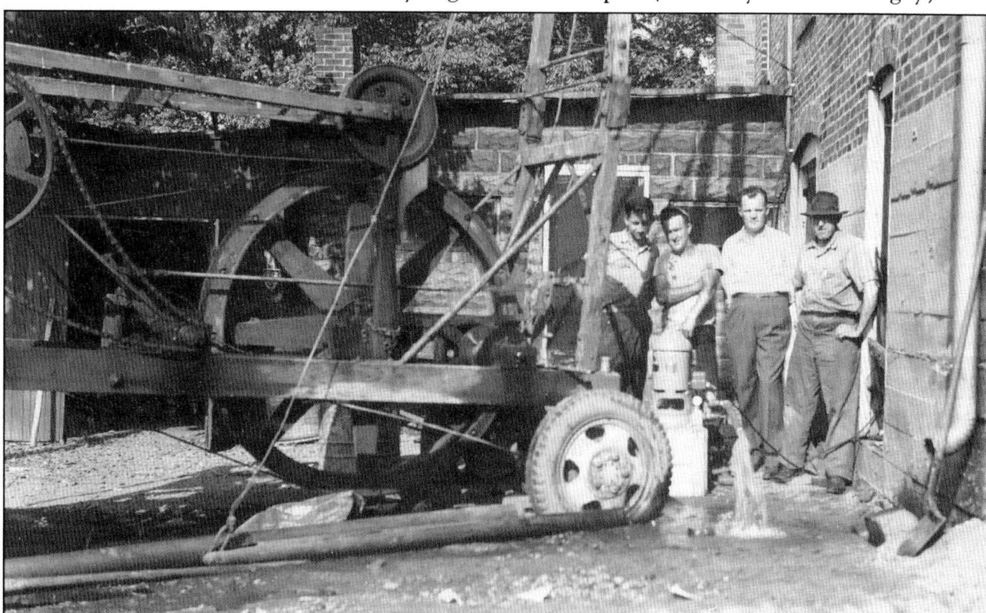

A crew stops for a photograph while drilling a water well behind the Gypsy Grill in Carrollton about 1947. From left to right are workers J.W. Wheeler, P.J. Maines, Gypsy Grill owner Joe DuVall, and Courtland Hanlon, of Hanlon Pump and Well in Ghent. (Courtesy of Darrell Maines.)

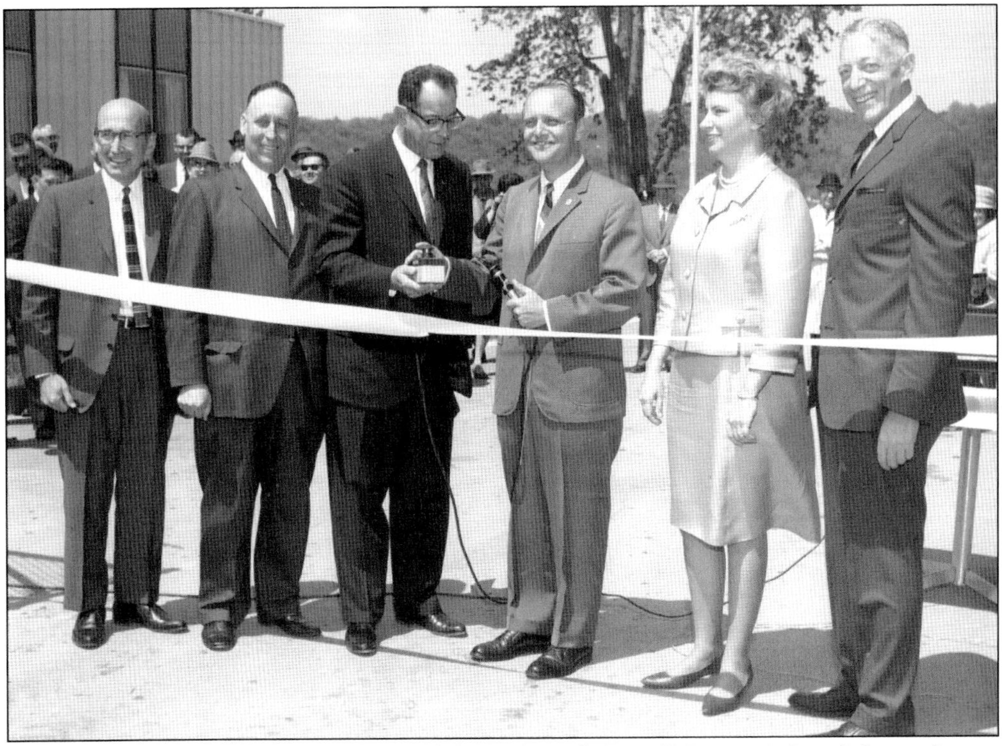

The Dow Corning Carrollton Plant was dedicated April 27, 1967. Pictured, from left to right, are Clarence "Bud" Lankton, plant manager; W.J. Louden, chairman of the Carroll County Industrial Development Foundation; Gov. Edward T. Breathitt; Dr. Shaler T. Bass, president of Dow Corning; Katherine Peden, Kentucky commissioner of commerce; and Earle J. Smith, general manager of the Chemicals Division of Dow Corning. (Courtesy of Carol Louden Shelton.)

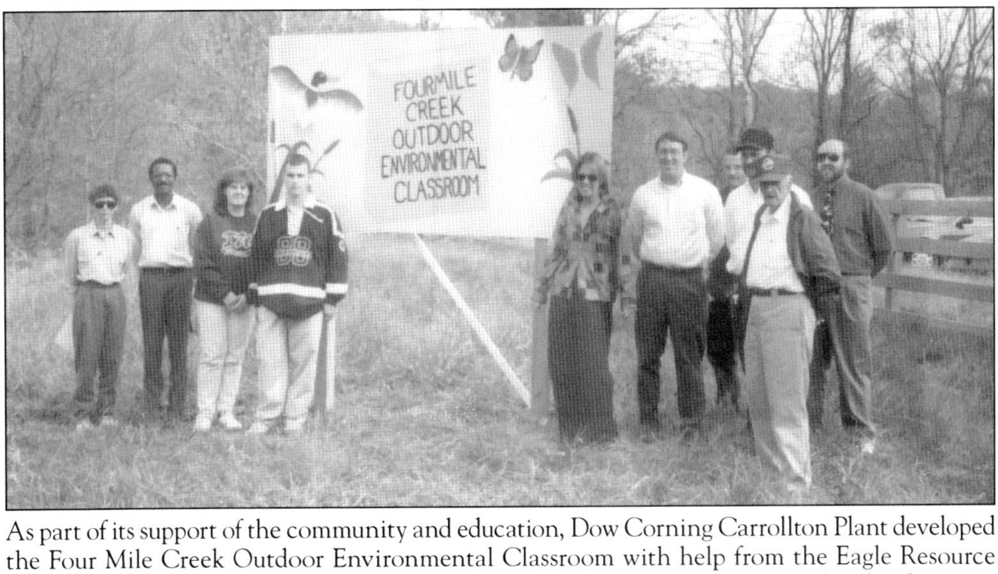

As part of its support of the community and education, Dow Corning Carrollton Plant developed the Four Mile Creek Outdoor Environmental Classroom with help from the Eagle Resource Conservation and Development Council as well as Carroll County Public Schools. The classroom allows teachers to take students into nature to study ecology and environmental protection. (Courtesy of *News-Democrat*.)

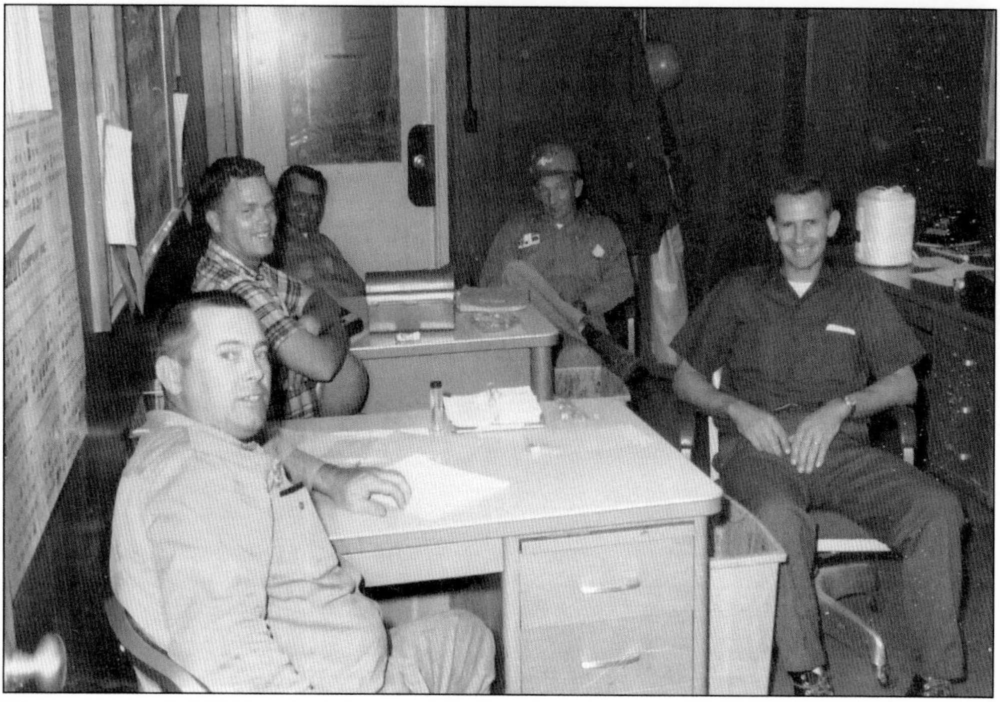

The foremen at M&T Chemical plant on US 42 in Carrollton take a break from their hard work. The plant has been sold several times since it was built in 1958, changing its name to Elf-Atochem, Atofina, and Arkema. Arkema, a French company, recently sold the facility to PMC Group of New Jersey. (Courtesy of Charles "Buck" Johnson.)

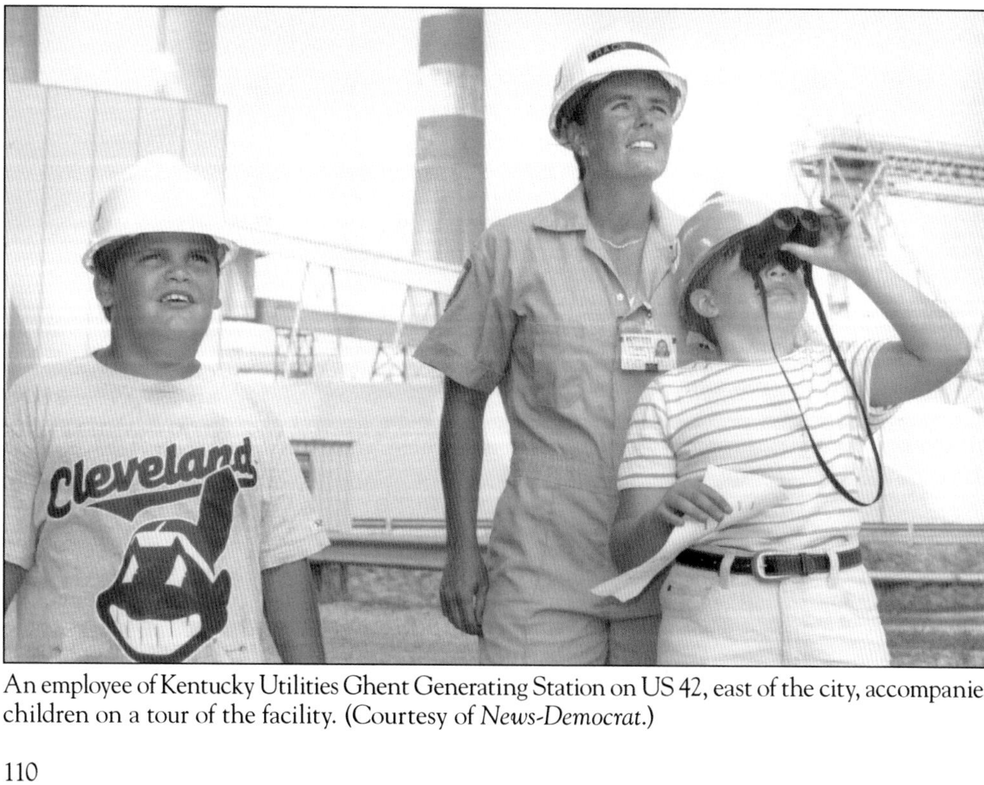

An employee of Kentucky Utilities Ghent Generating Station on US 42, east of the city, accompanies children on a tour of the facility. (Courtesy of *News-Democrat*.)

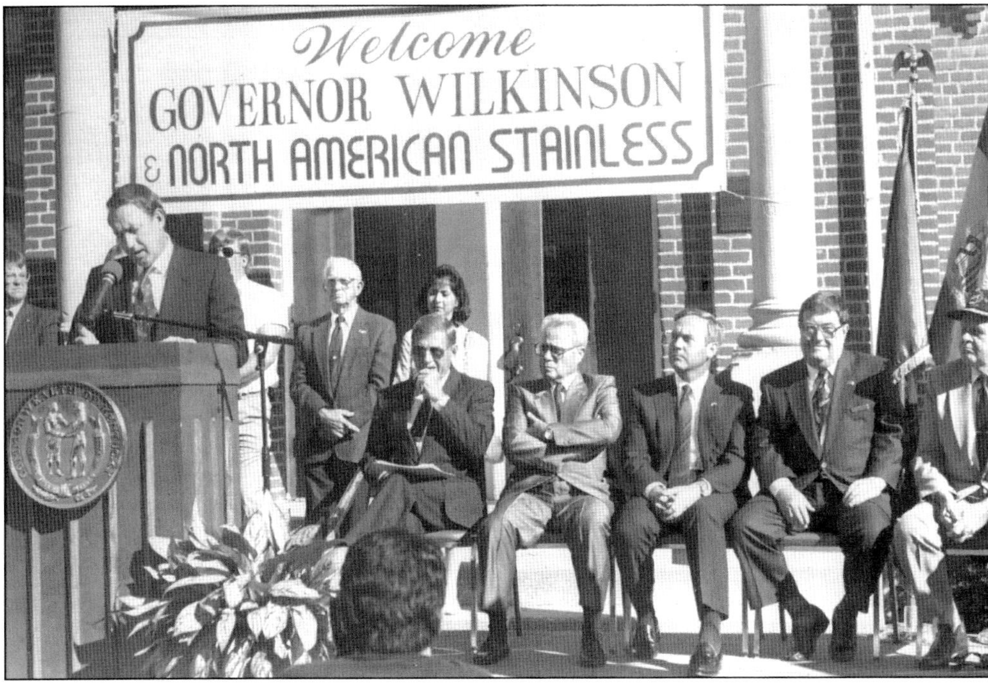

Kentucky governor Wallace G. Wilkinson came to Carrollton to help welcome officials from North American Stainless, which began building its Carroll County facility in 1990 on 1,400 acres just west of Ghent and continues to expand. The county's largest employer, with more than 1,700 workers, NAS makes flat and long stainless products. Below, guests are taken on a tour of one of the county's three plants, which also include Ghent Steel and Gallatin Steel, both east of Ghent near the Gallatin County line. (Both, courtesy of *News-Democrat*.)

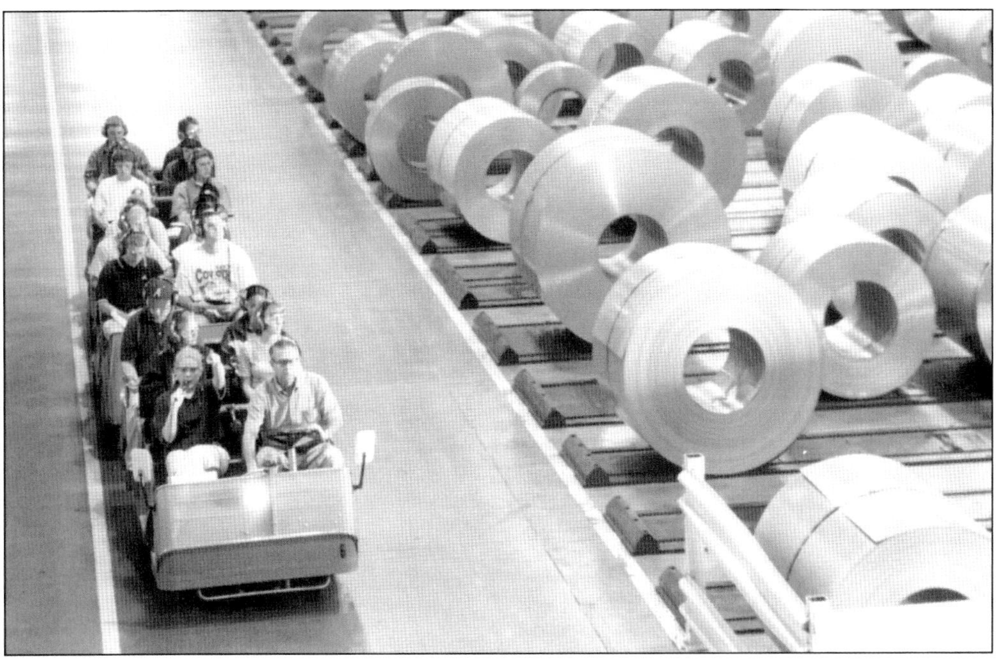

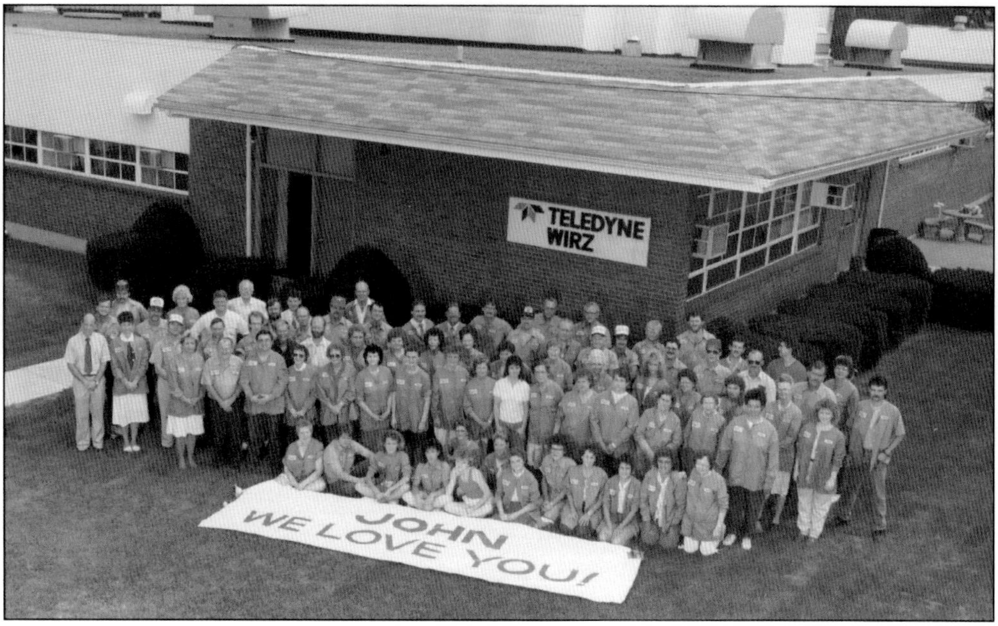

Employees at Teledyne Wirz gather for a portrait at the plant, which was located on the corner of Hawkins and Ninth Streets. Originally the A.H. Wirz Tube Plant, the facility produced metal tubes used for pharmaceutical creams, foods, chemicals, and cosmetics, including toothpaste. (Courtesy of Joan Jackson.)

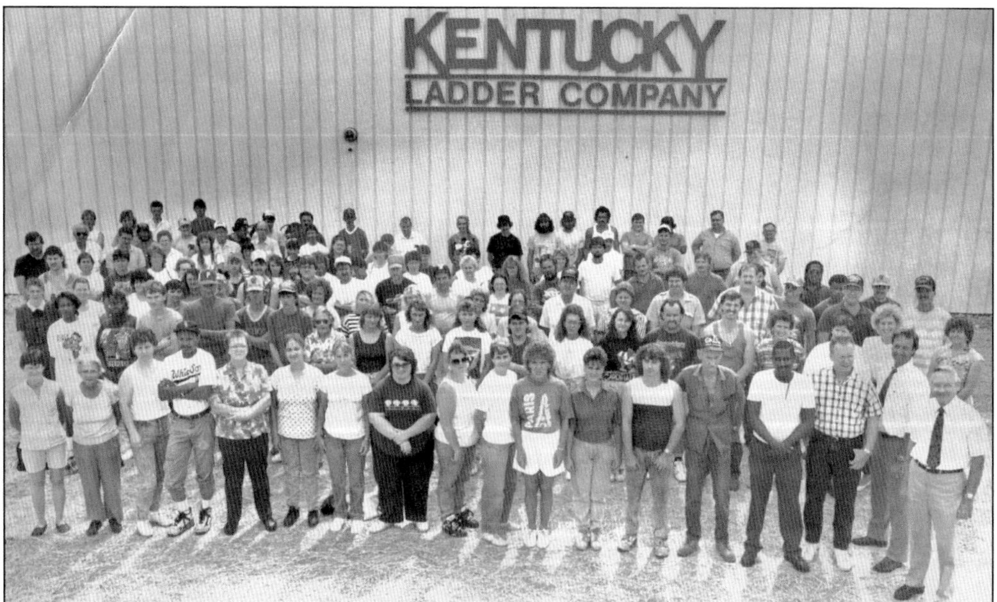

Kentucky Ladder Company, formerly Werner Ladder and H.B. Rich Company, was a longtime employer in Carroll County. In the 1960s, Louis Bunning moved his wife and family, including future baseball legend and US senator Jim Bunning, to Carroll County when he was named executive of the H.B. Rich Company. Senator Bunning maintained political connections with the county and helped funnel federal funding for numerous projects, including a regional wastewater treatment plant. (Courtesy of *News-Democrat*.)

Nine

PASTIMES AND PURSUITS

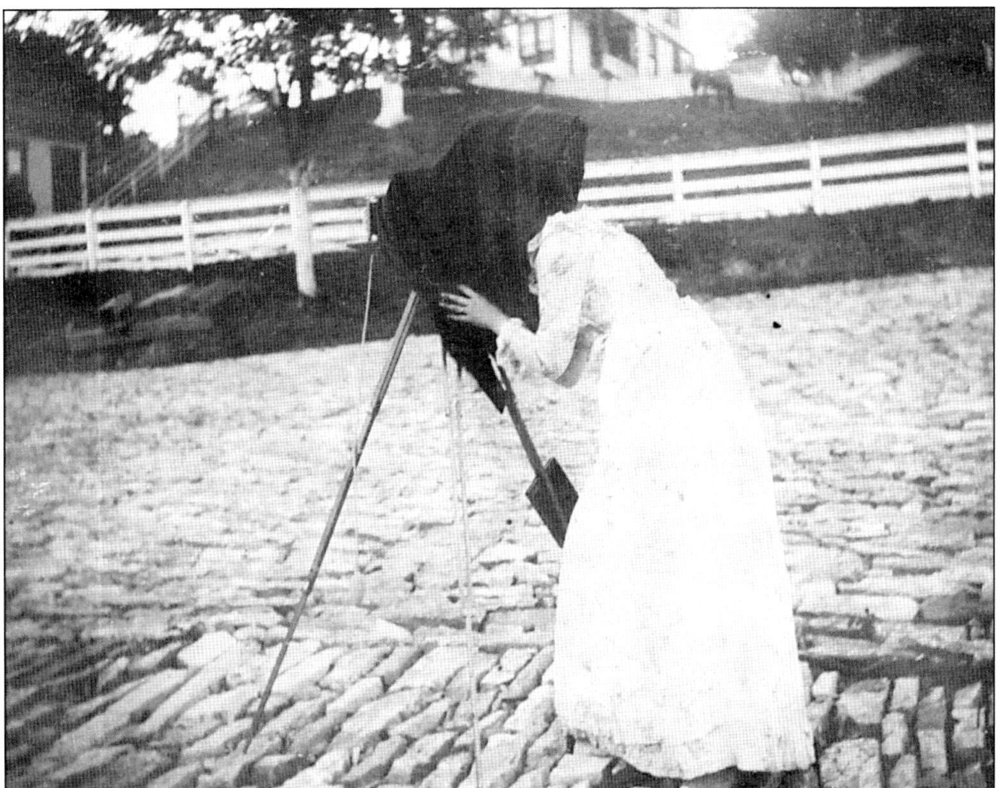

Ada Barker Fisher was an avid photographer in the early 1990s. She left behind a legacy of family photographs as well as images of the interior and exterior of her grand home, Pine View. Another of her favorite subjects was the view of the Ohio River from that home, which was destroyed by fire in the 1920s. She and her husband, William, were in the midst of rebuilding when Ada died. Her brother R.M. Barker took on the project, naming his new home Richlawn. (Courtesy of Don Mougey.)

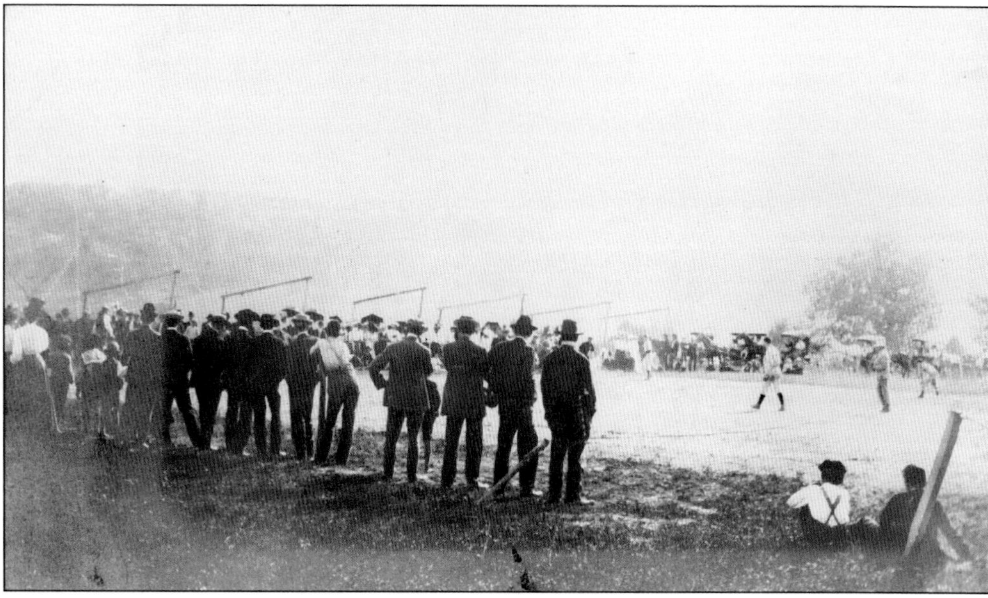

Baseball was another passion of Barker's, and he hosted numerous baseball games in one of the fields near his home, such as this one above in about 1900. He was a huge fan of the Cincinnati Reds. Below, Barker and two of his prized purebred Great Danes pose with members of the Reds team, whom he invited down for a weekend of bass fishing in September 1938. According to a *News-Democrat* article, guests were to include Johnny Vander Meer (kneeling at right), Whitey Moore, Lee Grissom, and Don Lang. (Both, courtesy of Don Mougey.)

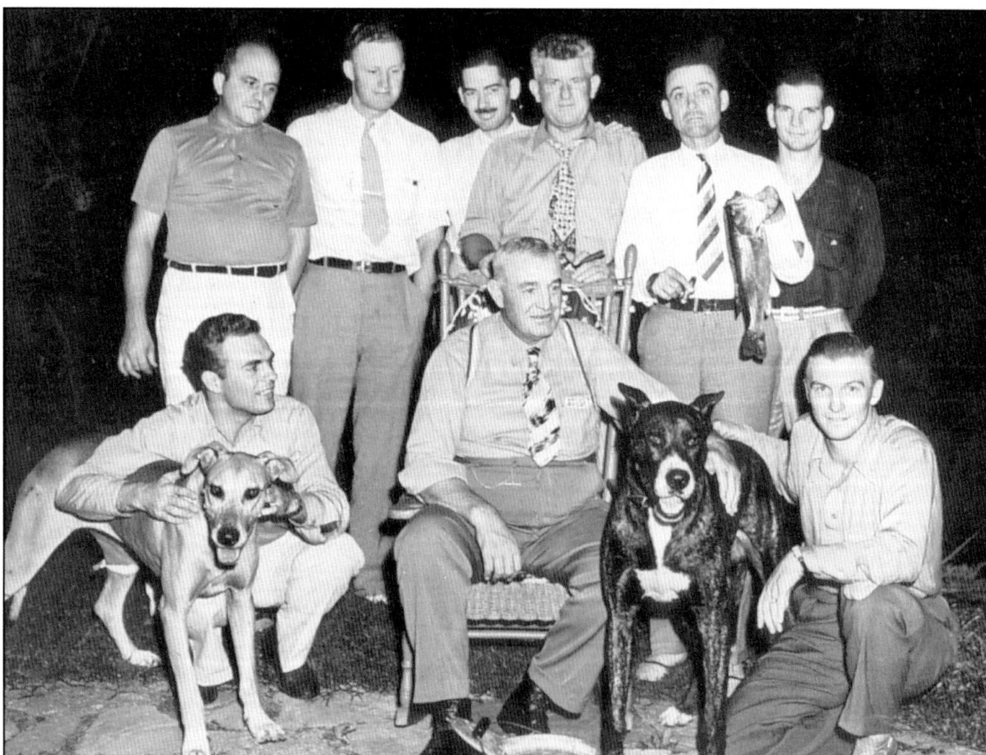

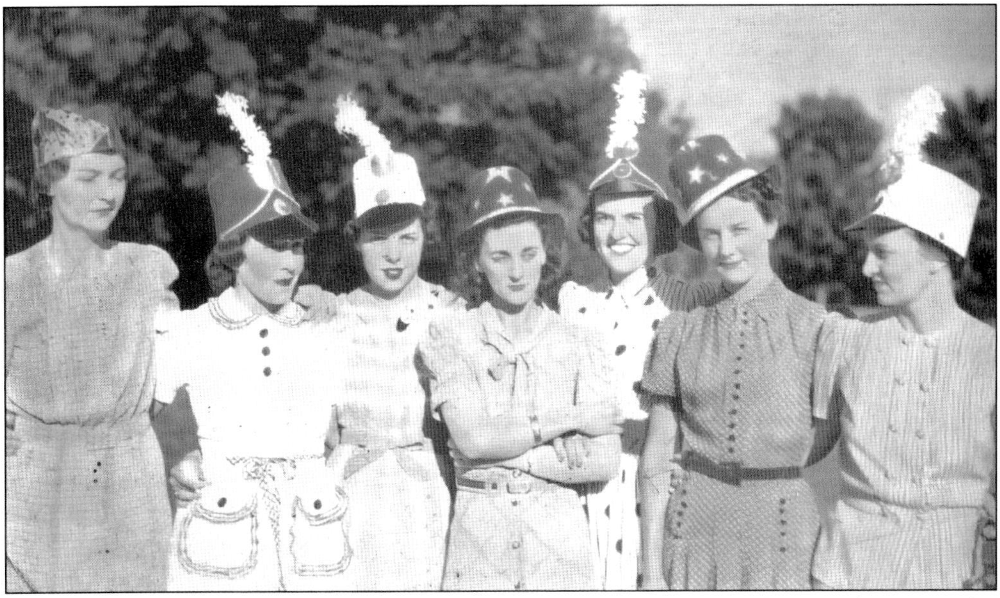

Ralph Malcolm Barker was not known just for being a major force in the tobacco industry. He also was known for his parties on the Fourth of July. Above, women in party hats pose for a photograph during one of the Independence Day events at Richlawn, Barker's house on US 42 East. In addition to installing thousands of Christmas lights on his home, which drew hundreds of visitors each year, Barker also had a live Nativity scene set up on his property, which the public was invited to see. Note the registration book on the far right. (Both, courtesy of Don Mougey.)

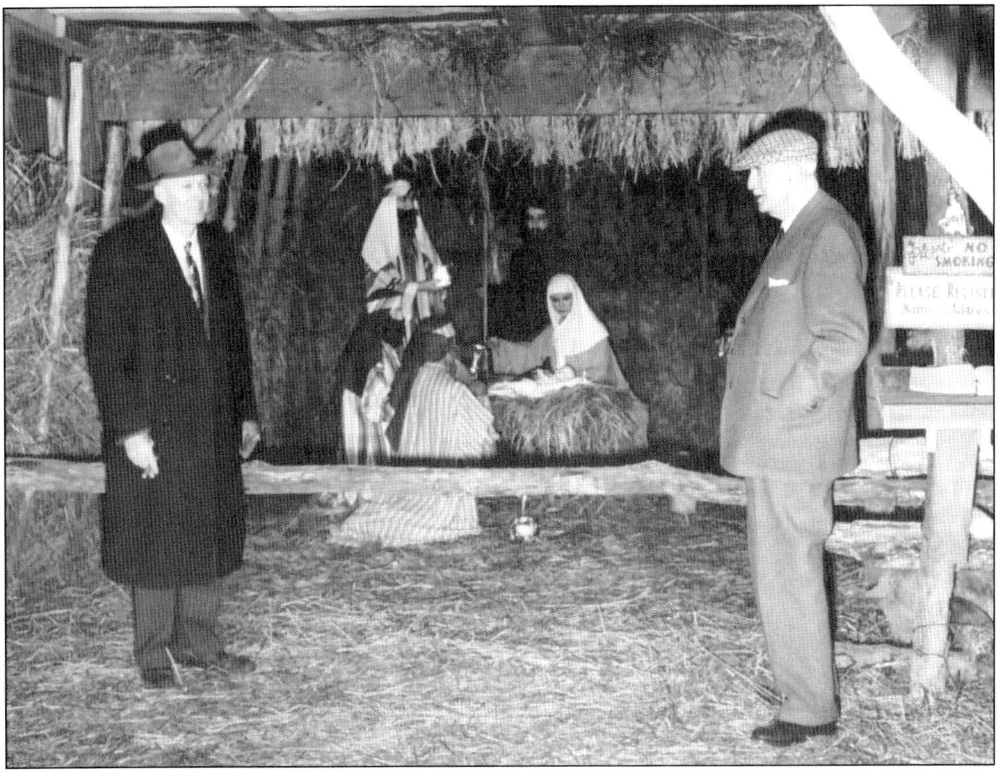

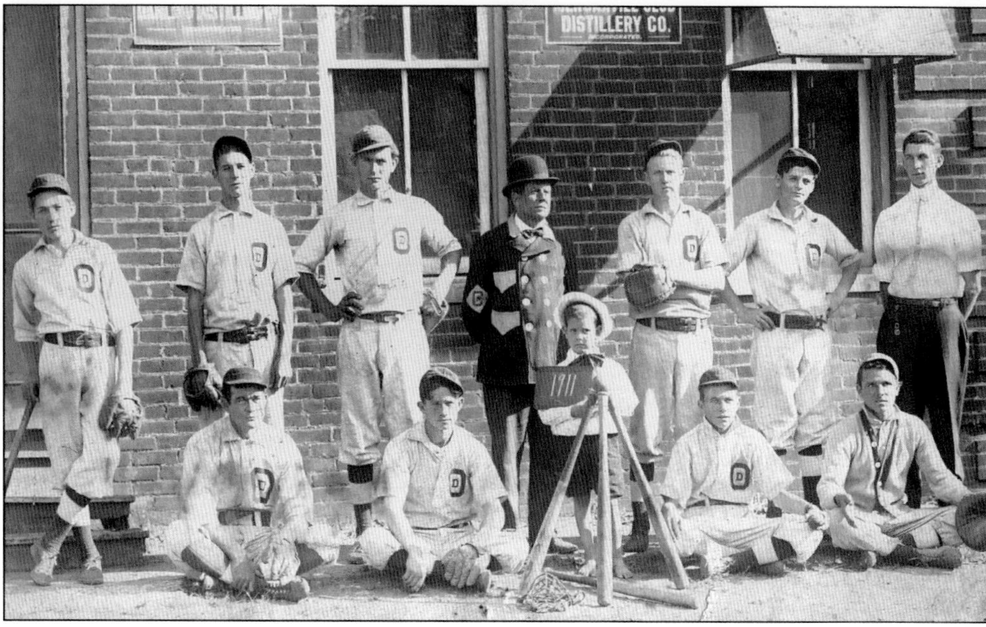

The Darling Distillery in Prestonville sponsored its own men's intramural baseball team. Pictured are members of the 1911 team. (Courtesy of Darrell Maines.)

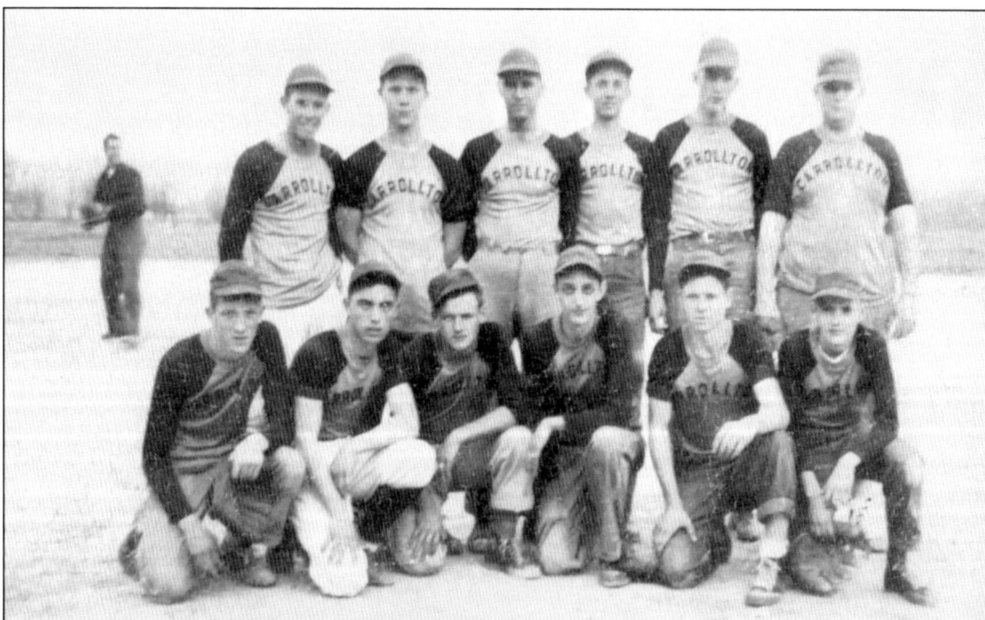

Members of the 1949 Carrollton High School varsity baseball team pose for a photograph. They are, from left to right, (kneeling) Pete Persall, Oliver Brunton, Logan Kring, Dickie Ellis, John Tilley, and Carl "Sonny" Wiese; (standing) Charles "Buck" Johnson, Jack Simonton, Coach Peck Perry, Carl "Sonny" Reese, Harold Schirmer, and Bill Fothergill. Getting ready to pitch, in the background, is Logan's brother Bobby Kring. (Courtesy of Charles "Buck" Johnson)

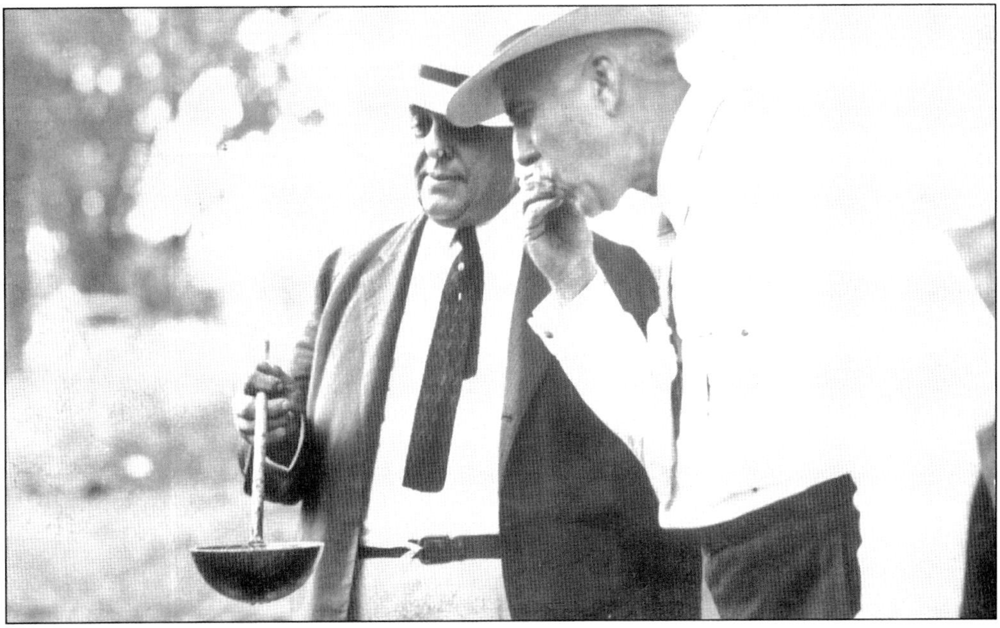

Author James Tandy Ellis of Ghent serves a taste of his famous burgoo to state senator Perry B. Gaines during the dedication of Butler Memorial Park on September 4, 1933. Tandy, who also served as adjutant general of the Kentucky National Guard, was famous for the dish, a kind of stew cooked outdoors overnight in a pot, containing whatever meats and vegetables were on hand. (Courtesy of *News-Democrat*.)

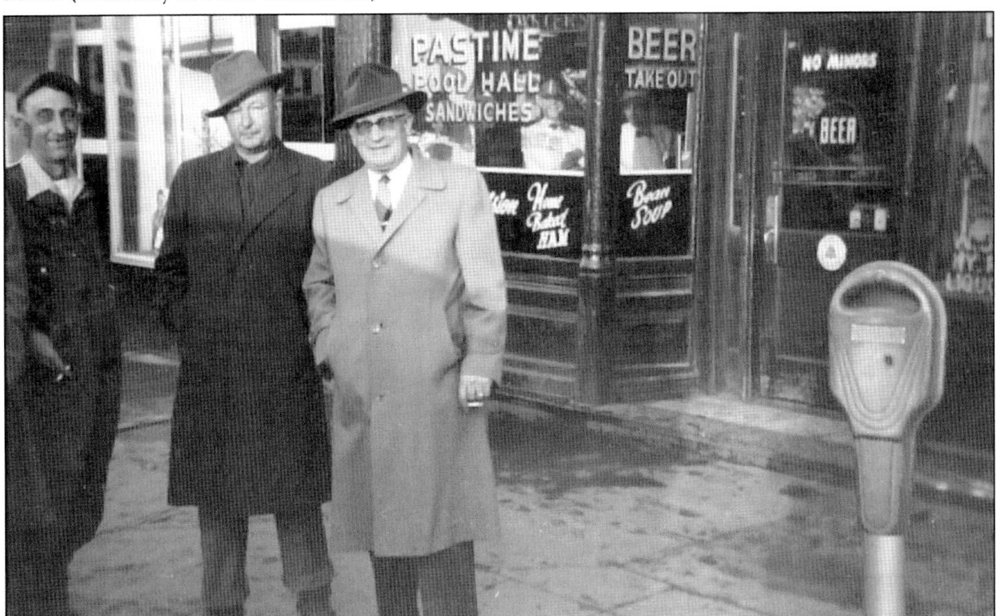

Standing in front of the legendary Pastime Pool Hall on Fifth Street, which was famous for its "Old South" bean soup and Fulton Fish Market breaded oysters, are Buford Hanlon (left) and Roy Adams (right). The man in the center is unidentified. Look closely for employees of the pool hall watching from inside as the photograph is taken, including original owner W.J. Louden. (Courtesy of Carol Louden Shelton.)

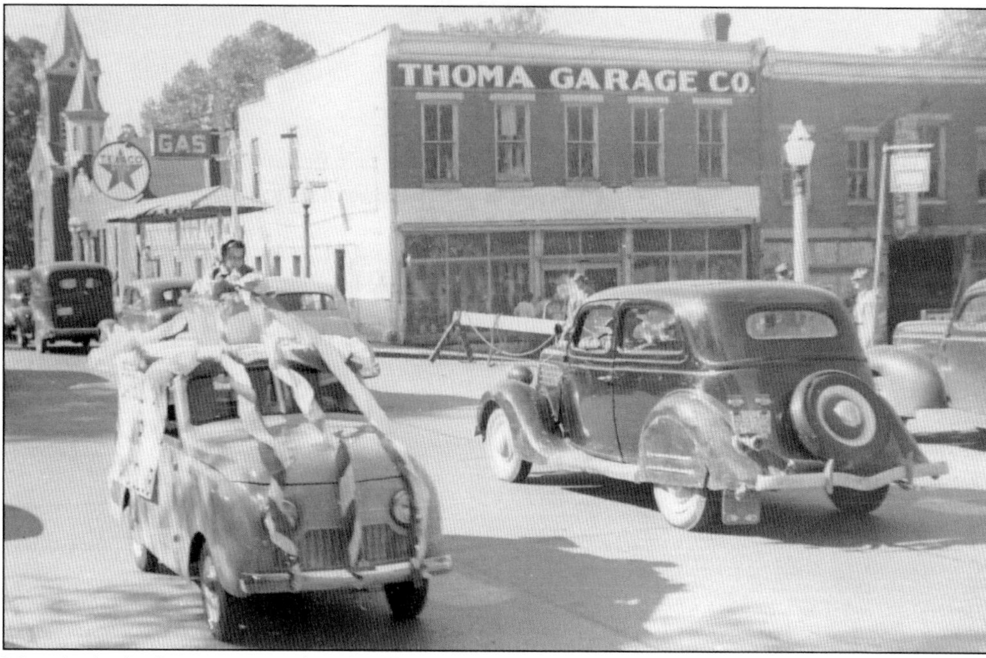

This funky little car was used as the float for the Carrollton Younger Women's Club during the first Tobacco Festival parade in 1948. In the background are the First Baptist Church and the Thoma Garage and Texaco station at the corner of Highland Avenue and Court Street. That building and the one next to it were razed in the early 1970s, and the site is now the parking lot for the Carroll County Public Library. (Courtesy of Amy Baglan.)

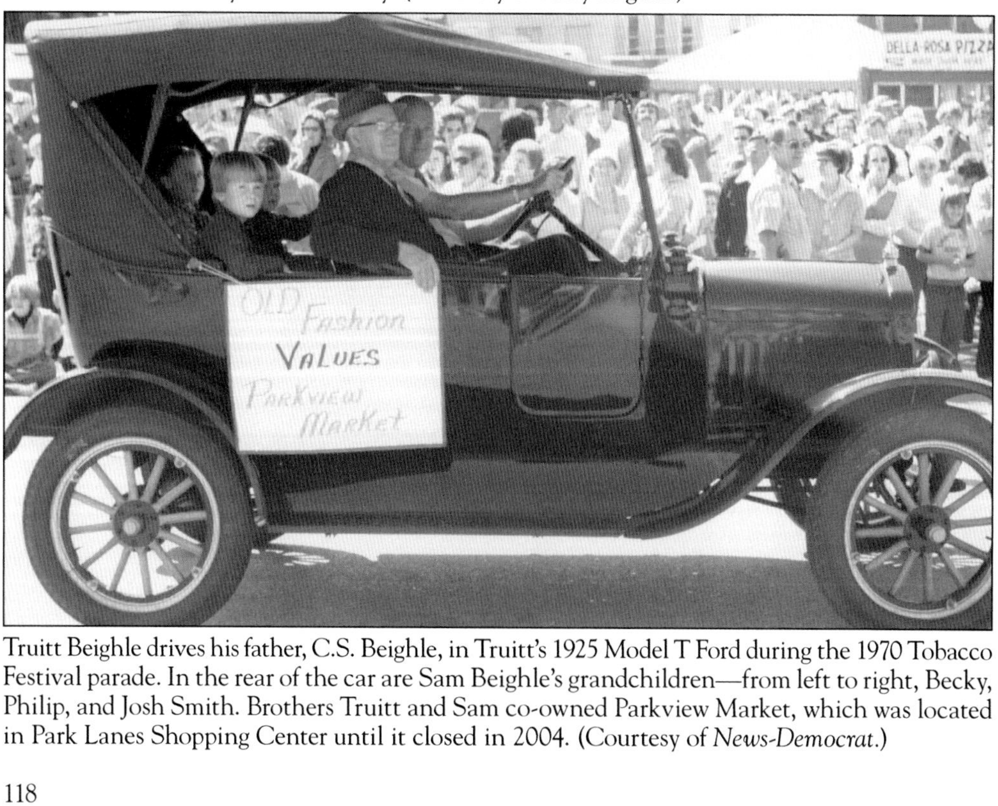

Truitt Beighle drives his father, C.S. Beighle, in Truitt's 1925 Model T Ford during the 1970 Tobacco Festival parade. In the rear of the car are Sam Beighle's grandchildren—from left to right, Becky, Philip, and Josh Smith. Brothers Truitt and Sam co-owned Parkview Market, which was located in Park Lanes Shopping Center until it closed in 2004. (Courtesy of *News-Democrat*.)

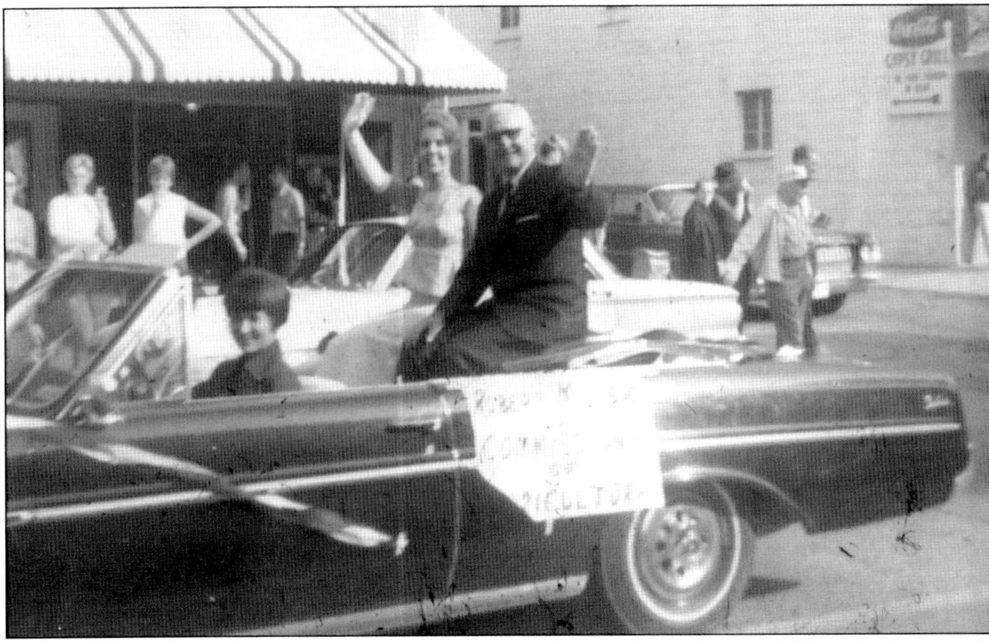

Amy Baglan accompanies the state commissioner of agriculture, Robert Miller, during a 1967 Tobacco Festival parade down Highland Avenue. (Courtesy of Amy Baglan.)

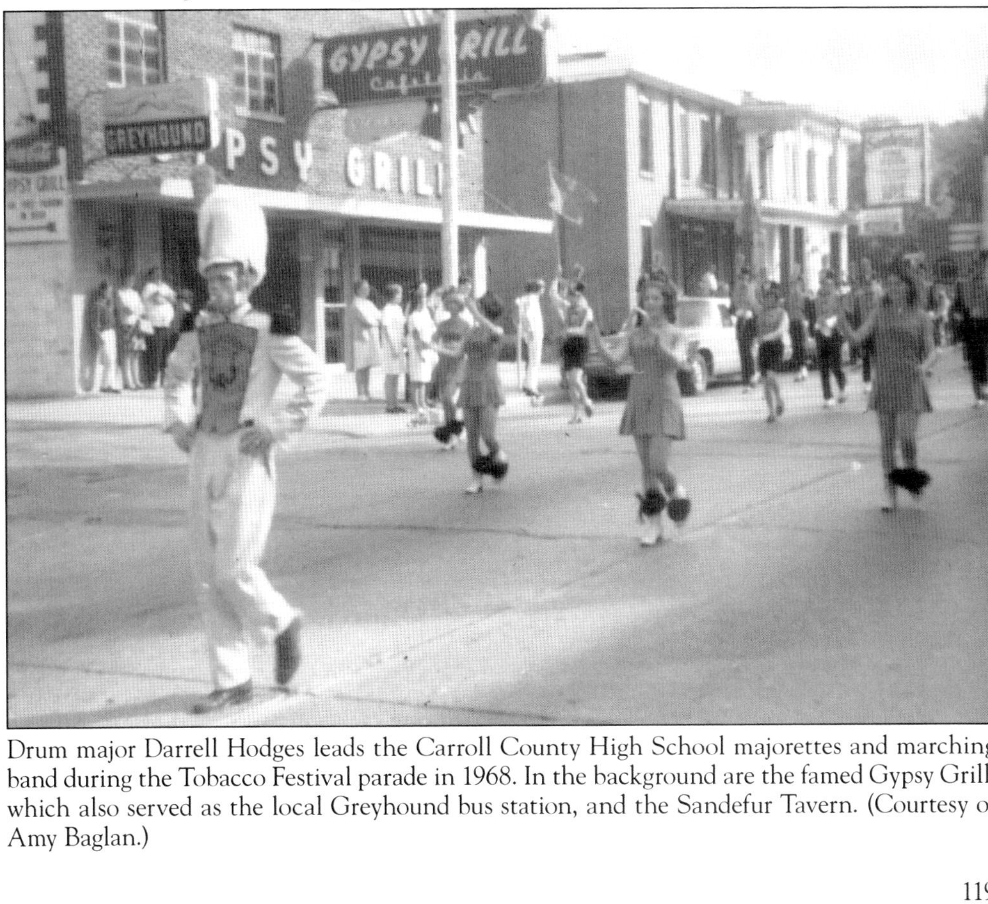

Drum major Darrell Hodges leads the Carroll County High School majorettes and marching band during the Tobacco Festival parade in 1968. In the background are the famed Gypsy Grill, which also served as the local Greyhound bus station, and the Sandefur Tavern. (Courtesy of Amy Baglan.)

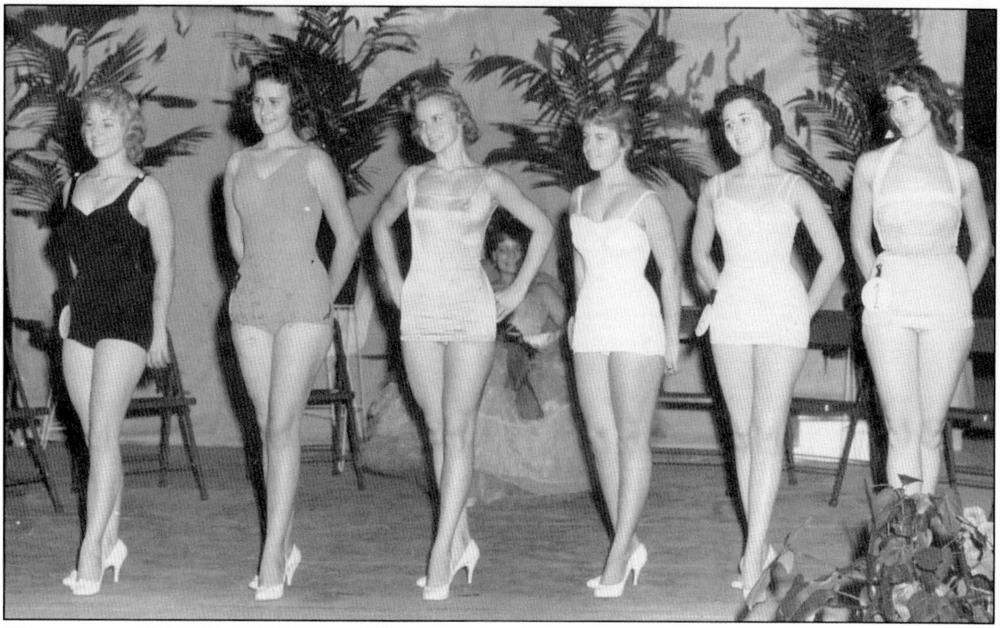

Women in the Miss Carroll County Tobacco Festival Pageant pose for the judges during the swimsuit portion of the competition. The pageant tradition in Carroll County is alive and well. Pageants are still the main attraction each year at the county fair and the Tobacco Festival. The first Miss Carroll County Fair was Lila Jo Gillock Shelton. (Courtesy of Carol Louden Shelton.)

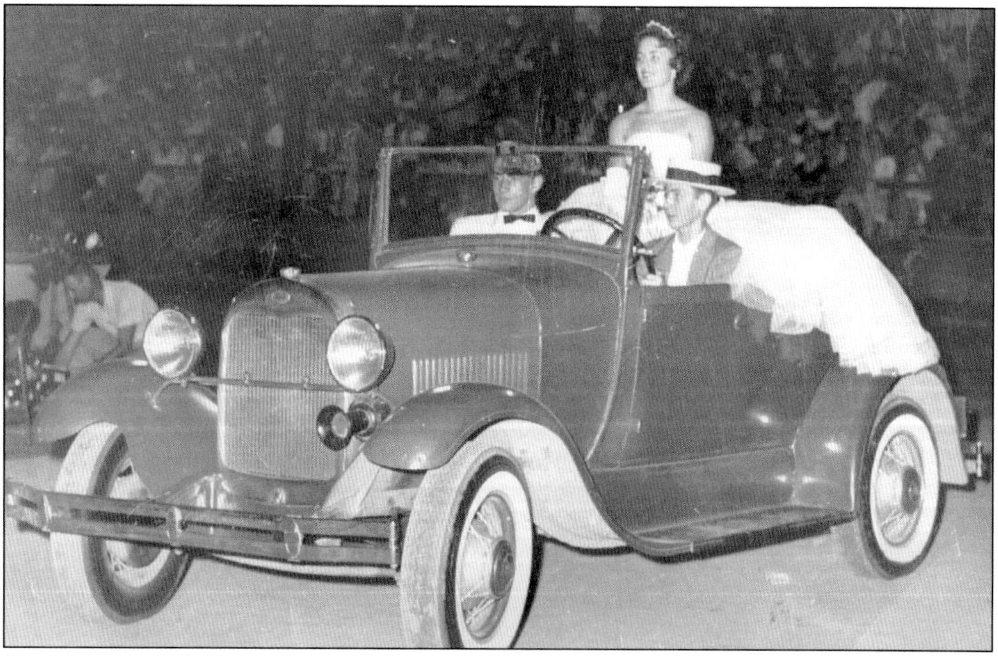

Over the years, rules have changed for county pageants, at times opening the event to candidates from other counties and sometimes limiting candidate eligibility to county residents. Gallatin County's Shirley Morgan was named Miss Carroll County Tobacco Festival in 1957. She and her escort, Owen Harris, ride with Ira Louden in Louden's Model A Roadster. (Courtesy of Carol Louden Shelton.)

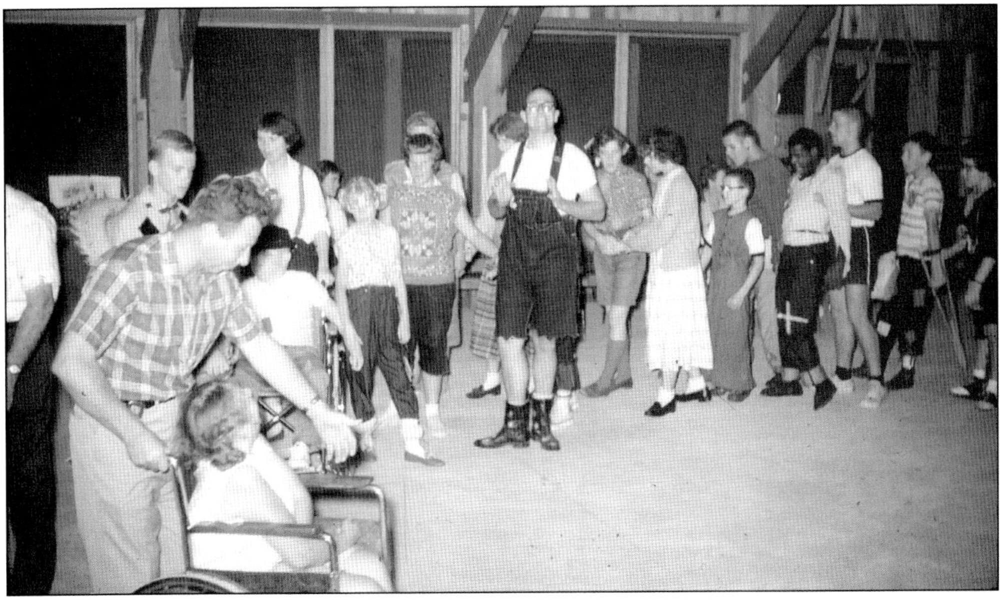

Above, Jim Montgomery (left) celebrates during a party with campers at Camp Kysoc, a summer camp for special needs children and adults, which opened in 1960. Montgomery was a fixture at the camp, helping to build the 27 cabins, trails, and footbridges within the camp's 124 acres. Below, Della West, a volunteer, helps during an Easter egg hunt for children involved with the Carroll County Association for Mental Retardation. Joyce Conway was an instructor for the younger children in the program; Jean Montgomery was instructor for teens and adults. The program was the predecessor of the Hope Workshop, now located at the corner of Fourth and Clay Streets. (Both, courtesy of Cathy Montgomery Gilbert.)

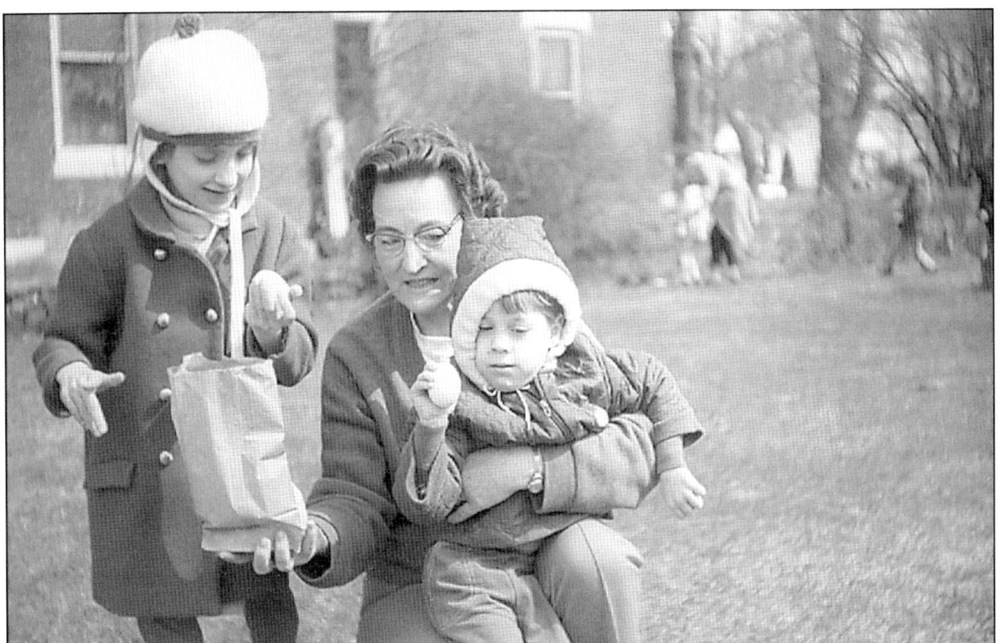

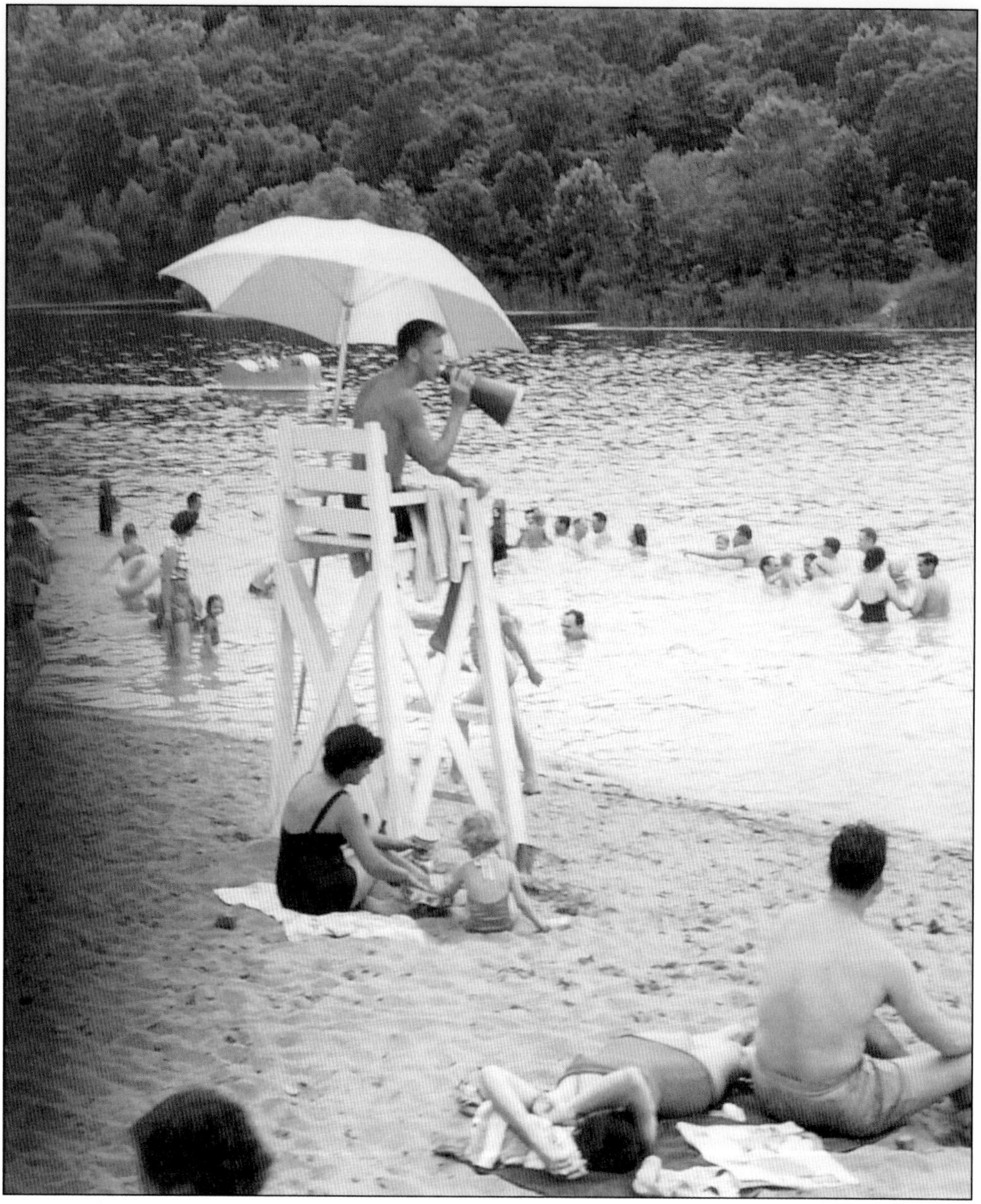

Sun worshipers from all over the tristate area flocked to the beach at the 30-acre, man-made lake at General Butler State Resort Park. Swimming is still an attraction at the lake, along with paddleboats and canoeing. Many people also come to fish along its bank. (Courtesy of General Butler State Resort Park.)

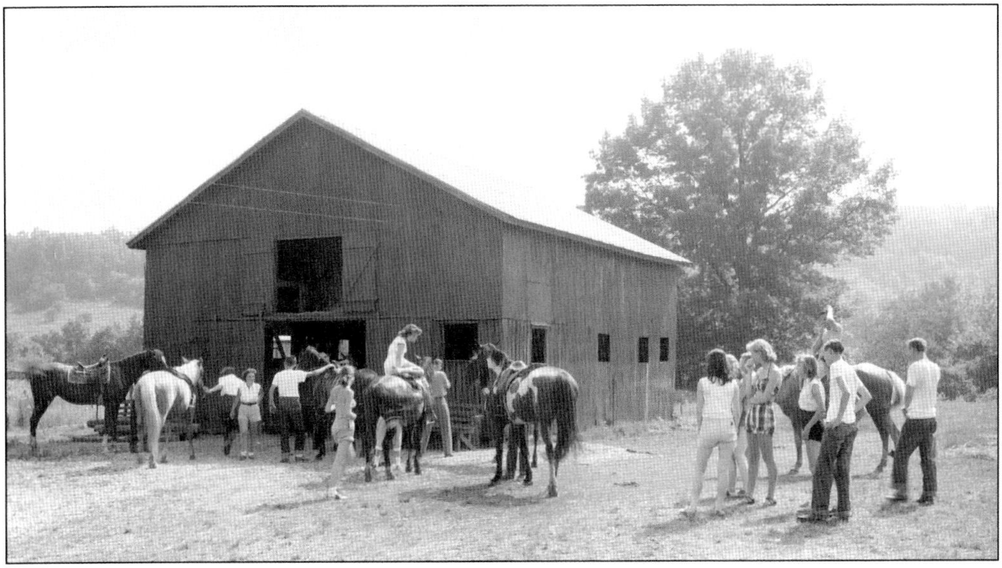

The riding stable was one of the main attractions at General Butler State Resort Park. The stables opened in May 1951. Other recreational facilities followed at the park, including the nine-hole golf course (added in 1961) and the Butler Park Lodge (opened in 1962). Today, the park includes tennis courts, basketball courts, miniature golf, and a swimming pool for lodge guests. (Courtesy of Darrell Maines.)

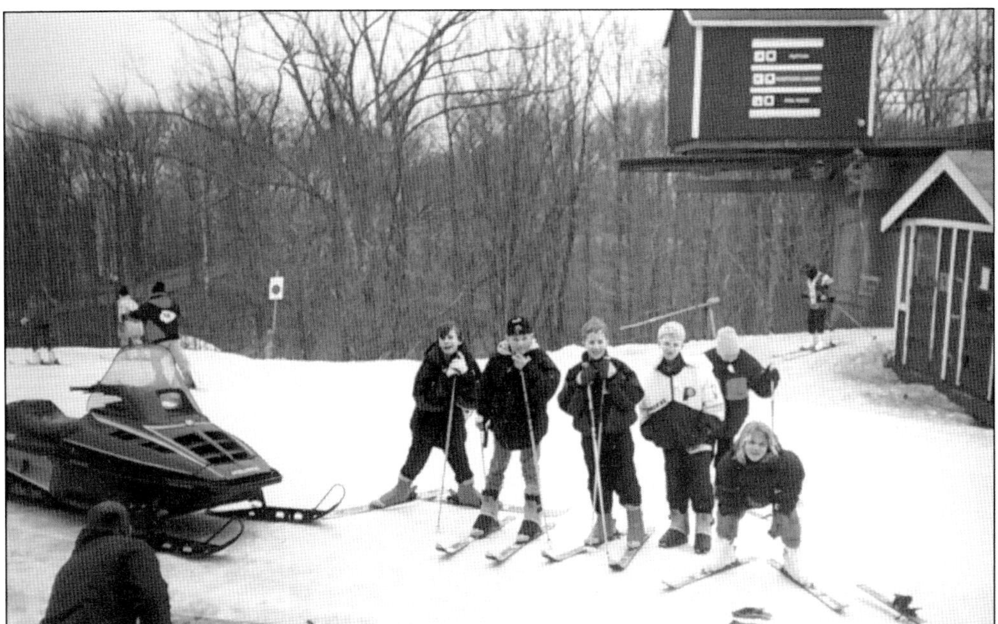

A group of children gets ready to hit the slopes at Ski Butler, a privately owned ski resort at General Butler State Resort Park in the 1980s and 1990s. Eventually, the endeavor failed due to a warming trend and less snow falling in the wintertime. (Courtesy of *News-Democrat*.)

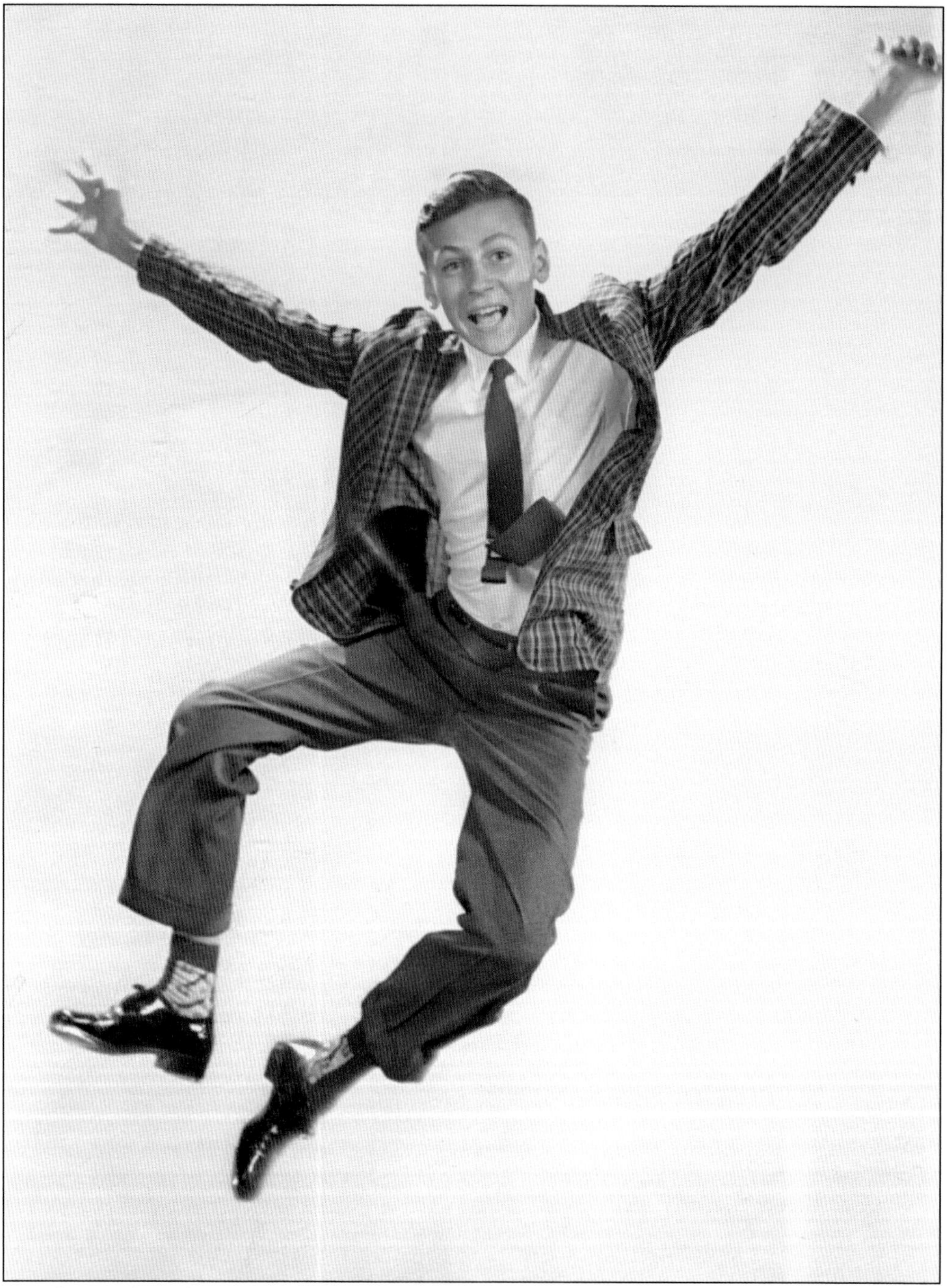

Dwight Louden, the youngest of the talented Louden family, clicks his heels in a publicity photograph. He and his older siblings Ira and Carol were involved in dance and musical acts throughout their childhoods. In the 1960s, Carol Louden taught in her own dance studio. Ira and Dwight both followed in the political footsteps of their father, W.J. Louden. Ira served several terms as a magistrate on the Carroll County Fiscal Court, while Dwight served on Carrollton City Council and as the city's mayor from 2006 to 2010. (Courtesy of *News-Democrat*.)

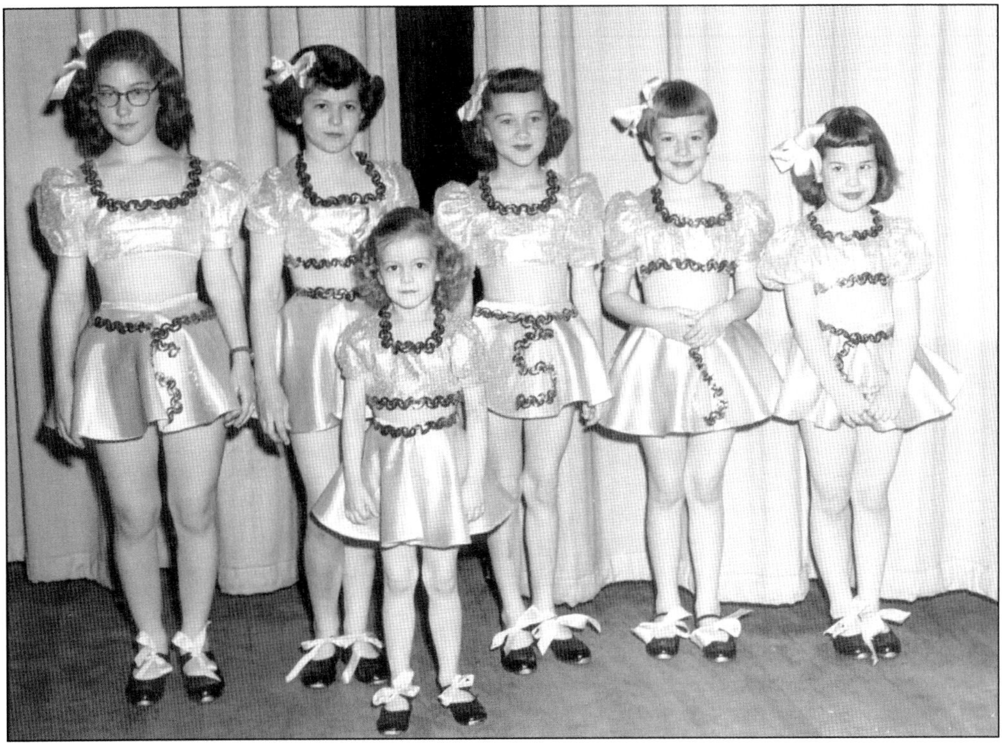

Dance class was a popular activity in Carrollton. Louisville dancer Bud Shelton, trained at the Courtney School of Dance, taught in the basement of the Independent Order of Odd Fellows lodge. These girls, believed to be some of Shelton's students, prepare for their April 1955 recital. Three girls are identified in the back row: Sherry Combs, far left; Sue Harris, center; and Karlene Kipping, far right. (Courtesy of *News-Democrat*.)

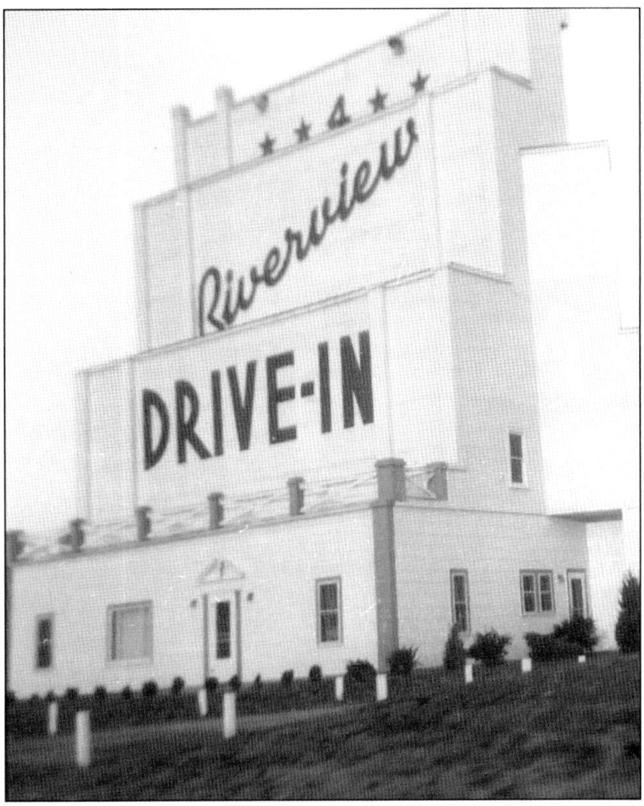

The Riverview Drive-In was built on US 42, between Carrollton and Ghent, in 1950 by R.L. Gaines. It was a popular spot for people of all ages for many years but was torn down when the property was sold to Dow Corning for the company's chemical plant. (Courtesy of Daisy Hughes.)

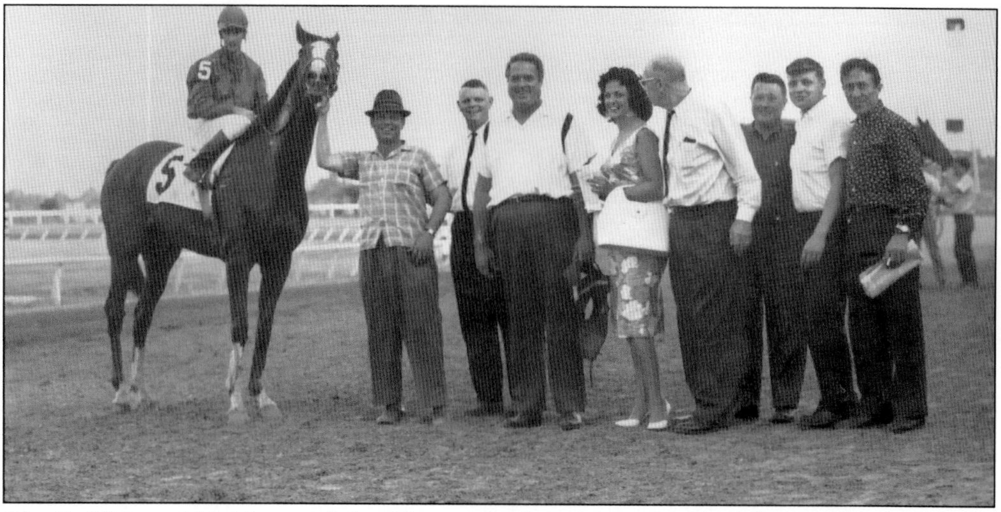

Charlie Webster (third from right) celebrates the first-place win of his Thoroughbred racehorse Thuries on June 14, 1963, at Miles Park in Louisville, Kentucky. The trainer was Kenneth Bright, and the jockey was Kenneth Knapp. (Courtesy of Carol Louden Shelton.)

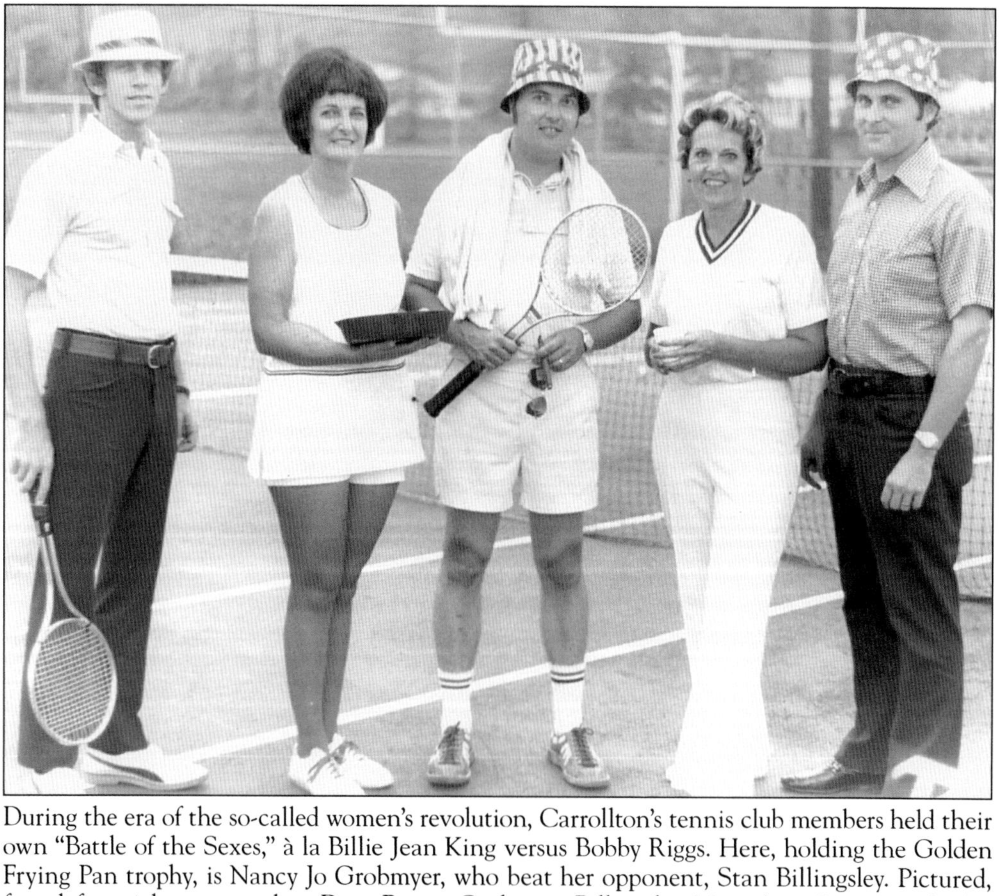

During the era of the so-called women's revolution, Carrollton's tennis club members held their own "Battle of the Sexes," à la Billie Jean King versus Bobby Riggs. Here, holding the Golden Frying Pan trophy, is Nancy Jo Grobmyer, who beat her opponent, Stan Billingsley. Pictured, from left to right, are members Doug Rouse, Grobmyer, Billingsley, Mary Ann Gentry, and John Newcomb. (Courtesy of Nancy Jo Grobmyer.)

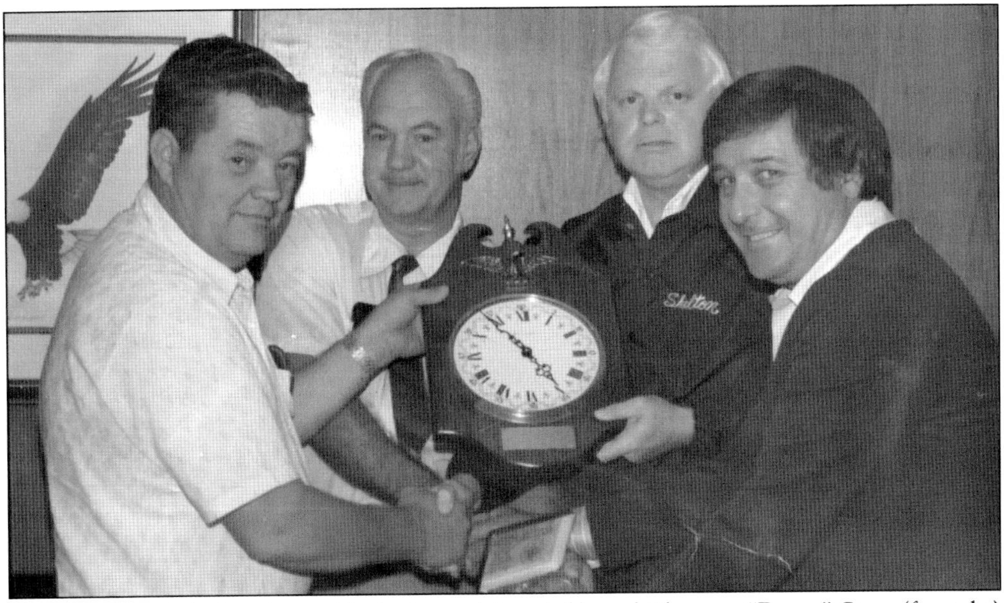

Robert Westrick (left), Marcus Tuttle (second from left), and Clarence "Duper" Craig (far right) present a clock and other items to Robert Shelton for his years of dedication to Carroll County's Little League baseball program. (Courtesy of Carol Louden Shelton.)

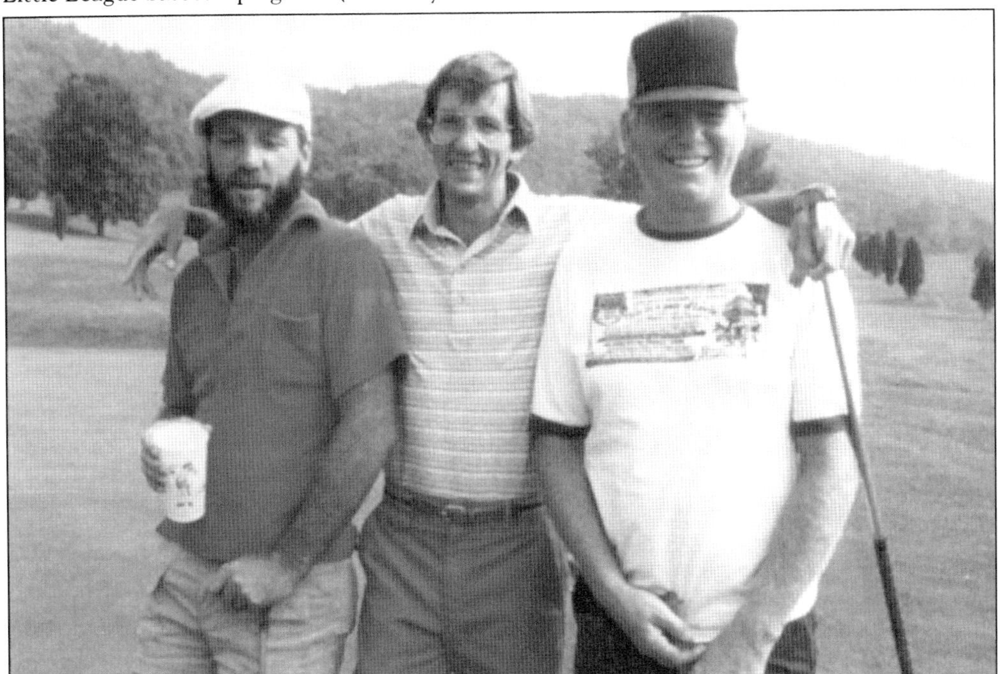

Charles Satterwhite (center) was from Owen County but served as the circuit judge for Kentucky's 15th Judicial District, which includes Carroll County. He presided over the 1990 trial of Larry Mahoney, who was convicted for his involvement in the worst drunk-driving accident on record in the United States, which occurred on Interstate 71 near Carrollton on May 14, 1988. Here, Satterwhite poses on the links with Floyd Lytle (left) and James "Sandy" Willhoite. (Courtesy of *News-Democrat*.)

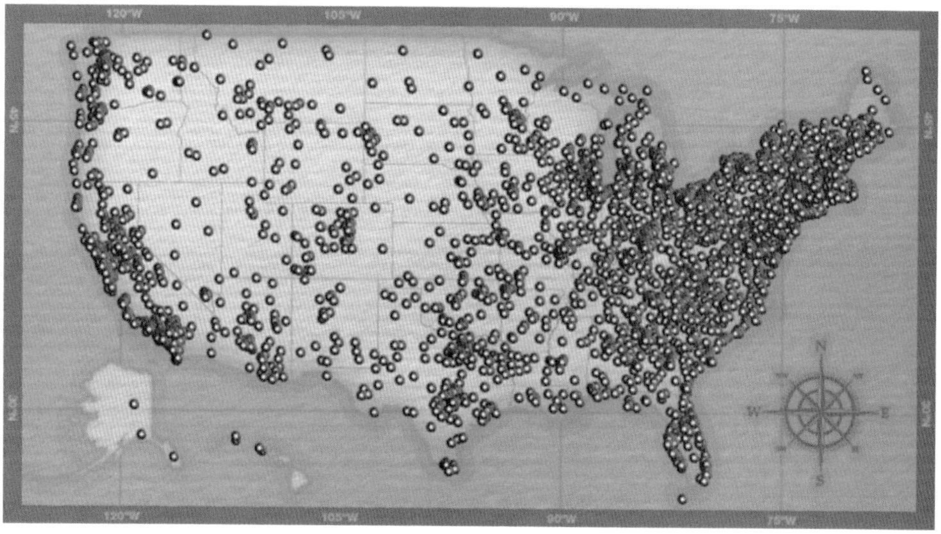